# TREVOR GRIFFITHS

## Plays One

*Occupations*

*The Party*

*Comedians*

*Real Dreams*

Introduced by
the Author

*faber and faber*
LONDON · BOSTON

This collection first published in 1996 by
Faber and Faber Limited
3 Queen Square London WC1N 3AU

Photoset by Parker Typesetting Service, Leicester
Printed in England by Clays Ltd, St Ives plc

A CIP record for this book is available from the British Library

ISBN 0–571–17742–5

2 4 6 8 10 9 7 5 3 1

# Trevor Griffiths

Trevor Griffiths's first full-length stage play, *Occupations*, was produced by the RSC; *The Party* was premièred by the National Theatre; and his 1975 play, *Comedians*, moved from Nottingham to the National Theatre at the Old Vic and later to Broadway. More recently, his work for the theatre has included *Piano* for the National Theatre; *The Gulf Between Us*, a controversial appraisal of the Middle East conflict from an Arab perspective; and *Thatcher's Children*, a damning indictment of the Eighties produced by the Bristol Old Vic.

Griffiths has also written extensively for television and was given the BAFTA Writer's Award in 1982. His 1976 political drama serial *Bill Brand* was followed by a wide-ranging series of pieces including the highly-praised *Country* and *Oi for England*, his anatomy of skinhead culture, as well as his adaptation of Lawrence's *Sons and Lovers* and his epic series about the race for the South Pole, *The Last Place on Earth*. *Hope in the Year Two*, a film for BBC Television about the French Revolution, was transmitted in May 1994 and seen in a stage version entitled *Who Shall Be Happy . . .?* at the Belfast Festival in 1995. His work for the cinema includes *Reds* with Warren Beatty, for which he received an Oscar nomination in 1981, and *Fatherland*, which was directed by Ken Loach and premièred at Cannes in 1986.

# Contents

# Introduction

*Occupations*, my first full-length play for the stage, was researched and written in 1969 and received its first production at the Stables Theatre in Manchester in the following year. Though the story of the play is bedded in a lost moment of European socialist history – the occupation of the factories in Northern Italy in 1920 – there are clear resonances with strategically similar struggles in Europe and Britain at the time of its writing. In spite of a fine, clear and impassioned chamber production by Gordon McDougall in Manchester and a powerful restatement of the piece by the RSC a year later under the direction of Buzz Goodbody, reviewers were, as is commonly the case with my work, predictably divided.

I wrote *The Party* in 1972, a first fast incomplete draft in Europe while researching a screenplay on the life of Strindberg, and a second revised and completed draft some months later. It was first produced by John Dexter at the National Theatre in 1973 and given a second completely new NT touring production by David Hare the following year. Both productions, compelling in their different ways, played to large and voluble audiences in London and around the country, together with a third major production of extraordinary clarity and great passion by Howard Davies and David Edgar at the RSC in the 1980s. All failed to persuade reviewers – though with important exceptions – that it was a piece worth doing. Some twenty years on with a dozen or so files of correspondence from students, teachers and literary critics from around the world about the play, I have little doubt that it was.

Set in a Manchester working-class evening centre in the

mid-1970s, the date of its writing, *Comedians* eschews political theory, professional ideologues and historically sourced discourse on political revolution – all the perceived hallmarks of those earlier pieces – in favour of a more or less unmediated address on a range of particular contemporary issues including class, gender, race and society in modern Britain. The luck the play had was not in its critical reception, divided as ever but on the whole supportive, nor in the response of theatre managements in London and elsewhere, but in its first founding production by Richard Eyre at Nottingham Playhouse. Good first productions (of which I have had my share) have never been easy to come by – not even back then in infinitely more propitious days – and are today grown rarer than the Norwegian fig. But great ones lie outside all laws of probability and distribution in any age. Such was Eyre's in the late winter of 1975 in Nottingham. The debt is immense and permanent.

*Real Dreams* was written in the spring of 1984 and produced at the Williamstown Theatre Festival later that summer. Based on a then unpublished short story by a long-time friend and comrade, Jeremy Pikser, it covers a day and a night in the lives of a group of student revolutionaries trying to learn about the lives of the people in a small squat in Cleveland, Ohio, in the summer of 1969. Reviewers, like the changing and increasingly treacherous times they squelched through, were on the whole hostile to its perceived content and largely blind to its form. Audiences, whether in Reagan's rebrutalized America or later in Thatcher's pantomime Britain, tended to find the play a journey worth the taking. It remains, for me, a favourite piece.

For all their faults, these plays have been continuously in print since their first productions. I greatly welcome this new extension of their licence to go on speaking.

Trevor Griffiths
Palestine, Summer 1995

# OCCUPATIONS

# In Defence of Occupations

*Shortly after completing its successful run at The Place, London,* Occupations *was featured in a two-page article by Tom Nairn in* 7 Days *(3 November 1971). Trevor Griffiths responded to this article with the following letter disagreeing with Tom Nairn's critical approach to theatre and answering his major criticisms of the play.*

It's important to respond to historical plays as art-works, not as selected documentary accumulations containing historico-political speculations evaluable largely in terms of a 'known', historical and political reality. And we must learn to look for 'historicity' more as Lukacs finds it in the histories of Shakespeare. As for example when Lukacs says: 'Shakespeare states every conflict, even those of English history with which he is most familiar, in terms of typical-human opposites; and these are historical only in so far as Shakespeare fully and directly assimilates into each individual type the most characteristic and central features of a social crisis.' Nairn's it's-either-historically-'accurate'-or-it's-purely-and-only-'symbolic' is just too crude and unfruitful a measure of the value of a play (or, indeed, of anything else).

Since he has established the parameters of the discussion firmly inside that approach, however, I have no option but to do likewise. He makes four major points, of varying weight and accuracy.

First, the 'historical' character of Gramsci is wrong; moreover, the characterization in *Occupations* is romantic, even sentimental. Second, the 'symbolic' meanings of Kabak, the Comintern representative, are deeply

3

ahistorical; the Comintern in late 1920 was never like this, though it may well have pursued foolish or even damaging policies. Third, the play's naturalistic form tended to undermine, even devalue, the promise of its content and themes. Fourth, the play is pessimistic, and therefore not revolutionary.

I'll respond to the last three points briefly, leaving the central question of the true 'historical' personality and character of Gramsci till last. Some conflation of 'different epochs of Communist history' does admittedly occur in the characterization of Kabak. For example, the Sovnarkom decree (and the seventy-two cleared concession items) that forms the basis of the final exchange with the Fiat boss was actually passed in November, some *five weeks after* the scene took place in the play's time scheme; though it's worth pointing out that the decree simply served to crystallize a whole strand of Soviet foreign policy that had been nursed (quite correctly in my view) since the summer of 1918.

After the autumn of 1920, however, with the failure of the Italian Revolution, the emphasis on the defence of Soviet national interests toughened, as the retreat from a policy hostile in principle to all capitalist government, (while the prospect of proletarian revolution remained alive) got under way. As far as I can see, the play simply states that emphasis as a pragmatic, unavoidable fact.

Perhaps the weight of compressed meaning upon Kabak in that final scene with Valletta is just too great (a 'formal' weakness; by no means the only one): his need to play a role *vis-à-vis* Valletta (brandy, jokes, cigars, portfolios, *business*) obscures the representative values of his actions by inviting a cynical and pessimistic response. But the *intention* is quite other; and it's an intention still substantially realizable in the text.

That Nairn should see that scene as conflating Stalinist adventures in Spain with sixties' deals for Fiat factories on the Volga is as much, one suspects, the result of his own grasp of the period as of the play's structural weaknesses.

As to whether the play is pessimistic and whether, if it is, it is therefore necessarily non-revolutionary, I would support Gramsci's assertion that 'It is a revolutionary duty to tell the truth', even where there is little comfort to be had from it. *Occupations* was written as a sort of Jacobinical response to the failure of the '68 revolution in France. *What it asserts* is that courage and optimism do not, of themselves, ensure the success of revolutions, unless they are harnessed, disciplined, tightly organized; in a word, *led*.

And what it *asks* – because it's a play that, characteristically, asks rather than asserts – is whether the courage and optimism aren't in some way necessarily damaged, distorted, in that disciplining process. (And that's a 'meaning' for Kabak that Nairn barely smells, he's so often away from the play's muscle, skin and sinew.)

But Gramsci; where to begin?

Nairn: 'In reality . . . all accounts agree . . . Gramsci was a hard, even a harsh, figure in most public situations.' Well, in the play, his second speech to the workers would rate as pretty harsh, I think; and in his first scene with Kabak, he's cold, suspicious, and unyielding for a long time, until Kabak's identity is finally established beyond doubt; certainly 'hard', one would have said.

But 'in reality', Gramsci was rarely ever *only* that. Nino Danielli: 'Good, almost sweet, with that large intelligent face on that greatly deformed body, quick to smile and every word full of thought, Gramsci was charming from the beginning . . .' Nino Bruno: 'He was a very cheerful fellow, laughing and joking all the time.' Carlo Bocardo: 'Gramsci let us talk . . . (he) never lost patience with us, he never acted like a theoretical know-all; he set great store by other people's opinions and was a good listener.' Nairn suggests that Gramsci's letter to Giulia, in which he refers

5

to himself as 'cross-grained' and 'spiteful' – one who made 'everything a matter of pure intellect and mathematical calculation' – is a good guide to the sort of person Gramsci was in September 1920 (when the occupations occurred).

If Nairn had read or remembered more of the letter than is printed in the English version of Fiori's *Life of Gramsci*, however, he would have known that the description refers to a *much* earlier period, to those 'sewers of my past' when he lived like a 'bear in a cave'. The 'bear in a cave' period, Fiori points out, ended around 1915. That he wasn't referring to 1920 when he spoke of his over-emphasis on 'pure intellect and mathematical calculation' is further suggested by his letter to Togliatti (27 March 1924) in which he argues: 'We must seek to rebuild an atmosphere like that of 1919/1920 . . . At that time, no project was undertaken unless first tested by reality and until we had sounded out in many ways the opinions of the workers. Consequently our projects always had an immediate and broad success and appeared as the interpretation of a widely felt need, never as the cold application of an intellectual scheme.'

'In reality', Gramsci moved, throughout his life, from states of deep depression to states of warm and generous sympathy. The image of Gramsci as consistently 'hard, even harsh' is founded in Lisa's and Lay's descriptions of him in prison in the thirties when Gramsci developed (understandably) personality problems not dissociable from physical suffering (TB, arteriosclerosis, angina, etc.); and, in its way, it's this myth that's damagingly romantic, sustaining, as it does, the notion that rebarbative personality is a necessary (or at any rate useful) prerequisite of serious revolutionary activity.

As to the 'sinewy intolerance inseparable from Gramsci's particular form of greatness', the evidence in refutation is so extensive as to require another article in itself to present. Gramsci's long dialogue with the anarchists, his sustained 'openness' towards non-communists and Catholic workers and intellectuals; his appointment of Gobetti, a liberal, as *Ordine Nuovo*'s theatre critic; his continued fight against Piedmontese working-class anti-clericalism all serve as evidence to the contrary. And even in prison, as Lay points out, Gramsci's costive testiness did not mean that he 'could not tolerate disagreement with his ideas. Athos Lisa was not in agreement with Gramschi's thesis . . . nevertheless, Gramsci esteemed and valued him.'

Gramsci's two factory speeches are a *device* for projecting two very different sets of theses developed by him in *Ordine Nuovo* essays at the time. Tasca and Degott are right: Gramsci was no great orator; nor are these speeches great oratory; nor are they delivered by a man who imagines he's a great orator. In the first one, he's constantly plagued by interruptions; in the second, he speaks to almost total, unsympathetic silence. But they *are* clear and concise accounts of some of his thinking at the time. And Gramsci did – incontrovertibly – address large gatherings of workers in the factories. Spriano notes that he spoke to a big meeting at Garrone Fiat on '*Domenica Rossa*' (I have him at Fiat Centro – another 'documentary inaccuracy'); Terraccini told me that Gramsci addressed workers' meetings, large and small, pretty well every day, sometimes three or four times a day.

There's no doubt that the workers responded very favourably to him (Terraccini spent a long time detailing the workers' response to Gramsci); little doubt, too, that since 1916, when he made his first public speeches, he had made considerable strides in overcoming his basic diffidence and reserve. Degott's view that Gramsci's appearance affected audiences unfavourably is not borne out by anything Terraccini had to say on Gramsci. According to him, the Turin workers 'loved him' ('*Molto,*

*molto, molto*'), they loved his untidiness, his raffish dress, his floppy hat – which they threw into the river, once, for a joke, then rescued – his jokes and fables. (Terraccini told me this against himself: *he* was not well liked by the workers, who detested his 'bourgeois correctness' of dress and manner.) Celeste Negarville refers to 'Gramsci's singular talent for talking with working people'.

Finally, though it would take too long to detail Gramsci's growing preoccupation with the relationship between public and private forms of experience, there is no doubt that 'love' was a basic reference for much of his social thought. He it is (not me) who asserts: 'One cannot divide oneself into fragments and make only one part function; life is a whole, and each activity is strengthened by all the others; love strengthens the whole of one's existence . . . it creates a new equilibrium, a greater intensity of all other feelings and sentiments.' Mucking about with love and Revolution?

All this notwithstanding, I'm truly grateful to your paper for printing such a long, detailed, and responsible piece. Of all the notices I've read, it's the one most likely to help me make the next play a better one. Is there any higher praise than that, from a writer?

# Characters

Polya
Kabak
Libertini
Angelica
Gramsci
D'Avanzo
Terrini
Valletta

**Occupations** was first performed at The Stables Theatre Club, Manchester, on 28 October 1970, with the following cast:

**Polya**  Clare Welch
**Kabak**  Richard Wilson
**Libertini**  Paul Williamson
**Angelica**  Katherine Barker
**Gramsci**  Richard Kane
**D'Avanzo**  John Flanagan
**Terrini**  William Simons
**Valletta**  John Horsley

*Directed by*  Gordon McDougall

**Occupations** was first performed in London by the Royal Shakespeare Company at The Place, on 13 October 1971, with the following cast:

**Polya**  Heather Canning
**Kabak**  Patrick Stewart
**Libertini**  Philip Locke
**Angelica**  Estelle Kohler
**Gramsci**  Ben Kingsley
**D'Avanzo**  John York
**Terrini**  Clement McCallin
**Valletta**  Sebastian Shaw

*Directed by*  Buzz Goodbody

# A Note on the Text

The version of *Occupations* printed here differs, in parts substantially, from the text first published in 1973. Such improvements as I've managed to make I owe to several key productions of the play during the last ten years: in particular, to the first production at The Stables Theatre; to Buzz Goodbody's at the RSC; and to a new and remarkable presentation of the play this year by the Dutch socialist theatre group, Sater.

What appears here represents a decade's intermittent but intensive effort to arrive at a definitive text of the play. And yet, notwithstanding, I publish the original final scene, now largely excised, in an appendix, impenitently unwilling to consign it wholly to the deliberations of scholars.

Trevor Griffiths
Boston Spa, Yorkshire
5 June 1980

# Act One

## SCENE ONE

*The stage is in total darkness. We hear, faintly at first, growing gradually louder and more insistent, a sung version of 'The Internationale'. A projected image slowly emerges: the famous* Tbi *('You – have you enrolled as a volunteer yet?' D. S. Moore, Russia, 1920). It's held, red and challenging, for several moments. Cut suddenly, as a fast spot reveals* **Polya** *bending over the bed to inject the writhing* **Angelica**. *Angelica shudders, quietens. Polya cools her brow with a cloth. Music down. Excited hubbub of conference. Take out spot a second after the* **Voice** *begins. Replace with Lizitisky's 1920 abstract,* With the Red Wedge Divide the Whites.

**Voice**  Comrade delegates to the Second Congress of the Third International; Lenin's promise is being fulfilled before your eyes. Denikin's treacherous hordes in the south have been quelled. Now it is the turn of Marshal Pilsudski and his reactionary Polish divisions to feel the bite of our revolutionary anger. Comrade Trotsky sends apologies for his absence – he is taking a short holiday in Poland, in the company of Generals Tuchachevsky and Buddenny and a few thousand comrades of the Red Army. (*Pause.*) Comrade delegates, Europe is little more than dry couch-grass and kindling, waiting for a spark. (*Fade up Internationale here.*) Waiting for *you*, comrades.

*Singing louder, more strident. The abstract fades. As it does, The Internationale shifts from march-time to slow waltz, the male choir to small twenties dance band. Fade up on hotel room, the play's single set. Take music out.*
*Hotel Fiorina: good, solid, tasteful, bourgeois. The set*

*represents these values without fully realizing them through committedly naturalistic design. (We have already used a wall for projection, and we'll use it again.) It's mainly furniture anyway: a solid bed and bed table, a divan, a table and three chairs, a couple of armchairs, a carpet, an upright phone. Two doors lead to adjoining rooms and the hotel landing respectively.*

*Angelica lies in bed. She wears a long and superb nightdress and négligé. She sleeps: lies wholly motionless.*

*Knock at door. Quiet, firm. Short silence.* **Kabak** *in. He stands in the doorway, a bag in each hand, for some moments, reading the room. He is big, very physical, with full beard and black hair. Dressed as he is in impeccable bourgeois style, there is something not quite right about him, as though the form were somehow at war with the content. He closes the door, puts down the bags, walks quietly to the bed, stares impassively at the sleeping face. Finally he picks up a used ampoule from a kidney bowl on the bedside table, smells it, lays it down, wipes his hand on the overlay. His face gives no sort of clue to state of mind or to any discovery he may have made.*

*He returns to his case, is bending to open it when Polya comes in, some sewing in her hands. She is young, sturdy, attractive in a heavy, peasant way. She gives a stifled yelp at his presence. He presses his palms downward on the noise, inclining his head towards the bed.*

**Polya** I'm sorry sir . . . Your letter said tomorrow . . .

**Kabak** (*crossing to the table with a work case*) I didn't want to waken . . . (*He's stuck for a word: he can't say 'Madam' or 'Your mistress', yet 'Angelica' isn't right either.*) . . . the Countess. If you insist on calling me 'sir' I shall insist on calling you Pelagia.

**Polya** I'm sorry.

**Kabak** Except when I need you to. And when I do, I'll tell you. And don't keep saying you're sorry.

**Polya** I'd forgotten, that's all.

*Kabak has opened the smaller of the two bags and removed some files and a black leather notebook. Polya stands uncertainly near the door. Kabak looks for an address and phone number in the notebook.*

(*advancing*) I'll take your bag through . . .

**Kabak** (*working on*) Leave it.

*Silence.*

**Polya** I could make you some tea . . .

**Kabak** (*absorbed*) No thank you. I had a late lunch at the station.

**Polya** (*bursting it out*) The mistress . . .

**Kabak** In a moment, Polya. Let me finish this first.

*Polya subsides grudgingly. There's a sharp outburst from the phone. Kabak crosses the room and picks it up, the black notebook open in his hand.*

Yes. (*Slight pause.*) Perfectly satisfactory, thank you. Yes, everything . . . Thank you, yes. (*quickly*) One thing. I'm expecting a visitor some time today. Send him up as soon as he arrives, will you. Gramsci. Yes, there is. (*checking notebook*) I want you to ring the Cavaliere D'Avanzo, that's right, at 271. 271. Do it now, I'll wait. (*Pause. He stands very still as he waits.*) Hello, this is Kabak. Yes, this evening. Hotel Fiorina. Room 2, first floor. Tonight would be very convenient. Good. (*He replaces the phone, turns to face Polya.*) What is it, Polya?

**Polya** It started last March. In Vienna. You'd left for Berlin . . .

**Kabak** April.

**Polya** April. I don't know, I don't know when it was. She started losing . . . blood. And, she didn't eat anything hardly. And, she wouldn't see a doctor, of course. Then the pain.

**Kabak** The blood came from where?

**Polya** It's a woman's . . . thing. It's . . . private.

**Kabak** And?

**Polya** (*stumbling*) She's going . . . she's going . . . she's going to die.

**Kabak** Did *he* say that?

*She nods, looks down at her sewing. Kabak stands up, paces the carpet a moment.*

Did he say when?

*There's a gentle knock at the door.*

(*fierce, but contained*) Damn. Damn. Damn. Damn.

*A second knock.*

You answer it, Polya.

*Polya rises to go, drying her eyes.*

And Polya.

*Polya turns.*

Sir?

*Polya nods and goes to the door to admit **Libertini**, the hotelier, a fine, delicate, artistic-looking man of fifty or so, with wavy silver hair and a smart moustache.*

**Libertini** (*expansive, pleasantly deferential*) May I come in, Mr Kabak? Thank you. I'm sorry I wasn't here to welcome you when you arrived. Turin is a city at war with itself, as I'm sure you realize, and there is much for a simple hotelier to do, if he is to survive the holocaust.

**Kabak** Please, Mr . . .

**Libertini** Libertini. (*advancing well into the room*) Now then, is everything to your liking, Mr Kabak? You have only to say, you know. We're honoured that you and your . . . wife, the Countess, should grace us with your presence.

**Kabak** Everything is perfect, thank you.

**Libertini** Sure? (*Waits theatrically for rejoinder that clearly isn't coming.*) Well then. I shan't take up any more of your valuable time. (*He dwells.*)

**Kabak** Is there . . . something else?

**Libertini** Well. I was actually wondering how long you intended . . . staying. The suite, I mean. Your letter from Vienna was somewhat . . . unspecific.

**Kabak** I'll let you know.

*Silence. Kabak looks at him for a moment. He might be staring at a grease stain on a wall.*

**Libertini** Mr Kabak, these are difficult times. The whole of Italy is but a push and a slip away from disaster. A man must pick his way with care . . . I, er, I understand you're expecting a visitor, a Signor Gramschi . . . (*Kabak says nothing.*) If I could give a stranger to our city some advice . . . This is not a good man. Indeed there are those who consider him the principal cause of our troubles here in Turin.

**Kabak** Mr Libertini. (*very patient*) What is it you are trying to say?

**Libertini** (*carefully*) Simply, Mr Kabak, if it became known to the authorities that revolutionary leaders were frequenting my hotel, I think it would be a close thing which I lost first, my clientele or my licence.

**Kabak** (*silent for a moment, then*) Aah. (*He crosses to his leather case, takes out a hand-sized satchel.*) Mr . . . Libertini. I have been in business, one way or another, since I was a boy. And I believe there is no more satisfying and inspiring a way of making a living. So we must accept its . . . distasteful aspects. There was a time when the world was calm and ordered, when men knew their class, their place, their limits. We now live in less comfortable times. Yet business cannot watch and wait: it has to be working. And if, in its course, I have to shake hands with anarchists and communists and revolutionary subversives of this sort or that, allow me to make my choice and do it.

**Libertini** But of course, Mr Kabak. I had no intention of . . .

**Kabak** (*ignoring him*) I have two things. First: a note, stamped with the Prefect Taddei's own stamp and signed by the Cavaliere D'Avanzo, Commissioner of Public Safety, authorizing me to move freely in pursuit of my work in Turin. (*He shows him the note.*) And . . . gold. (*Long pause. He takes out a small wallet, hands it to Libertini.*) Thank you for sparing me your time, Mr . . . Libertini. I think we can say a bargain has been struck? (*He takes Libertini's elbow and moves him to the door.*)

**Libertini** Yes, indeed, Mr Kabak. (*pocketing the wallet at once*) There's actually no need. No need at all. I simply wanted . . .

**Kabak** Thank you. And good evening.

*Libertini stiffens slightly, converts the gesture into a short formal bow, leaves. Kabak closes the door behind him. It's growing dark now, and Kabak walks round the room switching on the two standing lights but leaving the one by the bed – so that the bed area recedes visually. There is barely a clue as to his mental state, but there is a tenseness, a coiledness about his movements.*

**Kabak** No need at all! When did you last hear that?

**Polya** I don't know. Vienna? Munich? (*Pause.*) Don't you have . . . any fear?

**Kabak** Fear? (*Pause.*) No. (*Pause.*) Of what?

**Polya** Prison. Death.

**Kabak** I've been in prison. (*scratching his chest reflectively*) And death's a state of mind. A communist is always on leave from death. That little . . . eunuch has been dead for years.

*He turns involuntarily towards the bed and stares at Angelica. Polya stands up, gathers her sewing, and prepares to go.*

**Polya** Will you want food? (*Kabak doesn't answer.*) Let me know if you want food.

**Kabak** How long . . . has she been having cocaine?

**Polya** (*stopping, turning*) On and off, two or three months, I suppose.

**Kabak** And it *is* cocaine?

**Polya** That's what they say.

**Kabak** How long does it keep her . . . like this?

**Polya** It depends. Sometimes a day, sometimes less than an hour. It's not dependable.

**Kabak** Does she . . . do it herself?

**Polya**  I do it. But she knows how.

**Kabak**  Thank you.

**Polya**  Is that all?

**Kabak**  Thank you, yes.

**Polya**  Ring if you want me. Madame won't hear it now.

**Kabak**  Good night.

**Polya**  Good night, sir. (*She stops, turns.*) Sorry.

**Kabak**  (*gently*) Good night.

*She leaves, by the connecting door. Kabak stands looking at Angelica for a moment longer then uproots a bottle of vodka from his case and takes a long, rather violent pull from it, before fishing out a pair of knee-boots and an old, high-necked smock. He wanders round the room, removing jacket, waistcoat and shirt, pulling hard on the bottle from time to time; clicks off one light, another; carries a chair from the table to the bed and sits down facing Angelica, his face very close to hers. After a moment he clicks on the light by her bed. The bed area is now pooled, the rest virtually extinguished. He pulls again at the bottle, then drops his head on to his chest. Angelica half-wakes, enough anyway to recognize his presence, though the drug continues to separate perception and feeling, and to draw upon realities from different points in her person. She strokes his hair very gently.*

**Angelica**  You came.

**Kabak**  (*lifting his head*) Hello, my love.

**Angelica**  You said you'd come and you came.

**Kabak**  Shh. You'll tire yourself.

**Angelica** I couldn't believe it when your letter came. It's been so long.

**Kabak** Five months.

**Angelica** Five months. Five deaths. And I so wanted to be well for your arrival.

**Kabak** Now, now. We'll talk in the morning. Sleep.

**Angelica** Christo.

**Kabak** Mmm.

**Angelica** Say something.

**Kabak** Yes, I do.

**Angelica** That's good. That's good. Christo.

**Kabak** Shh.

**Angelica** I can't . . . love you . . . tonight.

**Kabak** I know.

**Angelica** It's . . . the time of the month.

**Kabak** Angelica . . .

**Angelica** Soon. (*taking his hand*) Soon.

**Kabak** Yes.

**Angelica** And you'll take me to the summer estate.

**Kabak** Of course.

**Angelica** This time you will. You really will.

**Kabak** I really will.

**Angelica** To be free of St Petersburg for a while. It can be quite stifling, even to one who loves it as I do. Tell me how it was.

**Kabak** (*pause*) Not . . . greatly changed.

**Angelica** (*faintly*) Tell me. Please.

**Kabak** (*playing by ear throughout*) The Tsar was in residence in the early spring. A ball every night for a month. Nights filled with the jangle of sleighs and the snuffling of horses. And then the greenness of leaf and grass over the city. The river *moving* again. (*He checks she's asleep, continues his narrative without a shift of tone or inflexion.*) And the revolution *moving* again. Soviets. An ecstasy of willed achievement. The Whites brought to their knees. The class enemy brought down like quail. The iron brain of Comrade Lenin hammering out the future.

*Angelica screams briefly, troubled in her sleep. Kabak continues gently.*

No place for you, my love. No place at all.

*He leans forward and kisses her forehead. She moans but sleeps on. Kabak stands, looks at the bottle but does not drink, and switches out the light.*

### SCENE TWO

*Lights up. Kabak sits in a chair staring at the landing door. He wears the full Bulgar dress – trousers, high boots, high-necked smock, a thick leather belt clasped round the waist. The bottle and two glasses are on the table by his right hand. Silence for some time. A quiet knock.*

**Kabak** Come in.

*The door opens and* **Gramsci** *enters. He is of dwarf-like stature, though not a dwarf, seriously hunchbacked – his spine was broken as a very young boy – with a* *heavy head, broad brow, thin lips, big lively eyes behind rimless glasses. His black hair is thick and bushy, his skin swarthy. He's 28. In spite of his deformity, he moves with grace, almost supplely. His hands are particularly fine: thin and elegant. His dress is careless, untidy, a little raffish, full of stains and patches: he could almost be a painter preoccupied with some important canvas. When he smokes – which is virtually continuously – he often leaves the cigarette between his lips the whole time, so that his coat and trousers receive the dropping ash. He carries a dark, wide-brimmed, very scruffy, soft felt hat in both hands.*

**Gramsci** Kabak?

**Kabak** Gramsci. Come in, comrade. I'm honoured you came so soon. Will you have a drink? I have only vodka here at the moment, but I could easily . . . send out for something else if you'd prefer it.

**Gramsci** (*interrupting*) Thank you, no. I don't drink. (*He has advanced into the room; he takes out a box of cigarettes, lights one abstractedly, stands staring at the Countess's bed.*) It has less far to go in me than in most, the doctors tell me. (*He stares on.*)

**Kabak** We could move into another room, if you'd rather.

**Gramsci** (*turning*) No, no. I hadn't expected . . .

**Kabak** Perhaps I should explain . . .

**Gramsci** Not at all. Please.

*A small silence. Kabak moves to the table, takes up the second glass.*

**Kabak** We won't disturb her.

**Gramsci** Good.

**Kabak** (*a little uneasy*) Won't you sit down? (*He gestures to the table.*)

**Gramsci** Thank you, yes. (*He takes a chair, back to the bed, eases himself on to it, very tired. He lights another cigarette, looks carefully round the room, does nothing about Kabak's unease.*)

**Kabak** Perhaps I could begin by explaining my presence here.

**Gramsci** (*a slight pause*) To be frank, I'd be happier if you would begin by furnishing some proof of identity. Forgive my caution, but the city is ringed with troops and every third hotel waiter is a police informer. I'm intrigued to know how you managed to penetrate the cordon.

**Kabak** Of course. (*crossing to briefcase on floor by table*) My name is Christo Kabak. Executive Member of the Communist Party of Bulgaria. Here, take this. (*Hands him wallet from briefcase.*) Representative of the Executive Council of the Communist International in Moscow. Please read it. It's all there.

**Gramsci** (*glancing briefly at the opened wallet*) I've no doubt. At least the picture's a likeness. (*a dry grin*) Regrettably I have no Russian.

**Kabak** (*at last*) All right, it could be a forgery.

**Gramsci** Civility did not permit. But the forging of papers of accreditation has grown into a major Italian industry. I've no doubt its workers will soon be demanding union recognition.

**Kabak** Well, then?

**Gramsci** Well, then. (*Pause.*) You came by train.

**Kabak** This morning.

**Gramsci** From Moscow?

**Kabak** No, from Rome.

**Gramsci** From Rome?

**Kabak** I had business there.

   *Pause.*

**Gramsci** Business. You are in fact travelling as a businessman. You arrived at Porta Nuova dressed as a bourgeois, not er – (*Waving hand at Kabak's dress.*)

**Kabak** Yours is a bourgeois country, comrade.

**Gramsci** (*smiling*) *Touché*. But we're working on it.

**Kabak** I saw Chiarini in Rome. He sends his regards.

**Gramsci** Does he?

**Kabak** (*reaching for wallet again*) And this letter.

**Gramsci** (*taking it*) Ah, Italian. Of a kind. (*Reads. Finally*) So you're Il Cuculo.

**Kabak** I believe so, yes.

**Gramsci** (*holding out hand*) Welcome to Turin, comrade.

   *Kabak crosses the room, draws Gramsci to his feet, kisses and hugs him unrestrainedly.*

**Kabak** Thank you, thank you. It's an honour to be with you.

**Gramsci** The honour is ours, Comrade Kabak. The factories will welcome your arrival with open arms.

**Kabak** Well, perhaps we should talk about that. I'm . . . my visit is not exactly . . . planned. What do I mean? It's not . . . official. I have no particular brief to conduct here in Turin . . . at least as far as you and the movement are concerned.

**Gramsci** (*pausing*) I see. That's an exaggeration. I don't see.

**Kabak** My mission in Italy is both delicate and . . . secret. I'm afraid I'm unable to say what it is. Except that I have to see a number of people. (*Pause.*) In Rome three days ago, nearing the end of my mission, I heard from Chiarini of the possibility of confrontation between employers and workers in the north. It . . . seemed right that I should come here and see for myself. That's all.

**Gramsci** You have no messages, nothing?

**Kabak** Nothing.

**Gramsci** And? (*Gesturing towards the bed.*)

**Kabak** From Vienna, two days ago, I think. She is, in a manner of speaking, my wife.

> *Gramsci gets up, walks about a little, goes back to the table, takes out a cigarette, lights it from the stub in his mouth.*

**Gramsci** How long will you stay?

**Kabak** As long as I think I might be useful.

**Gramsci** *You* think?

**Kabak** That's right.

**Gramsci** But you won't address the factories.

**Kabak** I don't know. Perhaps I'll be more useful doing other things.

**Gramsci** Like?

**Kabak** I have gold. I have . . . influence in the Prefect's office.

**Gramsci** D'Avanzo?

**Kabak** D'Avanzo.

**Gramsci** We call him 'the snake'. One day somebody will take a stick to him.

**Kabak** And . . . I have some experience . . . of revolution.

**Gramsci** Of course, comrade. I had not meant to . . .

**Kabak** Of course not. Please. (*A short silence. Kabak sits opposite Gramsci.*) I'd be deeply grateful if you would agree to give me the necessary background. I have seen the troop encampments outside the city. I have heard something about the work-to-rule. And I understand from tomorrow's *Avanti* that workers have taken over factories in Milan. Beyond that, very little.

**Gramsci** (*drawing deep breath*) It's hard to know where to begin. Whatever account I give will inevitably include elements you understand as well as much you don't. If you fall asleep, I'll know I've failed to get the balance right.

**Kabak** Tell me how we've arrived here.

**Gramsci** (*grinning*) You mustn't ask for the whole of Italian history. But . . . our situation is probably not greatly different from Germany's or France's or Austria's. That's to say, we suffered massively from a ruinous war. That's to say, the people suffered. The capitalist simply grew fatter. Prices soar, wages plummet. Inflation bites like a mad bitch, and Pirelli declares a profit of seven million lire – seven million lire – in 1917. And while thousands die of starvation and misery, our capitalist masters are working the rackets. In 1918 we discover a dozen top firms exporting silk by-products to Switzerland, whence they are re-exported to Germany – where else? – and used for munitions. And when Italian soldiers capture German trucks, whose tyres do you imagine they find on them? Pirelli. Only the best. The Socialist Party of Italy opposed

27

the war completely, of course. But we weren't immune to the suffering it created among the mass of our people.

**Kabak** But the Socialist Party of Italy was the first party to affiliate unequivocally to the Communist International.

**Gramsci** It depends what you mean by unequivocally. In Italy, there is always a considerable distance between form and content. We subscribe to the Third International and do nothing to further its aims. Perhaps we require another word.

**Kabak** And now?

**Gramsci** Since the war ended, the Party and the unions have sat on the revolutionary ardour of the organized workers and peasants. I'm sure it's a familiar story. We have pressed for reforms, not transformations. We have struck for better wages, better conditions; but we have led from the rear.

**Kabak** I heard Turin was different.

**Gramsci** From whom?

**Polya** Lenin.

*Pause.*

**Gramsci** You flatter us. Turin is very special. Turin is the industrial city *par excellence.* The proletarian city *par excellence*. The Turinese working class is compact, disciplined, mature, wise, different perhaps from any other in Europe.

**Kabak** And you lead them.

**Gramsci** (*laughing*) No, no. My God, no. I am an intellectual who works alongside them. They have leaders enough from within. Parodi, Boero, Forticchiari. Big men.

**Kabak** Go on. About Turin.

**Gramsci** Turin is the vanguard of the Italian revolution. But there is still much work of education, of preparation. We have suffered more than our share of defeats. We are still learning Lenin's lessons: a slow and painful process.

**Kabak** Do you have time?

**Gramsci** I don't know. We must make time.

*Pause.*

**Kabak** Are you so sure it isn't now?

**Gramsci** No. But I'm not sure it *is*, either. In each factory we have planted together a single seed of revolution: the factory councils. Free from Party direction; free from trade union interference. Not merely here in Turin, but throughout Italy. But they must sprout *together*, or there is no harvest. Merely a series of frail stems waiting for the scythe.

**Kabak** *Could* it be now? After Milan.

**Gramsci** Objectively, I fear not. The Party under Serrati offers no genuine revolutionary leadership. The unions are content to press wage claims. (*Pause.*) Olivetti is Secretary of Confindustria, the Employers' Federation. Do you know what he said last month, here in Turin? 'The future belongs to the organized classes.' What about that? In Italy, only the Marxist fails to recognize that as a self-evident truth.

**Kabak** What happened last April?

**Gramsci** (*surprised a little*) Last April? The strike, you mean.

**Kabak** Chiarini said something about it, before I left Rome. Not a lot. But he said it was important.

**Gramsci** He was right. (*Pause.*) In April we were forced

into a crippling strike in Turin, in defence of the factory
councils. We held out for *eleven days*: imagine that, a
general strike for eleven days. Half a million workers.
Peasants in surrounding areas even provided us with food
and money. After five days we asked the Party and the
General Confederation of Labour to extend the strike; to
make it national. Serrati, our national leader, answered
personally: 'We are not bound to accept battle every time
that the enemy provokes it. Apparently the leaders of the
Turin movement think differently. Let them not try to
burden the broad shoulders of the Party directorate with
the responsibility for a defeat that does not touch it at all.'
With socialists like that, who needs a bourgeoisie? For the
first time in our history, a proletariat undertook a struggle
for the control of production, rather than for economic
advantage. And they have their heads spat upon by their
leaders, who themselves understand history about as
profoundly as chickens understand soup. In Sardinia, we
tell a fable of a badger pursued by a hunter. Badger learns
that the hunter is sick and will die unless he can secure a
physic concocted from Badger's testicles. So, in order to
survive, Badger chews them off himself. And swallows
them. And survives. In a manner of speaking. I won't
labour the point.

**Kabak**  But the employers *are* going to take you on? After
Milan.

**Gramsci**  That's right.

**Kabak**  To smash your strength in the factories?

**Gramsci**  Yes.

**Kabak**  So what will you do?

**Gramsci**  We will fight.

**Kabak**  (*softly*) How?

**Gramsci**  The union has ordered factory occupations if there are lock-outs.

**Kabak**  And after?

**Gramsci**  We will run the factories. We'll rename them 'soviets' and continue production ourselves. That's what the factory councils are for, in the long run.

**Kabak**  And then?

**Gramsci**  I don't know. We shall have to see.

**Kabak**  You sound doubtful.

**Gramsci**  There are only two possible outcomes to the present situation. Revolution. Or the most horrendous reaction. No other possibility exists. If we fail, perhaps we fail utterly.

**Kabak**  (*searching the wallet*) Perhaps there *was one* message. Here. (*opening folded foolscap sheets*) I had it from Chiarini in Rome. (*reading*) To the Central Committee and all members of the Italian Socialist Party. To the Revolutionary Proletariat of Italy. (*reading hurriedly down the page, to himself*) Here. (*now he is translating*) 'The Executive Committee of the Third International knows that there are circumstances in which it is more advantageous for the proletariat to wait, until its own forces are stronger and those of the bourgeoisie weaker. But it should not be forgotten that every hour's respite will be used by the bourgeoisie in their turn to rally their forces, to form a bourgeois white guard.' And . . . listen . . . to this (*scanning page, turning it*) This is it. 'It is clear . . . quite clear . . . that nowhere in the world is the victory of the proletariat possible without suffering and deprivation for the workers. If the revolution does not come quickly in other countries, the Italian proletariat will have to travel the same hard and painful road as the

Russian proletariat. The Italian working class shows astonishing unanimity – it is as one *for* the revolution. The Italian bourgeoisie cannot count on their regular troops, who will at the decisive moment go over to the rebels, and the greater part of the peasantry are *for* the revolution. It is now up to the Italian workers' party'.

**Gramsci** Chiarini?

**Kabak** More. 'We repeat that we are opposed to artificially provoked putsches, we are opposed to actions that have not been thought out in advance. Equally, we are opposed to the proletarian party turning itself into a fire brigade, which puts out the flame of the revolution, when that flame is breaking through every crevice in Capitalist Society. (*placing deliberate emphasis on next three sentences*) In Italy there are at hand all the most important conditions for a genuinely popular, great proletarian revolution. This must be understood. This must be the starting point. This is the contention of the Third International. The Italian comrades must themselves determine the next steps. The decisive struggle is approaching. Italy will be Soviet.' Signed. G. Zinoviev, President; N. Bukharin and N. Lenin, Members, Executive Committee of the Communist International. Moscow. August 27th, 1920.

*Silence.*

It seems Comrade Lenin has already heard the story of the badger with no balls.

**Gramsci** It's a very old story.

*Telephone rings.*

**Kabak** Excuse me. (*lifts receiver*) Thank you. Ask him to wait. (*phone down*) D'Avanzo.

**Gramsci** (*rising*) I'll go.

**Kabak**  No, please. Let him wait.

**Gramsci**  No, I must. Talking tires me shamefully. (*Fiddles for pocket watch, inspects the time closely, brow furrowed.*) Tomorrow I might be helping to run Fiat Centre Plant. Tonight I should sleep. Good night.

**Kabak**  You'll . . . keep me informed.

*Gramsci turns at the door, looks steadily at Kabak.*

**Gramsci**  Of course. Comrade. (*smiling*) So long as you promise me the same. You know you can get me through the Chamber of Labour. And I know you're here. (*Turns to leave. Turns back, hand on open door.*) Watch out for D'Avanzo. He's most dangerous when he rattles.

*Gramsci leaves. Kabak stretches, aware of his own fatigue. He shrugs out of his tunic and stands for a moment, fingering a deep scar across his chest. Finally he takes a bathrobe from his bag and slips it on. At the table he drains the bottle of vodka, crosses to phone, picks it up.*

**Kabak**  Would you send the Cavaliere up now, please. Thank you.

*Kabak replaces phone, crosses to bed, stares down at Angelica, who stirs fitfully. **D'Avanzo** knocks and enters. Kabak turns quickly to face him.*

**D'Avanzo**  Mr Kabak? I'm awfully sorry, I didn't . . .

**Kabak**  Please. Do come in. It's good of you to call at such an hour. Won't you have a seat? (*gesturing to armchair*) Let me get you a drink.

**D'Avanzo**  (*sitting down*) Thank you. Anything will do. (*Mops neck with handkerchief.*) Did you ever know such a summer? Do you wonder the world's at sixes and sevens, in heat like this.

**Kabak** (*handing half-filled glass*) Vodka. Be careful. It's very deceptive.

**D'Avanzo** Thank you. Like most things Russian, I fancy. (*Looks around room.*) I couldn't help noticing you'd already been busy. (*looking finally at Kabak, who stares back impassively*) The dwarf. I saw him leaving. He's a dangerous man, that one. Pity. A brilliant brain.

**Kabak** (*holding glass up*) *Saluti!*

**D'Avanzo** *Saluti!*

*They drink.*

Mmm. That's good. That's very good.

*They stare at each other in silence. Finally.*

Well, Mr Kabak, could we get down to business. I take it you received your authorization permits in Rome.

**Kabak** I did, yes.

**D'Avanzo** And you had no difficulty with the troops outside the city.

**Kabak** None at all.

**D'Avanzo** Excellent. (*Pause.*) Did . . . Chiarini mention . . . the price?

*Kabak nods briefly.*

That's good. I find I haggle rather poorly. My dignity is a serious obstacle.

**Kabak** (*ironically*) I can imagine.

**D'Avanzo** (*still mildly, unoffended*) You must not think dignity is the unique preserve of the poor or the professional revolutionary, Mr Kabak.

**Kabak** (*drily*) I'll try not to. What else can you do for me?

**D'Avanzo** You have only to ask. If it is within my power, I will do it. For a price.

**Kabak** Good. I take it you have no especial objection to being paid in gold, Cavaliere?

**D'Avanzo** (*very seriously*) None at all, Mr Kabak.

*Kabak gets up and paces the room. Turns.*

**Kabak** How long before they catch you?

**D'Avanzo** Catch me? At what?

**Kabak** This. Corruption. Treason.

**D'Avanzo** My dear Kabak, this is Italy. I doubt if there's a civil servant in the country who isn't taking something home each week for services rendered. I just happen to have given more time and thought to the matter than most of my colleagues. That's why I'm here now.

**Kabak** Go on.

**D'Avanzo** Italy will have its revolution. In an uncertain world, that is one certainty I am prepared to stake my future life and prosperity on. Despite which, most of my state functionary colleagues continue to support the bourgeois cause, with a kind of lemming blindness that would be quite touching if it weren't so appallingly pathetic. Since the end of the war I have made it abundantly clear, in a thousand practical ways, that I will be available for duty *the morning after* the revolution takes place. (*Pause. Drinks.*) I'm not a revolutionary, Mr Kabak. I'm a realist. You will have need of us the morning after.

**Kabak** And the Prefect?

**D'Avanzo** Taddei? Pure as snow. Impeccable, innocent, honest, loyal, boring. Show him a brothel and he'd think it

35

was a shrine to the Virgin Mary. He's no problem.

**Kabak** (*decisive*) All right. Answer me this. Could the factory occupations in Milan trigger off a revolution throughout the country? And if so, which person or group is likely to direct it?

**D'Avanzo** (*holding glass out*) Could I have another?

**Kabak** (*taking glass, filling it*) Certainly.

**D'Avanzo** Thank you. It's funny, I thought you'd have heard from Gramsci.

**Kabak** Heard what?

**D'Avanzo** The owners have declared lock-outs in almost every major town in Italy. Here in Piedmont alone, apart from Turin, over a dozen large towns are affected. Alessándria, Asti, Novara, Vercelli, Acqui, Arquata Scrivia, Novi Lígure, Casale, Tortona, Callarate. In Lonbardy, besides Milan, of course, there's Bergamo, Cremona, Crema, Pavia, Legnano, Como, Lecco, Varese, Brescia. In Veneto there's Verona, Udine, Padua, Venezia, Treviso, Castelfranco Veneto, Battáglia. Do you want more? There's plenty yet. In Emilia: Bologna, Modena, Ferrara, Reggio, Piacenza. In Tuscany: Firenze, Pisa, Siena, Pontedera, Piombino, Portoferráio, Livorno, Arezzo, Pistoia, Grosseto, San Giovanni Valdarno, Castelfiorentino, Lucca. In Marche: Ancona. In Umbria: Terni and Perugia. In Campania: Napoli, San Giovanni, Castellammare, Torre Annunciata. In Sicily: Palermo. (*Pause.*) I imagined he'd have told you.

    *Long silence.*

**Kabak** (*very quietly*) Go on.

**D'Avanzo** Two things. Turin will occupy the factories tomorrow morning. Within two days there will not be an engineering factory in Italy that is not in the hands of the workers.

**Kabak** And?

*Long pause.*

**D'Avanzo** The government has at present no intention of using troops to eject the workers and repossess the factories on behalf of the owners. Our illustrious prime minister is keen to appear impartial in the matter. Besides which, he has a pathetically inadequate military force; and he can't be at all certain that what he does have won't defect to the side of the workers if matters get out of hand. (*Long pause.*) Does that answer your question?

**Kabak** Not quite. You suggest that the objective conditions for revolution might well exist. But revolutions must be led. The question still is: by whom?

**D'Avanzo** I'm not a politician, Mr Kabak, I'm a poor state bureaucrat trying to survive in rather difficult times. If I were a gambling man, I should put my money on the Socialist Party Directorate being unable any longer to damp down the revolutionary ardour of the glorious Italian proletariat. Serrati will be a revolutionary hero in spite of himself, I shouldn't wonder.

**Kabak** What about Gramsci?

**D'Avanzo** Strong enough in Turin, I understand, but without a power base nationally. I doubt it, quite honestly. For one thing, he's uncommonly modest, for one so arrogant in other ways. Personally diffident, if you know what I mean.

*Kabak goes to the table, begins scribbling rapidly on a piece of paper. Finished, he folds it and hands it to D'Avanzo, who opens it and looks at it with furrowed brow.*

37

**Kabak** (*while he now takes small wallets from case*) It won't make too much sense to you unless you read Russian. I want you to send it to Moscow – I've put the address in Italian at the bottom, can you see it? Here. (*handing two hand-sized pouches over*) You'll find twice the sum you agreed with Chiarini. And there is more.

**D'Avanzo** (*taking the pouches*) This could prove extremely dangerous, Mr Kabak.

**Kabak** (*hard but quiet*) But you'll do it none the less.

**D'Avanzo** (*getting up*) I shall do my best.

**Kabak** And your best will be good enough. That telegram must reach Moscow by the end of the week.

**D'Avanzo** I shall do everything in my power to see that it does.

**Kabak** (*tossing another small pouch at him*) Do that. Good night, Cavaliere.

**D'Avanzo** (*stiffening formally*) Good night, Mr Kabak.

> *D'Avanzo leaves. Kabak drains his glass slowly, sways just a little with fatigue and the effects of the alcohol, finally walks to the bell and rings it, quite loudly. He stands by the table until Polya arrives, struggling into her dressing gown.*

**Polya** (*tired*) Yes.

**Kabak** (*taking bathrobe off, again scratching scar*) Have you got any goose grease?

**Polya** Any what?

**Kabak** Goose grease. Goose grease.

**Polya** Goose grease? Where would I get goose grease from? What would I be doing with goose grease anyway?

**Kabak** (*sharply*) All right. You haven't got any goose grease.

**Polya** (*a bit sullen*) What is it for?

**Kabak** I'm stiffening up. Here and here. (*pointing to bullet wound across pectorals and another in shoulder. Grinning*) I suppose it means it's going to rain.

*She still stares on.*

I wanted you to rub it on me. Massage. Never mind. Go to bed.

**Polya** There's some oil.

**Kabak** What kind of oil?

**Polya** Oil. Olive oil, I think.

**Kabak** Would that do?

**Polya** I don't know. Can't imagine it being any worse than goose grease.

**Kabak** All right. Fetch it.

*She goes. He takes his boots and socks off, stands naked save for trousers. He sits down in the chair facing out and rests head on arms on the table. Polya returns with the bottle.*

**Polya** It's olive oil. You'll smell like a waiter when I've finished.

**Kabak** All right. Just rub it in.

*She starts the massage.*

**Polya** (*examining the scar on his shoulder*) Uushh! Just look at that. That's really ugly. Uushh! Was it a bullet?

**Kabak** Two bullets. Can you see, lower down?

*She traces down with her finger.*

That's it. Came out under the arm here. (*Showing her.*)

**Polya** I can't imagine why you do it.

**Kabak** I don't suppose you can. Any more than I can understand why you consent to being a personal maid all your life.

**Polya** (*laughing*) Well, nobody's shot at me yet.

**Kabak** You have your scars, Polya. (*Leans back, so that she can begin to massage the front of his neck and down across his pectorals. He's now looking up at her.*)

**Polya** Just look at that. I don't know how you survived, I don't really.

**Kabak** Because I wanted to, Polya. Needed to.

**Polya** Well, an inch to the left and all the wanting in the world wouldn't have saved you. (*She rubs on, gradually becoming aware of his steady stare.*)

**Kabak** (*finally, low voice*) Polya.

*Polya ignores him, continues the massage.*

Polya.

**Polya** What?

**Kabak** Polya.

**Polya** Please, just, please let me just . . . do this and go back to bed.

**Kabak** (*stretching arms up and back to clasp her upper arms*) Polya, Polya.

**Polya** (*she freezes*) Please don't. Please. Please don't.

*Kabak gets up quickly, tries to take Polya in his arms.*

*She resists, but very unsurely, aware of her position as
servant.*

Please don't. Please. Please don't, sir.

**Kabak** Polya, listen. Polya. Polya, listen.

*He quietens her with the palm of a hand. She is in some
disarray. Her eyes glare above the hand.*

Listen. I don't want to force anything upon you. I . . . I
want to sleep with you. I'm lonely. I want to love
somebody. I want . . . to love somebody. That's all. (*He
removes his hand gently. She still stares at him like a small,
frightened night animal.*) That's all. That's all.

**Polya** (*shaking her head*) No. No I couldn't. I couldn't. No
I couldn't. I love my mistress and I couldn't do that to her.
No. I couldn't.

**Kabak** Then don't. It's all right. (*Pause.*) Look, she's going
to die. Right? It doesn't matter what you do, she's going to
die. *Think* what that means to you. Hunh? Just think of
that. Go on.

**Polya** I couldn't. I couldn't. I don't care. She trusts me and
I love her.

*They stare at each other for a long moment. Then.*

**Angelica** (*not moving, but clearly awake*) Polya.

**Polya** (*startled*) Madame?

**Angelica** Do it.

**Polya** Madame?

**Angelica** Do it, Polya. Do what Mr Kabak asks.

*Silence again. Kabak has frozen, his back to the bed.
Slowly Polya begins to unbutton her dressing gown,
takes it off, unbuttons her nightdress, removes it. She*

*stands naked before Kabak, her eyes cast down, her
body slightly crouched. He looks at her very carefully,
then picks up his bag and leaves through the adjoining
door. Polya stands staring ahead of her at the bed.
Angelica makes no move.*

## SCENE THREE

*Stage completely black. Bring up factory sounds,
machinery. Men's voices, in meeting. Fade up, centre, and
take out again, the following: pictures of workers
defending factory gates; preparing food; tramway strike;
railway strike at Mantua; communist group at Lancia
(Turin) during occupations; Red Guards on factory roof,
armed with rifles, pistols, machine guns (all available
through Centro Gobetti, 6 Via Fabbro, Turin). As this last
image appears, the men begin singing 'Bandiera Rossa',
the mood jubilant yet disciplined. The image remains
throughout the 'factory meeting' that follows, but is taken
out for the Gramsci–Kabak exchanges.*

*Gramsci walks hesitantly forward as the singing ends.
There is cheering, whistling, jocularity as the crowd
catches sight of him. (The interjections from the men may
be done on tape, or by actors in the auditorium.) As
Gramsci reaches a sort of lectern at the front, the side
walls of the auditorium are gradually lit to reveal blow-up
photographs of this actual meeting (available at Centro
Gobetti). The theatre is now the factory; the audience, the
workers.*

**Gramsci** Comrades. (*Noise begins to die down gradually.*)
Comrade workers, representatives of the factory councils
of Fiat Centre, Fiat Diatto, Fiat Brevetti, Scat, Acciaien
Fiat, Lancia, Itala, Lingotto Fiat, Industrie Metallurgiche,
representatives of the Turin Chamber of Labour and of the

Turin section of the Socialist Party of Italy. Perhaps I should begin by thanking the owners for the use of the hall.

*Laughter.*

I mean it, comrades. I mean you. You are the owners now. And you must never forget it. Sunday, September 5th, 1920. Red Sunday. Our first. And we choose to celebrate it . . . by working, first of all; and then, by discussing, sensibly, seriously, above all honestly, what we have done and what is left to do. That's as it should be. You are right to feel happy. You are right to feel exhilarated. But it would be a sort of treason, comrades, to let that euphoria blind us to the gravity of our position or to the enormity of the task that confronts us.

**Voice** Cheer up, Nino, it might never happen.

*Laughter.*

**Gramsci** (*drily*) Precisely, comrade. It might never happen. It's that that makes me sad.

**Voice** It will, Nino, it will.

*Great cheer.*

**Gramsci** (*as they subside*) What we have done. We asked for better wages and conditions. They said it wasn't possible. We applied a work-to-rule. They applied a lock-out. We occupied. The industrial strength of Turin, of all Italy, is in the hands of the Italian working class. Production continues. Despite difficulties of materials supply, transportation, capital, markets for finished products, and the defection of technical support, we continue to produce. Our first great lesson, comrades: we are learning how to become producers, active, vital, controlling, instead of mere consumers, passive, inert, controlled. You will have heard of peasant uprisings, in

43

Sicily, in Lucania, in support of our cause. Peasants supporting workers, just think of that, comrades! It could almost be Russia!

*Laughter, cheers. Somebody begins singing The Internationale, others join in.*

The state, meanwhile, stands by. The Old Fox hasn't even bothered to come back off his summer holiday. He's still at Bardonecchio, sunning himself.

*Laughter.*

The army stands by. We wait. Italy waits. Europe waits.

*Somebody sings 'Why are we waiting'; others join in, amid laughter and cheers.*

Meanwhile, we make a few discoveries. In the director's safe at Fiat Centre, for example, mountains of anti-Russian propaganda, a blacklist of militant workers, and details of an espionage service against the labour movement that would make the work of the carabinieri seem gentle horseplay between young lads of the same village. On the blacklist, every factory council member, almost without exception. Though the exceptions are interesting. As well as others: in particular, Matteo Dotta and Domenico Arduina, who died at the hands of the fascists in this year's May Day parade. At last, at last we can get a clear and undistorted picture of our employers, not as individuals, not as people with particular skills and functions, not as loose arrangements of reciprocal needs and interests, but *nakedly, as a class*, organized against us, an army in a war, capable of any heroism or treachery in the defence of their motherland. And we can see, too, that this motherland is not Italy, that fat-headed, sore-arsed sow: the motherland is Capital, sleek, dark-eyed, bright, warm, passionate Capital. Who wouldn't defend her, the young, delicious whore! Well, perhaps one or two of us.

*Laughter.*

**Voice** She's got the pox anyway, Nino.

*Laughter.*

**Gramsci** Well, that's what we've done. We've taken power into our own hands. And we have shown that workers' control is a reality. The question that now concretely confronts us is the question Lenin posed many years ago: simply, what is to be done? Between *here* and *there*, the whole of our history trembles. Our leaders are in little doubt. Even now, Buozzi and D'Arragona are in a huddle with the employers, 'seeking solutions'. But in this new situation, where remote trade union leaders no longer direct, where the moral position of the worker assumes a different form and value, it is *you*, comrades, who will decide. And if I say, honestly and clearly, what *I* think should happen, I do so in the knowledge that you will listen – (*twinkling*) with no more respect than I deserve of you – and then make up your own minds, on the evidence confronting you. (*Pause.*) There are many possible lines of march. But make no mistake, comrades: if you want revolution, you must take it for yourselves. It will not be handed to you, on a plate. (*consulting watch*) I have spoken too long already.

*A few shouts of 'Aye', quickly followed by a thunder of No's.*

They may be right, comrades. Intellectuals always imagine words win wars. And they don't. Let me finish with three slogans, the simple signposts of *my* line of march. One: create urban soviets. Two: prepare for insurrection. Three: forge links with the peasants. If we are to win, we must break out of the factories, wage war on the state as well as the employer. If we are to win, we must arm ourselves for a prolonged *offensive*. Merely defending the factories against attack is not, in itself, an insurrectional act. And if we are to win, we must eat, and that means we must involve the peasants in our struggle.

*Cheering, applause.*

One last word. You are my comrades, in the deepest sense that history allows for that word. You are the best disciplined, most mature working class in Europe, in the world. Soon you will be invited, by your enemies, I'm afraid to say, to put up or shut up. No other city proletariat will have the experience or the deep courage to act as insurrectional vanguard. All I want to say is: decide for yourselves. It is no cowardice to say no, if by saying it you survive to fight more fruitfully another day. It is no heroism to say yes, to be mown down by overwhelming force of opposing arms, while your party and your unions stand by with folded arms and watch you destroyed. Find your courage where it is. Beware rhetoric! Even mine!

*He steps down. Cheering. Applause. Singing* 'Bandiera Rossa', *deep and melodic. Fade to black.*

### SCENE FOUR

*Stage in complete darkness. Kabak snaps on light on table. Gramsci walks into the light, throws his hat on to the table and sits down in the chair opposite Kabak. A cigarette hangs from his lips. He is tired but wide awake. Kabak has been drinking but isn't drunk.*

**Gramsci** Did Palmi ring?

**Kabak** Nobody rang.

**Gramsci** He said he'd ring as soon as the meetings broke up.

**Kabak** Relax. It's barely nine. In any case, you know what will happen. Togliatti will tell you nothing you don't know already. D'Arragona will urge moderation. Bordiga will urge intransigence. Everyone else will urge a compromise. When reformist leaders talk to capitalist employers, what else can happen?

*Silence. Gramsci lights another cigarette from the stub of his current one. Kabak tops up.*

**Gramsci** Any word from Moscow?

*Kabak shakes his head. Another silence.*

You place extraordinary faith in D'Avanzo.

**Kabak** Faith? (*a short bark of a laugh*) I place faith, extraordinary or otherwise, in nobody. Believe me, Nino. It is not a question of faith. It's just the nature of the occupation I'm embarked on. Help I must have. Whether I win it or buy it isn't important. But I cannot choose whether I have it or not.

**Gramsci** Perhaps it's Moscow.

**Kabak** (*finally*) Perhaps it is.

*Pause.*

**Gramsci** Have you spoken to D'Avanzo?

**Kabak** Just the once. Seven, eight days ago. Just after I met . . .

**Gramsci** Yes, I remember.

**Kabak** Not a word since. Not a peep. He might be just a little out of his depth, the way things have blown up.

**Gramsci** Your gold could keep him afloat for a while.

**Kabak** (*gravely*) My gold will take him to the bottom.

*The phone rings shrilly. Kabak unhooks it.*

Yes. Just a moment. For you.

*Kabak hands receiver to Gramsci.*

**Gramsci** Hello. Hello, Palmi. (*silence as he listens*) Go on. (*silence again*) D'Arragona did? Ahunh. And what did you say? Yes, surely, surely. Look, Palmi, I'm with our friend. Can I ring you back? Just a moment. (*Fishes pencil and pad from pocket.*) Go ahead. 792. Got it. Thanks, Palmi. Half an hour at the most. All right. (*He hangs up*). The meeting continues. Recessed for an hour.

**Kabak** And?

*Pause.*

**Gramsci** The Directors of the General Confederation of Labour want to know whether the Turin section will be prepared to lead an insurrection.

*Silence. Kabak pours another drink, takes a long swig.*

**Kabak** What hangs on the answer?

**Gramsci** Perhaps nothing. Perhaps everything. They don't say. They don't commit themselves at this stage to any course of action. They simply want to know if we are prepared to present them with one more possibility, before they make up their minds.

**Kabak** (*mildly, as though remarking on the weather*) Then you say yes.

**Gramsci** (*quietly*) No. We say no.

**Kabak** (*low*) You cannot say no. If there is no insurrection, there is no revolution.

**Gramsci** And if we lead the insurrection and there is still no revolution, there is no longer a working class in Turin.

**Kabak** Jesus God, man, this is warfare you're talking about. Of course there are dangers. Somebody, sometime, must be moved up to the front. Surely you can see it!

**Gramsci** But is it now? And is it us?

**Kabak** (*searching for words and patience*) Look . . . Holy Christ . . . look, erm, isn't it this way? The Party and the unions, like the state and the employers, want peace. Revolution is not on the agenda. The Party and the unions are currently meeting in Milan to see how negotiations with the employers might be reopened. That's right isn't it? All right. Now, only one thing stands in their way. The working class of Italy. *They* don't want peace. Perhaps they don't know yet what they do want. But as yet it isn't peace. The Confederation knows it. The Party knows it. You know it. The workers are forcing their national leaders into increasingly more radical postures. At length, those miserable men are forced to consider the possibility of an insurrectionary thrust. Not surprisingly, they look in your direction. Now, Nino . . . if you say no, they have called you out, make no mistake, comrade, they have called you out and from now on in we'll have only rhetoric to fall back on, because the real action will be OVER. You'd better be oh so clear about that, comrade, because that's the way it will be. Now I'm telling you. (*He is angry, trembling a little. He takes a drink, rather hastily, spills a bit on his shirt front, begins dragging at it with the palms of his hands.*)

**Gramsci** (*very quiet*) Have you finished?

**Kabak** (*not looking, still wiping his front*) I've finished.

**Gramsci** It's possible you're right . . .

**Kabak** (*interrupting; fierce*) I *am* right.

**Gramsci** It's just possible we're both right. That's to say, both wrong as well. Neither yes nor no, I mean. From where we are, there is no answer to make that will advance the cause of a communist revolution.

**Kabak** Metaphysics, Nino. They don't become you.

**Gramsci** You know what happened last April. We led the Italian proletariat, the Party and the unions in a general strike. Unfortunately, though not by accident, they did not follow. So we were isolated, our supply lines cut, our carefully nurtured alliance with the Piedmont peasants smashed. We crawled back to work on our hands and knees. The compact between capital and labour couldn't have been more complete. Bosses, union and Party leaders conspired to fill our mouths with soil. Now, the same people are inviting us to put ourselves at total risk, in all-out confrontation, without any commitment on their own part to support us.

**Kabak** It is a risk you must take. It's September now.

**Gramsci** We have risked too much already. I will not allow that class to be wiped out. I could not survive it.

**Kabak** No sentimentalisms, please. You must not confuse revolutionary duty with bourgeois conscience.

**Gramsci** Nor shall I, comrade.

**Kabak** You cannot say you love your working class too much to put them at risk, and then imagine you're saying something profoundly revolutionary.

**Gramsci** That *isn't* what I'm saying. I am saying that they are too important to the world revolutionary movement to squander on a dubious adventure that could well have been concocted precisely to produce their annihilation.

**Kabak** And you . . . could not survive it? Do you mean . . . you love them?

**Gramsci** Yes I do. That's exactly what I mean.

**Kabak** I see.

**Gramsci** What?

**Kabak** You cannot *love* an army, comrade. An army is a machine. This one makes revolutions. If it breaks down, you get another one. Love has nothing to do with it.

*Gramsci is overwhelmed by this. He gets up, walks away from the table, comes back to it, lights another cigarette.*

**Gramsci** (*finally*) Oh, comrade. Oh, comrade. Listen. (*very quiet, very gentle*) There is nothing more relevant than love. There is nothing in the world more relevant than love. When I was a child – inside this . . . body – I imagined I could never be loved. For many years, the thought that I could be loved seemed an absolute, almost fatal, impossibility. So perhaps I came to the masses with the same mechanical view of them, and my own relation to them, as you have just propounded. Use them. Tool them up. Keep them greased. Discard when they wear out. But then I thought, how can a man bind himself to the masses, if he has never loved anyone himself, not even his mother or his father. I thought, how can a man love a collectivity, when he has not profoundly loved single human creatures. And it was then I began to see masses as people and it was only then that I began to love them, in their particular, detailed, local, individual character. You would be wrong to see this . . . love . . . as the product of petit-bourgeois idealism. It is the correct, the only true dialectical relationship between leaders and led, vanguard and masses, that can ensure the political health of the new order the revolution seeks to create. Treat masses as expendable, as fodder, *during* the revolution, you will always treat them thus. (*Pause.*) I'll tell you this, Comrade

Kabak, if you see masses that way, there can be no revolution worth the blood it spills. (*Long silence. Gramsci picks up the phone.*) Yes. Milan. 792. Thank you. (*He holds the receiver in his hand, fishes for a cigarette and lights it with the other.*)

**Kabak** You are wrong, Comrade Gramsci.

**Gramsci** I think not, Comrade Kabak. (*to phone*) Hello. Hello, Palmi. Yes. (*Long pause. He listens gravely for some moments.*) No, say what we agreed. 'We in Turin cannot assume the responsibility of an armed struggle without assurance that the rest of Italy would also fight, without assurance that the Confederation and the Party, in their usual way, would not let all the military forces of the state concentrate on Turin as in April.' Do you have it? Good. That's fine, Palmi. Good luck comrade. (*Puts phone down.*)

**Kabak** (*finally*) So?

**Gramsci** (*very tired now*) I don't know. Palmi says he smells a deal. D'Arragona and the Party are pressing for a referendum.

**Kabak** Of whom?

**Gramsci** The General Confederation of Labour.

**Kabak** On what issues?

**Gramsci** Basically, to stay here or move to there.

**Kabak** (*bitter*) This isn't a revolution, it's a bloody Italian farce. Jesus God, revolution by referendum. You could almost laugh. (*Takes another drink.*) Well, comrades, what do you think, eh? Shall we have a revolution, or shall we just play silly buggers for a bit and see what happens? Now it's up to you, so take your time, don't hurry it now.

*There is a high shriek from the bed, a babble of words.*
*Kabak strides swiftly over, clicks on the bed light. He*
*begins to swab Angelica's face with a wet cloth from the*
*bed table.*

**Angelica** It's here. Underneath. Under the skin. It's not a part of me. It's foreign. I can feel it moving. Underneath. In the hands. In the legs.

**Kabak** Hey, hey, hey, hey, hey, hey, hey, hey. (*He mops her brow with the cloth.*)

**Angelica** Russia *is* in Europe. You'll have to tell them. They don't appear to know. Underneath. Not a part. But *there* all the same.

**Kabak** Yes love. Now sleep. Come on. Sleep. (*He soothes her.*)

**Angelica** I saw a soldier. He was crawling in the snow and . . . he had something . . . in his hand. And . . . when the carriage . . . got closer. . . I saw it was his . . . boot. As we passed him, he raised the boot in the air. And I saw it still had . . . his foot in it. We . . . drove on . . . and . . . I didn't look back.

**Kabak** Sh, sh, sh. Hey, hey, hey. You must sleep, love. Try to sleep. Try to sleep.

**Angelica** Yes. Yes. (*Drowsing.*)

**Kabak** There . . . now. There . . . now.

**Angelica** (*eyes closed; very rational voice*) Why do you do it, Christo?

**Kabak** Do what, love?

**Angelica** Why do you kill? And maim?

**Kabak** Please. Sleep.

**Angelica** Tell me.

**Kabak** It would take too long.

**Angelica** Longer . . . than there is, you mean.

**Kabak** Yes. For both of us.

**Angelica** Say it, Christo.

**Kabak** Yes, I do.

**Angelica** (*low, fierce*) *Say* it.

**Kabak** I love you. I love you.

**Angelica** Why is it always so hard?

**Kabak** It isn't. It's just . . . so pointless.

*She sleeps suddenly, the cocaine reasserting. Kabak stands up, waits a moment longer, clicks off the light, returns to the table.*

**Gramsci** I think I should leave you.

**Kabak** (*a lot of emotion just held under*) She's dying. She has a cancer in her womb. A lonely fruit for a womb. We occupied the family estate in Kiev. 1918. Her husband fled, she . . . remained. We've been . . . (*He stops suddenly, turns his back on Gramsci, swivelling in the chair.*)

**Gramsci** Is there anything you need?

*Kabak doesn't answer. He sits staring into the darkness. Gramsci rises.*

I'll say good night. (*Pause.*) Comrade.

*He leaves. Kabak turns to the light. He weeps quietly and hopelessly. Finally he clicks off the light.*

# Act Two

## SCENE ONE

*Project factory slides. 'Bandiera Rossa', now muted, over. At the end, very unexpectedly, the distant thud of marching boots, and a slide of fascist guards holding Roman daggers aloft (Moro, Milan). This holds the stage, unexplained, for half a minute, then fades. Lights up on hotel bedroom. Night. Kabak is at the telephone. The bed is empty.*

**Kabak** (*who's been holding*) I see. Do you know where he is? Yes, I know he's a busy man but . . . yes, I know that too. Milan? With Taddei? But you're not sure. Ahunh. Well, thank you. (*Depresses receiver rest several times.*) Hello. Hello. (*Pause.*) Yes, do you happen to know the Prefect Taddei's number? That's right, the Prefect. All right, I'll wait.

*He takes out a large black revolver from the table drawer, breaks it, takes aim at the connecting door through which Polya arrives suddenly, carrying the sleeping Angelica in her arms. She stops in the doorway. Kabak lowers the revolver slowly, replaces it in the drawer.*

**Polya** Is it safe?

**Kabak** (*to phone*) Good. Try it please. Now. I'll wait.

*Polya carries the Countess to the bed, places her in it, covers her solicitously. She does it with stolid power, not unlike a peasant carrying a calf.*

**Polya** She's clean.

**Kabak** But dying.

**Polya** She'll die clean.

**Kabak** Good.

**Polya** It's not bad.

*They look at each other hard. Finally Polya breaks the gaze and leaves.*

**Kabak** (*to phone*) Hello. Good evening. I wonder if you could tell me whether the Cavaliere D'Avanzo is there at the moment. (*Listens briefly.*) Yes. My name is Kabak. I'm here on business and . . . there is a matter I have to settle with the Cavaliere. Thank you.

*He holds receiver away again, holding. He looks casually at the bed. Angelica lies stone white in it. She could be dead already. Polya comes back in .*

**Polya** I've made coffee. Do you want some?

*Kabak nods. Polya withdraws.*

**Kabak** (*to phone*) Yes. (*listens*) I see. Perhaps in Milan? Well, thank you anyway. No, no message. Goodbye.

*Kabak puts phone down, stands, stretches, walks round room, looks out of window. Polya carries tray in, places it on the table, pours coffee.*

**Polya** Sugar?

**Kabak** No.

**Polya** (*turning*) Anything else?

**Kabak** Polya. Stay a minute.

*She stands, impassive.*

Sit down. Please.

*Polya sits stonily on one of the hard chairs by the table.
Kabak moves from the window towards the centre of
the room.*

(*uncertain*) I'm . . . not very sure . . . how long I'll be able
to remain in Italy.

*Polya stares ahead, totally unresponsive.*

I've lost contact with Moscow. The man who was to have
helped me appears to be more interested in helping
himself. And my comrade in Rome has gone to ground. In
any case, it looks as though things're through here . . .
(*Silence. Polya doesn't reply.*) There is the question . . . of
the Countess. (*Another silence.*) I can't take her with me.

**Polya** (*very quiet and tight*) Can't you?

**Kabak** You know I can't. I never did . . . not even when
she was . . . well.

**Polya** That was when she was well.

**Kabak** (*very patient*) Polya, listen to me. Your mistress
will die. In a week. In a month. She *will* die.

**Polya** And you should be with her.

**Kabak** Perhaps. But I can't stay here. And she should die
in a bed, not a couchette between nowhere and nowhere.

**Polya** It would not be nowhere if you were there. (*Silence.*)
What do you want me to do?

**Kabak** Just stay. Be with her.

**Polya** You insult me to imagine I would do otherwise.

*Knocking at door.*

**Kabak** I'm sorry, thank you.

*Polya crosses to the door, opens it. Libertini enters,*

57

*carrying a small package. Polya closes the door.*

**Polya** Will that be all, sir?

**Kabak** Thank you, yes.

*Polya leaves by the connecting door.*

**Libertini** (*curious, looking round*) Good evening, Mr Kabak. A fine evening. I think things are at last looking up for us all, in Turin.

**Kabak** I'm glad you think so, Mr Libertini.

*They look at each other for a moment. Libertini remembers the package.*

**Libertini** Ah, This package arrived by special messenger from Berlin. From . . . I happened to notice the sender's name here . . . a Signor Chiarini.

**Kabak** (*taking it*) Thank you. It's good of you to bring it yourself.

**Libertini** Not at all. A pleasure.

*Silence again.*

**Kabak** Was there something else?

**Libertini** No. No, no. I . . . er . . . I simply wanted to know how you were faring in our city. I seem to have seen very little of you, since you came.

**Kabak** I'm faring very well. Thank you.

**Libertini** Well. I won't disturb you any further then.

**Kabak** Thank you.

**Libertini** I take it he's a . . . business associate of some sort.

**Kabak** What?

**Libertini** (*pointing to the package in Kabak's hand*)
Chiarini. I take it he's a business . . .

**Kabak** Yes.

**Libertini** It really is amazing, you know. All this conflict
and turmoil and destruction, and anarchy, and yet
somehow, we manage. We manage to keep the wheels
oiled, the pumps primed. Somehow we manage. We will
not be stopped, will we, Mr Kabak?

**Kabak** (*a tired irony somewhere*) We will not, Mr
Libertini.

**Libertini** At the office of the Prefect only yesterday,

*Kabak looks at him sharply, momentarily startled.*
*Libertini rambles on, seemingly unaware.*

waiting for my licence to be renewed, they were laying 5 to
1 on a full return to work by the end of the month. I
suppose you had heard that the results of the referendum
are due very soon.

**Kabak** Yes, I had.

**Libertini** I think we have a victory on our hands, Mr
Kabak.

**Kabak** Very likely. (*Long pause. Neutral, final*) Well.

**Libertini** (*fiddling in waistcoat pocket*) Ah. While I
remember. There is the matter of the . . . telephone. (*Finds
paper; takes it out; studies it.*) I'm not sure how you would
care . . . to pay. I have had a list of . . . outgoing calls
drawn up by reception. Would you care to check it? It's
simply . . .

*Kabak stretches a slow hand for it, looks hard at*
*Libertini as he takes the paper back, finally looks down*
*at it, studies it for a long time. Libertini stands very still,*

*tense; a tiny exultancy is working to get out, but his control is supreme.*

**Kabak** (*finally*) Yes. You appear to have it all there. Would you prefer I paid you now?

**Libertini** As you wish, Mr Kabak. Entirely as you wish.

*Kabak takes out a wallet, riffles 1000-lire notes, looks at Libertini, who smiles rather sweetly at him.*

**Kabak** I imagine . . . ten thousand lire might cover it?

**Libertini** Amply, Mr Kabak.

*Kabak hands him the notes. Libertini smiles, counts them, places them gravely in his own wallet, holds out his hand once more. Kabak hesitates.*

The list, Mr Kabak.

*It registers. Kabak hands it to him.*

I shall need it for the accounts. Well, that's . . . er . . . that's very good. I've enjoyed our little chat. I always find foreign businessmen. . . . curiously invigorating. You will let me know if there's anything more I can do for you.

**Kabak** There is one thing.

*Libertini turns back.*

It's possible I shall be called away rather suddenly in the next few days.

**Libertini** Ah. I'm sorry to hear it.

**Kabak** However, I should like to rent the rooms for, say, another month. Long enough for . . . my wife to recover her health.

**Libertini** Delighted to accommodate you.

**Kabak** (*smiling*) Yes. (*He draws his wallet out.*) Ten

thousand lire, how does that sound?

**Libertini**  It sounds excellent, Mr Kabak.

**Kabak**  (*handing him the money*) Good. Thank you very much.

**Libertini**  Thank *you* very much. (*Pause.*) Will you be returning to Bulgaria?

**Kabak**  Does it matter?

**Libertini**  (*quickly*) No, no. I simply wondered . . .

*Libertini begins to move towards the door. Kabak begins to tear open the package, read its contents, his back now half-turned, his body tensing as he reads. As Libertini opens the door, he discloses* **Terrini** *framed in the doorway. Terrini makes a small silencing beckon to Libertini, who offers a small and rather scruffy smile in return, bows, looks once at Kabak, and leaves. Terrini stands unannounced for a moment longer; reads the room; looks hard at Kabak's back; then knocks, very deliberately, on the jamb.*

**Kabak**  (*sharply*) Come in. (*He turns towards door, seeing Terrini in already.*)

*Terrini is tall, slightly stooped, about 40, hardfaced, sombre, tough. Though he is a commendatore, his dress is sober, unflamboyant. In some ways, he is the physical and moral counterpart of Kabak: the state's professional guardian of the status quo.*

**Terrini**  Mr . . . Kabak?

**Kabak**  That's right.

**Terrini**  Terrini. Commendatore.

**Kabak**  I'm sorry, I don't think . . .

**Terrini** From the office of Prefect Taddei.

**Kabak** I see. Won't you come in?

**Terrini** Thank you.

**Kabak** Have a chair.

**Terrini** Thank you. (*Sits in armchair.*)

**Kabak** Can I get you a drink?

**Terrini** Thank you, no.

Silence. Kabak looks at Terrini, who looks back with composure.

**Kabak** What can I do for you, Commendatore?

**Terrini** Your presence in Turin this past three weeks hasn't gone entirely unnoticed, Mr Kabak.

**Kabak** I'm flattered. I can't imagine why the Prefect's office should be interested in an obscure Bulgarian businessman.

**Terrini** Can't you? Come now, Mr Kabak. Of all your possible deficiencies, I shouldn't have thought imagination was among them. Can't you really?

**Kabak** I'm supposed to have done something? Infringed a business code, perhaps? Even so, it's hardly a matter for the Prefect to concern himself with.

**Terrini** Not . . . business, Mr Kabak. Not, at least, the sort of business you are ostensibly here to pursue.

**Kabak** Look, Commendatore. I'm perfectly prepared to play mouse to your cat for as long as it amuses you. But if you could devise some speedier means of arriving at your substantive point, I'm sure we'd both appreciate the time you saved.

**Terrini** Brevity has never been our strong suit, Mr Kabak. To an Italian, arrival is anti-climax. The only excitement is the journey itself. (*feeling inside coat for wallet, opening it, taking out folded piece of paper*) However. Since you appear to be in something of a hurry. Here.

*Hands Kabak paper, which he reads.*

Yours I think. Your telegram. Russian *and* code. It kept us busy, I can tell you. (*Pause.*) D'Avanzo really isn't to be trusted.

*Kabak stands up quickly.*

Oh, I don't mean to say he betrayed you. Not that he wouldn't have, mind, if he'd seen more gold in it for himself. No, it's simply that we've had the Cavaliere under scrutiny for some time now. His every move has been monitored since the beginning of the year. Quite an impressive dossier it makes too. You should read it sometime.

**Kabak** Perhaps I'll get the chance to, one day.

**Terrini** I really do doubt that Mr Kabak. I really do. We . . . er . . . didn't arrest him because . . . well, frankly, he was more use to us where he was. Attracting all the sordid deals and all your sort of . . . business . . . into one small, manageable cesspool. Couldn't have worked better.

**Kabak** So what do you want of me?

**Terrini** Well, it did occur to me you might quit Turin rather soon. Say, tomorrow morning? There's a good train for Berlin leaves at 10.15. I'd consider it a personal favour to me if you'd agree to be on it.

**Kabak** And if I refuse?

**Terrini** You won't refuse. You've nothing to keep you here now. The . . . revolution is over. Or didn't you know. The

63

workers are about to ratify the national agreement. And that particular book is closed for ever, I fancy.

**Kabak** I wouldn't count on it, Commendatore.

**Terrini** I'm afraid I have to, Mr Kabak. My life will be spent in the service of the Republic. And this Republic will not sanction a communist revolution. You're not playing games with children, Mr Kabak.

**Kabak** Am I allowed to send a telegram? I shall need . . . instructions.

**Terrini** Leave it be. Comrade Lenin has enough problems. Just take the train.

**Kabak** I have no choice.

**Terrini** Precisely. What an enviable state.

**Kabak** My wife is sick. She can't be moved.

**Terrini** The Countess can stay. She won't . . . embarrass us.

**Kabak** (*finally*) All right then.

**Terrini** Splendid, splendid. I knew you'd see it. (*standing*) Oh, in case you oversleep, I have arranged for a couple of my aides to be in attendance to . . . run you down to Porta Nuova.

**Kabak** You're too kind.

**Terrini** Not at all. It's the least we could do. (*Pause.*) The power is coming back, Mr Kabak. It's a good feeling, after all that . . . anarchy. The man Gramsci. I understand he's planning to address factory meetings tonight, when the final results of the referendum are through. Have a word with him, there's a good fellow. Make him see reason. Turin can't go it alone. It makes no sense to remain in occupation when the rest of the country has pulled out.

**Kabak** Gramsci doesn't need my advice, Commendatore.

**Terrini** Well, perhaps not. (*moving to door*) I'll take my leave of you, Mr Kabak.

> *Kabak stands unmoving in the middle of the room. Terrini gives an ironic bow.*

I'm sure we shall not meet again.

> *Terrini leaves. Kabak walks nervously about, then rings bell for Polya. After a moment she arrives, begins clearing up crockery.*

**Kabak** It's tomorrow.

**Polya** What's tomorow?

**Kabak** I leave tomorrow.

> *Long silence. Finally Polya begins to stack coffee things on tray.*

I'll leave you gold. The room will be yours for another month. That should . . . I'll need my bag packing tonight.

**Polya** (*loudly*) It's not . . .

**Kabak** (*fierce*) Shut up. I'm not concerned with your stupid peasant loyalties and your . . . sentimentalisms. Do what I say. Is that clear? Just . . . do what I say. (*calming*) I'll leave you an address poste restante. If you need me . . . you can contact me there. All right? All right.

> *Polya walks out, eyes lowered, face set. Kabak picks up phone, bumps rest up and down impatiently.*

(*eventually*) Yes. 442. That's right. (*Waits, still tense.*) Hello. Chamber of Labour? Yes, is Comrade Gramsci there, please? Where? I see. Do you know . . .? No, it doesn't matter. Thank you. Oh, just a minute. Yes. Have we had the results of the referendum yet? Ahunh. Could

you tell me what they . . .? (*listening*) Ahunh. Ahunh.
Thank you very much indeed. Thank you comrade. And
you. (*Puts phone down. He paces a moment, rubbing
palms together, then returns to the phone.*) Can you find
me the number of Signor Valletta? Valletta. That's it. Of
Fiat, that's right. No. I'll wait.

*Lights out.*


## SCENE TWO

*Total darkness on set. The factory-meeting slides slowly
reappear (cf. page 42). This time there is no music, no
gaiety, no excitement. Men's voices are muted, anxious. A
spot on front of stage, into which Gramsci walks, carrying
papers in his hands. His floppy hat is on his head. He is
deeply tired, apparently beaten. But his eyes are still fierce,
uncontained, behind the rimless spectacles. A small
cheering and drumming set up, as he appears; but they
quickly subside. And still there is no singing. He takes up
the position, stage left, he had in the first factory scene.*

**Gramsci** Comrades.

*Noise dies quickly.*

I have to announce the results of the national referendum
of all workers in occupation of the factories. *For*
acceptance of the agreement negotiated by the union with
the employers: 127,904. *Against* the agreement: 44,531.

*Some slight cheering, tailing swiftly off.*

Abstentions: approximately 210,000. You cheer too soon,
friends. We will see what there is to cheer about. (*Pause.*)
The agreement this vote has ratified is as follows: ONE, an
increase of 4 lire a day across the board throughout the
industry, equivalent to an average 10 per cent wage

increase; TWO, half of 1 per cent increase on overtime rates; THREE, six paid holidays a year for all workers in the industry; FOUR, payment to be agreed by negotiation for all production undertaken and completed during the occupation; FIVE, no victimization of militants, and particularly those who took leading roles on the factory councils; SIX, under pressure from government, the employers have agreed to implement a policy of workers' control . . .

*Big burst of cheering.*

. . . in principle, comrades. IN PRINCIPLE. No details have been worked out. No minimum conditions imposed by our union leaders. This big empty clause simply offers 'workers' control' at some unspecified date in the future. (*Long pause.*) That is what you have voted for today, comrades. That's the 'package' they offered and you accepted. Now, think back to that first wonderful heady Red Sunday, and of what we talked and hoped for, and ask yourselves again what it is we have to cheer about. (*Pause.*) All right. Perhaps our optimism was unwarranted. Perhaps we should have been able to predict all along the precise way in which our leaders would betray us with this massive act of class collaboration. For that is what it has *been*, comrades. And perhaps we should have prepared ourselves in advance for that most perfect tool of such collaborative acts: I mean, of course, the referendum. What an exquisitely democratic, deeply counter-revolutionary form the referendum is! For what is its main, its essential function? To strengthen the shapeless mass of the population and to crush the vanguards that lead those masses and give them political consciousness. So that even here, in Turin, the vanguard's vanguard, it has worked.

*Shouts of 'no'.*

Of yes, comrades. The figures are unequivocal. (*consulting*

*papers.*) For the agreement: 18,740. Against: 16,909.
Abstentions: 1,024. (*Pause.*) Even here, comrades. (*Pause.*)
Well, we will see. Perhaps your determination to be the
last to go back will help. But it is perspective, not pride,
that we are in need of now. (*Pause.*) It might be that the
working class can chalk up a great leap forward. Certainly
as a mass, shaped and disciplined in the factories by its
*direct* representatives, it has shown itself vibrantly capable
of running its own affairs. And that, *as a fact*, may have
consequences of incalculable social importance. Only half
a century ago – a single tock of time in the long history of
class struggle – that same class was still, in Marx's phrase,
a sack of potatoes, a . . . generic unknown, a . . . shapeless
gathering of individuals, without ideas, without will,
above all without perspective. It was, if you like,
comrades, a blind boil on the arse of capitalism: annoying,
but hardly fatal. (*Pause.*) Today, it appears to be the
entrepreneurial class that has become a sack of potatoes,
an aggregation of the useless and the idiot, powerless,
nerveless, will-less. (*Pause.*) If we find this; if we find that
*this* action, these occupations, have advanced the
proletariat as a ruling class; if we find, too, that this new
political situation is a spring driving irresistibly towards
the conquest of power –

> *Cheering has begun earlier in this speech, but*
> *sporadically, a sort of nervous punctuation to Gramsci's*
> *political syntax: now it begins to reach for a full period,*
> *more certain of itself, happier with the drift of the*
> *rhetoric. Gramsci waits in silence till it subsides.*

WHAT THEN? (*Long pause. Gathering passion, bitter
vehemence*) Why doesn't it happen? Why has no genuine
attempt been made to reach our goal? We must find
answers, comrades, or these questions will outstare us for
ever. (*Long pause.*) All right. Let us look at the 'tactics'
pursued by our 'leaders', culminating in today's

referendum. The 'leadership' of our movement boasts that it bases itself in the 'masses'. What does that mean? It means, comrades, that it asks the 'masses' for prior permission to act; and it 'consults' those 'masses' when and how *it* chooses. (*Hardening. Very emphatic*) Learn this, comrades, and teach it to your children. A revolutionary movement cannot be led in this way. A revolutionary movement can only be led by a revolutionary vanguard, with no commitment to prior consultation, with no apparatus of representative assemblies. (*Pause. Then very big*) Revolution is like war: it must be scrupulously prepared by a working-class general staff, as a national war is prepared by the army's general staff. (*Long pause. Some coughing, mumbling, muttering*) Comrades, Comrade Trotsky said, between the revolutions of '17: 'We shall not enter into the kingdom of socialism with white gloves on a polished floor.' Comrades, Comrade Trotsky was right. For Italy as for Russia. Today, the proletarian vanguard stands rocked, disillusioned, threatened with fragmentation, dispersal, even rout. Why? Because we have consistently failed to face up to the major problem of revolutionary movements; I mean, the problem of political organization. Examine our base, inside the General Confederation of Labour, inside the individual unions, inside the Socialist Party of Italy. What do you find? Nothing worth crossing the street for. *That's* the real situation, comrades. And it won't be oaths and reproaches that change it, it will be tenacious, patient and ruthless preparation. In this way, we will make it possible for a revolutionary general staff to emerge, capable of carrying out wide-scale collective action with intelligence and with daring. (*Long pause. Gathering himself for the final assault*) Today, we have the referendum. It must not be made the occasion for despair and dissolution. Rather we must see it as an urgent lesson from history; as a call for tighter, even more disciplined action. The liberation of our class is not a part-time hobby, and it isn't the work of small minds and feeble imaginations. When disillusion prospers like malaria in a southern swamp, when a cause has been recklessly squandered by those to whom it should never have been entrusted, only he who can keep his heart strong and his will bright as steel can be regarded as a fighter for the working class; can be called a revolutionary. *Evviva* Lenin! *Evviva il rivoluzione!*

*The men take up the slogans, which boom like tribal chants. Gramsci's light fades slowly.*


## SCENE THREE

*Lights up. Kabak, in suit, white shirt, tie, sits by the table staring at the landing door. Polya in, with brandy and cigars. She places them at the table. A quiet knock at the door. Polya crosses to open it. Kabak stands. In the doorway,* **Valletta,** *personal assistant to Giovanni Agnelli, Chairman and Managing Director of Fiat. Valletta is about 60, a very fine example of old-style, courteous, bourgeois gentleman; civilized; very cultured; gentle.*

**Kabak** Please do come in, Signor Valletta. It's very good of you to agree to see me like this at such short notice.

**Valletta** (*moving into room*) Not at all, Mr Kabak. No trouble at all. Business never is.

*Polya closes door, leaves.*

**Kabak** Have a seat, won't you.

**Valletta** (*taking an armchair*) Thank you.

**Kabak** Some brandy, perhaps.

**Valletta** Well, perhaps just a little.

**Kabak** Good. Good. (*He begins to pour.*) You've worked for Fiat a long time, I take it.

**Valletta** Since it became Fiat. This is my twenty-second year with the company. Sometimes I think you don't *work* for Fiat, you live for it. What is important is that I am able to speak for Fiat. (*Pause.*) That's to say, as Chief Executive Assistant to Giovanni Agnelli, founder and Chairman of the company. I have his personal authority to present your . . . propositions to the board for their scrutiny.

*Kabak opens the table drawer and removes a slim case, from which he draws a file. He hands the file to Valletta.*

**Kabak** My portfolio. There's a summary of proposals on the first page.

*Valletta opens the file, flicks through it, quickly, then settles to read the summary. Kabak prepares two cigars, hands Valletta a glass.*

**Valletta** Ah. Thank you.

*And a cigar.*

Thank you. (*Lights it deftly.*) Mmm. Mmm.

**Kabak** (*the toast*) To business.

**Valletta** To business.

*They drink. Valletta settles into the file. Kabak resumes his seat opposite, sits very still, glass in hand. There is a long silence while Valletta reads.*

(*Finally*) I take it you have . . . credentials.

*Kabak begins to get up.*

No, no I would . . . have to see them, I mean, before we parted.

**Kabak**  Of course.

**Valletta**  (*purposefully*) I think I can say we would be interested.

**Kabak**  Good.

**Valletta**  Naturally, I should need to read the portfolio more fully.

**Kabak**  Naturally.

**Valletta**  Perhaps you would be good enough to fill in some of the background now.

**Kabak**  By all means. (*Pause.*) More brandy?

**Valletta**  Just a little.

*Kabak stands to take Valletta's glass. Pours, speaking as he does.*

**Kabak**  It has taken our government some time to make up its mind on concessions to foreign capitalists. Our major problem is simply to prime the industrial pump. We have, as you no doubt know, vast natural resources. Timber in the north – 2,000 miles of it, from the Yablonovi Mountains in the east to the Finn of Karelia in the west. In Siberia there's tin, iron, coal, copper. And a whole range of non-ferrous metals. In the south and east, enormous agricultural concessions. (*Hands Valletta his glass; resumes seat; homes in now.*) And of course, we have oil; particularly in Kamchakta. You'll see that forms the basis of a separate protocol in the portfolio. (*Pause.*) There are those inside the Soviet government who would argue – still, I fear – that the granting of concessions in return for capital, or capital equipment, credit and services, is the kiss of death to revolutionary socialism. Comrades who have never understood the first thing about capital or its uses have imagined we can, in some magical 'communist' way, run a state and a society without it. Fortunately, they look to have been defeated. Our central economic planning authority has recently issued a major decree broadly supporting a concession policy. You will find, as an appendix to the portfolio, a list of seventy-two items already cleared. (*Pause.*) Is there anything further I can tell you, Signor Valletta?

**Valletta** Well, you might indicate, however tentatively at this stage, what it is your government would require of Fiat, in return for . . . concessions.

**Kabak** Certainly. First, capital.

**Valletta** Difficult. We are ourselves currently negotiating a massive capital loan from America.

**Kabak** But not impossible, I fancy. Particularly if you can reinvest at a higher rate than the interest on the original loan.

**Valletta** (*smiling*) As you say, not impossible. You'll make a good capitalist, Mr Kabak.

**Kabak** (*laughing*) I've been trained to regard that phrase as a necessary contradiction in terms, Signor Valletta. But I thank you for the compliment.

**Valletta** What else?

**Kabak** Equipment. Plant. Marine and stationary. Cars. Lorries. Tractors. Locomotive boilers. Machine tools. Maintenance and repair. Three-quarters of your product, in fact. (*smiling*) You can keep your aeroplanes for the time being.

  *Longish pause.*

**Valletta** What would happen if we wanted, say, for example, to set up a Fiat enterprise in Russia?

**Kabak** You'll find it clearly taken care of in the portfolio. The decree sets it all out, I think: remuneration, exporting rights, agreed proportions to host state. It's all there.

**Valletta** What about duration?

**Kabak** Long enough to ensure an adequate return on investment. In addition, a cast-iron guarantee against nationalization or confiscation.

**Valletta** There would have to be. (*Pause.*) And labour?

**Kabak** Available under the conditions prescribed in the Soviet labour code.

**Valletta** That's a code I'm not exactly . . . familiar with. Could you . . .?

**Kabak** You have nothing to fear from it, Signor Valletta. It's all in the portfolio, of course, but after the events of the last few months in Italy, I fancy you would find labour relations in our country a distinctly welcome change.

*Silence for a fair bit.*

**Valletta** (*eventually*) Good. I'm glad I met you, Mr Kabak. May I take the file with me?

**Kabak** By all means. (*Phone rings.*) Will you excuse me for a moment. Please help yourself to brandy.

*Kabak answers the phone, Valletta pours himself a small drink, sits down again, browses through the file.*

(*into phone*) I said I wasn't to be disturbed. (*Pause.*) I see. No, tell him . . . ask him to wait. That's right, wait. No, down there. Thank you. (*Puts phone down.*) I'm sorry about that. Somebody has arrived to see me.

**Valletta** (*rising*) Well, since we appear to have done our business . . .

**Kabak** (*signalling him down*) Please, Signor Valletta . . . I would be offended if you left. Please.

*Valletta subsides, smiling.*

Thank you. (*Kabak pours himself another drink.*) In any case, you haven't seen my credentials. (*He opens the drawer, removes an envelope, takes a small book like a passport from it, which he hands to Valletta.*) I think you'll find it all in order.

**Valletta** (*studying it*) I'm sure I shall, Mr Kabak. I'm sure I shall. Yes, that seems perfectly proper. (*handing it back*) Thank you very much.

**Kabak** Thank you, sir. (*raising his glass*) Your health, Signor Valletta.

*They drink.*

**Valletta** Thank you. I'd like to propose another toast, but I fear you'd find it in dubious taste.

**Kabak** Please.

**Valletta** My toast is: business as usual.

*A beat.*

**Kabak** (*raising his glass*) Why not? Business as usual.

*They drink. Kabak sits down again.*

**Valletta** Why did you leave it so long?

**Kabak** I don't . . .

**Valletta** Before seeing me, I mean. I heard of your arrival almost a month ago.

**Kabak** I see. I . . . there were other pressing matters I had to deal with.

**Valletta** Yes.

**Kabak** Personal. You understand.

**Valletta** Of course. It did just occur to me you might have been awaiting the outcome.

**Kabak** I wouldn't say that. The outcome never really seemed in much doubt, I regret to say.

**Valletta** I must confess, I would have enjoyed a little of your sang-froid at the time.

**Kabak** I prefer to call it . . . professionalism, Signor Valletta.

**Valletta** Call it what you will. We were trembling in our boots, I can tell you.

**Kabak** I know. Unfortunately, so were we. At least, our leaders were.

   *Silence.*

**Valletta** I have read some Marx, you know.

**Kabak** Really.

**Valletta** At university. Here, in Turin. He makes a lot of sense.

**Kabak** We think so.

**Valletta** But there *is* a flaw.

**Kabak** Ah.

**Valletta** There is. He underestimates us. The bourgeois. He underestimates our passion. He underestimates our intelligence and our discipline. Above all he underestimates our ability to adapt. (*Pause.*) Today, I was putting the final touches to our plans for a new social welfare programme. You'd have been impressed, Kabak. We're establishing a new Central Training School. It will offer free training to all apprentices between 14 and 18 who gain admission. We're establishing a health organization, to care for the health not only of employees, but of employees' families too. It will begin as a mutual benefit society, but I can see a day when our workers will receive, free of charge, every kind of medical, dispensing and hospital treatment; when Fiat will provide sick pay; even grants in aid to cover funeral expenses. We'll provide convalescent homes; recreational facilities; sanatoria in the hills; holiday camps for workers' children. I can see a day when Fiat workers will live in Fiat houses; when every Fiat worker will live Fiat, when every Fiat worker will *be* Fiat.

**Kabak** (*finally*) And God said, '*Fiat Lux*'; and there was Fiat.

**Valletta** My vision amuses you.

**Kabak** No. Not amuses. (*Pause.*) Not . . . amuses.

*Long pause.*

**Valletta** We *will* adapt, Mr Kabak. *We* will become the comrades of the future. (*He gets up, places his glass on the table, stubs his cigar.*)

**Kabak** Once again, thank you for coming.

**Valletta** Not at all. My pleasure.

**Kabak** I can be contacted through Chiarini in Rome. I look forward to your decision.

**Valletta** I'll do what I can. (*He's at the door.*)

**Kabak** Signor Valletta.

*Valletta turns. Kabak crosses to a small cupboard, takes from it a small wallet.*

I'd like you to take this, as a personal gift from my government. As an earnest of our sincerity and good intentions.

**Valletta** What is it?

**Kabak** Gold.

**Valletta** No. I mean, what is it for?

**Kabak** I told you. It's a gift.

**Valletta** (*smiling bleakly*) I've already said I'll do what I can. Good night, Mr Kabak.

*He leaves. Kabak places the wallet on the table, drains his glass, pours another drink, crosses to the phone, picks it up.*

**Kabak** Hello. Yes, send him up now, please.

*He replaces the receiver, crosses to the table, takes the revolver out of his jacket pocket and places it in the table drawer. A knock at the door.*

Yes.

*Gramsci enters. He is drawn, tired, very slow in his movements.*

Gramsci. Come in. I'm sorry you had to wait. I had someone to see me.

**Gramsci** (*remaining in doorway*) I saw him leaving. Vittorio Valletta.

**Kabak** That's right. Come in, rest your feet.

**Gramsci** (*standing firm*) I can't stay. I've work to do. (*Pause.*) I heard you were leaving.

**Kabak** That's right. Tomorrow. The Prefect's booked my ticket. One-way to Berlin.

**Gramsci** I see. I wondered if there was . . . anything . . . (*He gestures towards the bed.*)

**Kabak** No, comrade. That's . . . taken care of.

78

**Gramsci** Right. That's . . . all right, then.

**Kabak** Ahunh.

**Gramsci** Did you hear about D'Avanzo?

**Kabak** No.

**Gramsci** Shot. They dragged him out of the canal this evening.

**Kabak** An occupational hazard. Perhaps he had simply outlived his usefulness.

*Long silence.*

**Gramsci** I'll say goodbye then.

**Kabak** Oh, while I remember. Chiarini sent me details of a letter from Moscow to the Italian workers. Did you see a copy?

*Gramsci shakes his head.*

It's here somewhere. (*fumbling in overcoat across chair-back*) Here it . . . is. It's in Russian, so I'll have to translate . . . Let's see now. (*rushing opening*) 'From the Executive Council of the Communist International to the Italian Proletariat, 22nd September, 1920. Comrades, strike after strike, rising after rising, are breaking out in Italy. Matters have gone as far as the mass seizure of factories, houses, etc. by the workers. The labour movement in Italy is faced by decisive . . .'

*He looks at Gramsci, who leans against the door jamb, eyes closed.*

I don't suppose it says anything you didn't already know.

**Gramsci** (*struggling to stay awake*) Please . . . go on.

**Kabak** (*skimming*) It's all . . . fairly familiar, really. Seizure of factories and workshops to continue . . . scope of the movement to be extended and generalized . . . the whole of Italy to be covered with workers', peasants', soldiers' and sailors' councils . . . Begin at once to arm . . . prepare for genuine insurrection . . . drive out reformist leaders . . . mobilize all the genuinely revolutionary forces of the country. (*Pause. Very deliberately*) Et cetera. Et cetera. Et cetera. Signed. Lenin. Bukharin. Zinoviev.

**Gramsci** A nice irony. Right but late.

**Kabak** Yes. I thought you should . . . know.

**Gramsci** Yes.

*Pause.*

**Kabak** What will you do?

**Gramsci** (*toneless*) Build. Prepare for the backlash. There'll be fascists at every street corner from now on. First I have to go to Sardinia. My sister is dying.

**Kabak** I'm sorry.

**Gramsci** Hundreds die every year. Emma just happens to be my sister. It's a kind of malaria. You don't actually have to *dig* the ditches to have a chance of contracting it. And it's not always fatal. Just another of capitalism's little lotteries. (*He straightens.*) But we'll win, comrade. Go well. (*He starts to leave.*)

**Kabak** (*softly*) You still love them too much, comrade.

*Gramsci turns, looks at Kabak for a long time, leaves without answer. Kabak drains his glass, sits in a chair, tries to sleep.*

## SCENE FOUR

*Daylight. A brilliant day. Kabak is dead asleep, sprawled like a drunk, legs thrust right forward. Angelica is awake, upright in the bed, two pillows stiffly propping her. She is drained. Her face is garish with rouge and lipstick, which she is still applying. Polya enters through the connecting door, a small kidney bowl in her hands. She stops when she sees Angelica.*

**Angelica** Not now, Polya. Later. I'm feeling much better.

**Polya** (*looking at the sleeping Kabak*) I'm not sure you should be sitting up like that, Madame. Remember what the doctor said about . . .

**Angelica** (*snapping compact firmly to*) Thank you, Polya. That will be all.

*Kabak stirs. Stretches. Polya looks at him again, unsure. Finally.*

**Polya** (*turning*) Very well, Madame.

*She leaves. Kabak stretches, yawns, stretches, stands – clothes in disarray – back more or less to the bed, stretches again, begins to button shirt and do up cravat. He sorts a watch out from his waistcoat, checks time, returns it. In the middle of this he turns and sees Angelica.*

**Angelica** Good morning.

**Kabak** Good . . . morning. Should you be . . .?

**Angelica** Don't, please. You're worse than Polya. I'm feeling better. How do I look?

**Kabak** (*recovering; crossing the room to the bed*) Radiant.

*He kisses her forehead. She holds him by shoulder and*

*neck, kisses him full on the lips with surprising strength and passion. Kabak is kissed; his lack of response is almost palpable.*

**Angelica** You don't have to lie, you know. It hasn't affected my eyes yet. (*Indicating compact.*)

**Kabak** And it hasn't affected mine. Radiant.

*Pause.*

**Angelica** Thank you.

**Kabak** (*bowing slightly; ironic*) Not at all. My pleasure, ma'am. (*He gets up, moves towards the chair he slept in, slips his coat from the chair-back, puts it on. He begins smoothing his hair with flat palms.*)

**Angelica** You're beautiful. Do you know that?

**Kabak** It's not important.

**Angelica** Christo.

**Kabak** Mmm.

**Angelica** You know what I'd like?

**Kabak** (*looking for boots*) What's that, love?

**Angelica** Winter in Carlsbad.

*Kabak stops fractionally, back to her, then continues the search.*

**Kabak** I can't find my boots.

**Angelica** We could go to Darmstadtbaden. There's still a staff there of sorts. I think I could grow well again, there. Christo.

**Kabak** (*ringing bell*) Yes, love. I've got to have boots.

**Angelica** Christo.

*Polya comes in.*

**Kabak** Have you seen my boots?

**Polya** Yes. I had them cleaned.

*Kabak looks hard at Polya.*

**Kabak** Did you? (*Pause.*) Would you mind . . . bringing them then.

*Polya looks at Angelica, back at Kabak.*

**Polya** Certainly. (*She leaves.*)

**Angelica** Christo.

*Phone rings. Kabak answers it.*

**Kabak** Yes. That's right. Oh. (*Pause.*) Tell them I'll be down in five minutes. (*Pause.*) I know what time the train leaves. Tell them five minutes. (*Bangs phone down.*)

**Angelica** Christo. Who is it? What train?

*Polya comes in. She carries the boots on one arm, Kabak's grips in the other hand. She stands about a yard inside the door. Kabak and Angelica look at her in silence.*

**Angelica** (*finally*) Put them down, Polya.

*Polya puts them down; leaves. Kabak crosses the room, picks them up, places the grip near the landing door, takes the boots to an armchair, sits to put them on.*

Christo.

*Kabak concentrates on his boots.*

(*struggling to quit the bed*) Christo?

*Kabak gets up, stamps his boots snug.*

**Kabak** I haven't much time, so listen carefully. I have been ordered to quit Turin. They have sent men to escort me to the station.

**Angelica** (*not listening; yowling rather*) Oh why? Christo? Oh why? Oh why?

**Kabak** (*fierce*) Listen. I have . . . Listen will you . . . I have made arrangements . . .

**Angelica** Why? Why? Why?

**Kabak** (*shouting*) I couldn't. How could I? You're dying.

**Angelica** (*standing; very still*) Do you think I don't know that?

*Long silence.*

**Kabak** (*finally*) I've made arrangements with the hotel. When you're . . . you can join me in Berlin. I've left an address with Polya.

**Angelica** I don't want to die on my own.

**Kabak** Polya will be . . .

**Angelica** I don't mean that. Oh God. I don't *mean* that.

**Kabak** I must go. (*He approaches her.*)

**Angelica** No. No.

*Kabak stops. Looks at Angelica.*

**Kabak** Love. I must.

**Angelica** (*turning her back; small and quiet*) No.

*Kabak waits a moment longer, then turns, picks up the grip at the door. Leaves. Angelica finally sits on the bed, head on hand, back to audience. She sobs. At length she opens the drawer, takes out syringes and capsules, prepares one, draws up her nightdress, plunges needle into thigh. She then repeats the process. For a moment she sits upright, very stiff, then rings the bell for Polya and lowers herself slowly into the bed. Polya comes in quickly.*

**Polya** (*crossing room*) Are you all right?

**Angelica** Yes. Draw the curtains, will you.

**Polya** (*complying, solicitous*) Try and sleep. There's nothing a good sleep won't put right.

**Angelica** Thank you. Now. Go downstairs and see whether you can get me a morning paper.

**Polya** I can ring down . . .

**Angelica** (*sharp; eyes closed*) Go. Please.

*Polya goes finally. Angelica is very still for a moment longer then surrenders to a voluptuous spasm, and another, and another. She screams slightly, on the upthrust. It is a little orgasmal: intense, powerful, almost an ecstasy. Words tumble from her, shredded from her life.*

The Tsar was in residence in the early spring a ball every night for a month Faberget swore he'd never seen such costumes such diamonds such . . .

*She screams once, sharp, anguished, then holds her breath. The scream cues an image on the wall behind her: the corpse of Nicholas II. Cut the image as she speaks again.*

(*shouting*) Bolsheviks Bolsheviks Bolsheviks bread riots strikes bread peace land they were there underneath here now here . . .

*She screams again, cueing a second image: Lenin embalmed in the catafalque. The image is cut on her next word.*

85

All things will bend all things the iron brain of Lenin
hammering the future will will will what will stop them
stop them who . . .

*She screams again:* Tato's March on Rome. *She screams*
*again: Mussolini embracing Hitler. She screams again:*
*Stalin in profile stares across a black gap at Hitler, who*
*stares back. She screams again: the gap is filled with an*
*image of Molotov and von Ribbentrop signing non-*
*aggression pact. She screams again: cut to black.*

# Appendix

*Polya goes finally. Angelica is very still for a moment longer, then surrenders to a voluptuous spasm, and another, and another. She screams slightly, on the upthrust. It is a little orgasmal: intense, powerful, almost an ecstasy. She is shouting now. Gradually her words begin to make a little sense.*

**Angelica** . . . *My* estate. *My* estate. Darmstadtbaden. A good winter. Hear the snow hiss past the carriage. Steady, Mikhail. Coax him. Raska won't submit to bullying. You should know that. (*Pause.*) Another winter. '15. '16. Grigor looked so handsome in his uniform. Was Deniken there? Grigor came from Turkey, I remember. Did Deniken come? Perhaps he didn't. (*Pause.*) But who wasn't there! Tsar Nicholas. Her. The Friend. Tchernikov. Pterepnin. All the princes. Bankers. Heads of the Commissariat, industrialists, ballerinas of the Tsar and the Grand Dukes, prelates, ladies in waiting, deputies, generals, lawyers, mandarins, innumerable nephews and nieces. (*Pause.*) Faberget swore he'd never seen such costumes, such diamonds, such settings . . . (*Pause.*) Not a word about the war. Not a word. (*She screams with pain.*) Or those . . . Bolsheviks. (*Pause.*) Was that the last winter? (*She sits up stiffly, hugs her stomach.*) But they were there all right. They were there. Bread. Riots. Strikes. They were there. Here now. You can't see them, but they're here now. Underneath. Under the skin. (*Stretching hands*) There. Underneath. Erupting there. There. And here. (*clutching stomach*) Oh God. Oh Blessed Theodosia, save me from these . . . foreign bodies. Save me from these . . . intruders.

Protect me, Blessed Theodosia, patron saint of lost causes,
protect my estate in Kiev, protect my lands in
Darmstadtbaden . . . They moved her bones, Christo. Did
you know? Grigor took them, very solemnly, from the
shrine at Kiev, and led the honour guard to Moscow,
where the blessed bones were solemnly laid in the Basilica.
Nicholas said the bones should stay in Kiev. The Germans
would not dare touch them, he argued; and if they did, so
much the worse for the Germans . . . A raspberry-coloured
shirt he wore. In the Pripet Marshes. Canoeing. Shooting
crows. Walking. Where the Dnieper meets the Beresina.
Was it breeding, I wonder, that . . . calmness? Or simply
poverty of the spirit? A weakness of the will? You used to
call him something, Christo. What was it? (*She is racked
by a huge spasm. From this point her fit becomes
apocalyptic.*) Grigor saw it. The last winter. They were
there, under the skin, waiting to . . . consume us. Waiting
to consume Europe. Our Europe. What . . . appetite they
displayed! And we are powerless. Our skin needs them
perhaps. We must share the same pelt. Even Theodosia. By
the sea. Even Theodosia they took. They erupted from
under the skin of Theodosia; they confiscated even *that*.
And they will. They will. What did Christo say? All things
will bend to Lenin's iron will. They will. They will.
Nicholas. Her. The Friend. Grand Dukes, bankers,
ballerinas. They've all had their last winter. Everywhere.
They will. Will. Will. Will. What will stop them? Will
anything stop them?

> *She slides gently to the floor. Lies very still. Fade slowly
> to black. We hear the sound of jackboots, very clear,
> close. On the screen, Tato's* March on Rome. *After a
> while, it is replaced by* Fascismo (*an anti-Fascist poster,
> c. 1921). This in turn is replaced by the picture of
> Mussolini's bodyguard (Moro, Milan). A fourth slide –
> Mussolini embracing Hitler – replaces this. Its place is*

*taken by a picture of Stalin. Then a slow mix to Molotov and von Ribbentrop signing the German–Russian non-aggression pact. This fades to black. In its place, the factory-roof slide from page 42. The theatre walls are lit. We are in the factory again. Factory noises. A hooter sounds. Silence.*

# THE PARTY

# Characters

Angie Shawcross
Joe Shawcross
Eddie Shawcross
Milanka
Malcolm Sloman
Susie Plaistow
Kate Stead
'Grease' Ball
Richard Maine
Jeremy Hayes
Kara Massingham
Louis Preece
Andrew Ford
John Tagg

The Party was first performed in Great Britain at the National Theatre, London, on 20 December 1973. The cast was as follows:

**Angie Shawcross**  Doran Godwin
**Joe Shawcross**  Ronald Pickup
**Eddie Shawcross**  John Shrapnel
**Milanka**  Sarah Atkinson
**Malcolm Sloman**  Frank Finlay
**Susie Plaistow**  Anna Carteret
**Kate Stead**  Rachel Davies
**'Grease' Ball**  Desmond McNamara
**Richard Maine**  Nicholas Clay
**Jeremy Hayes**  Gawn Grainger
**Kara Massingham**  Gillian Barge
**Louis Preece**  Ram John Holder
**Andrew Ford**  Denis Quilley
**John Tagg**  Laurence Olivier

*Directed by*  John Dexter
*Designed by*  John Napier

# Prologue

*Black stage. Track of very bad theatre orchestra playing
'The Internationale' in spry waltz-time. Fade up huge,
stage-high pic of Marx; mix to pic of Lenin; mix to pic of
Trotsky (last days in Mexico). Take pic down to black.
Single roving spot in centre. Music up, cymbally. An
ancient Groucho Marx on – moustache, cigar, tails, bent
back, fish eyes. He carries a clipboard of papers and a
trail-mic, which he places in the mic-stand that squirts up
from the boards. He looks at the darkness behind him.*

**G** Good evening. (*to audience, but ignoring them*) So
what happened to the happy guy with the whiskers.

*Trotsky pic up.*

Come on, come on, you think I don't know Abie the
Fishpedlar when I see him? Give me the guy with the nests
in his face.

*Marx appears.*

Poppa. So what's tickling you, pa – apart from the flora on
the face, that is? (*to audience*) Which reminds me, did you
ever hear the one about the 150,000 supporters of De
Gaulle who marched through the streets of Paris on 30
June 1968 shouting 'France aux français!' and 'Cohn-
Bendit à Dachau!'? You what? Oh, you were there. Well,
well, well. Why don't I keep my big trap in my pocket?
That way I could smile while I counted my money. But to
our story, as they say. Captain Hugo C. Hackenbush, at
your service. Explorer, adventurer, natural scientist, *bon
viveur, homme moyen sensuel* bordering on the priapic

and pretty nearly totally irrelevant to the rest of this play.
But to our story. And talking of talkies I've been asked to
put you in the picture with a few choice epigraphs. Sit
down, madam. Your turn will come, I promise you.
(*riffling papers on the board*) I have here a miscellaneous
collection of choice quotations that I understand – nay, am
authoritatively assured – has a more than glancing
relevance to what follows. (*He looks at the giant Marx.*)
Pity you can't be here to do it yourself, hunh. Eh? You old
. . . boulevardier, you. Hummm. (*turning page, reading*)
'The bourgeoisie . . .' Wake up, madam, I'm talking about
you. Give her a nudge, will you, sir? Thank you so much.
May your back never buckle under the strain. 'The
bourgeoisie cannot exist without constantly
revolutionizing the instruments of production, and thereby
the relations of production, and with them the whole
relations of society. Constant revolutionizing of
production, uninterrupted disturbance of all social
conditions, everlasting uncertainty and agitation
distinguish the bourgeois epoch from all earlier ones. All
fixed fast, frozen relations, with their train of ancient and
venerable prejudices and opinions, are swept away, all
newly formed ones become antiquated before they can
ossify. All that is solid melts into air, all that is holy is
profaned, a man is at last compelled to face with sober
senses his real condition of life and his relations with his
kind.' Nobody's writing like that any more, believe me. (*to
pic*) O.K.?

   *Pic of Lenin appears.*

Ouch. Or as they have it in Russia – Ilyich! (*turning pages*)
Steady as she goes! (*Deep breath*) 'Revolutionary phrase-
making is a disease from which revolutionary parties
suffer at times when the course of revolutionary events is
marked by big, rapid zigzags. By revolutionary phrase-
making we mean the repetition of revolutionary slogans

irrespective of objective circumstances at a given turn in
events, in the given state of affairs obtaining at the time.
When people are seized by the itch of revolutionary
phrase-making, the mere sight of this disease causes
intolerable suffering.' (*He begins scratching his elbow.*)
No, madam, that's a flea. I'm just a petty-bourgeois funny
man with quasi-anarchic tendencies; it says here.

*Pic reverts to Marx.*

And talking of money – and if we weren't, by God we
should have been – is he back? They do hug the stage these
boys, don't they – talking yet again of money, see how this
grabs you? Or indeed where. (*clipboard again; cough,
sniff*) 'Money . . .' My, how straight you're sitting now.
Me too, folks. 'Money, since it has the property of
purchasing everything, of appropriating objects to itself, is
therefore the object *par excellence*. The universal character
of this property corresponds to the omnipotence of money,
which is regarded as an omnipotent essence. Money is the
pander between need and object, between human life and
the means of existence. But that which mediates my life,
mediates also the existence of other men for me. It is for
me the other person . . .'

*Another spot up, side of stage. An Olivier as Timon.*

O  Gold? Yellow, glittering, precious gold? No, gods,
I am no idle votarist: you roots, you clear heavens!
Thus much of this will make black white; foul fair;
wrong right; base noble; old young; coward valiant.
. . . Why, this
Will lug your priests and servants from your sides;
Pluck stout men's pillows from below their heads:
This yellow slave
Will knit and break religions; bless th'accurst,
Make the hoar leprosy adored; place thieves
And give them title, knee and approbation,

With senators on the bench; this is it
That makes the wappen'd widow wed again;
She whom the spittal house and ulcerous sores
Would cast the gorge at, this embalms and spices
To the April day again. Come, damned earth,
Thou common whore of mankind, that putt'st odds
Amongst the rout of nations, I will make thee
Do thy right nature.

*'O' light fades. 'G' light up.*

**G** There's nobody speaking like that anymore, believe me.
'The power to confuse and invert all human and natural
qualities, to bring about fraternization of incompatibles,
the *divine power* of money, resides in its *essence* as the
alienated and exteriozed species – life of men. It is the
alienated *power of humanity*.' (*big breath*) Yeah, well. If I
had the choice between you and a bedful of money,
madam, you'd have trouble making second.

*Pic of Trotsky asserts itself. He turns round.*

All right, Abie, your turn will come, as the albatross said
to the gannet.

*Trotsky pic fades. Only black now.*

Well, don't say I didn't tell you. If you see anything that
looks like a ten-dollar bill – for instance, a hundred-dollar
bill – don't hesitate to bring it round back, will you? You'll
know it's mine because it'll have . . .

*Pic of hundred-dollar bill.*

Well there you go. (*muttering, leaving*) I really must do
something about these *pockets*. How a man's supposed to
keep a quiet mouth in there I'll never know, slipping down
around your ankles, getting trodden underfoot.

*Black.*

*Caption: 'Je Suis Marxiste, Tendance Groucho'.*
*Black.*
*Caption: 'Nous Sommes Tous Juifs Allemands'.*
*Black.*
*Caption: 'Violez Votre Alma Mater'.*
*Black.*
*Burst of sound; film of Paris students marching,*
*demonstrating.*
*Black.*
   *Left screen:* BERLEIT *across a picture of the factory.*
*Letters leave the left screen one by one:*
LIBERTE;
*and reform on the right, over a pic of a clenched fist.*
*Chords of Archie Shepp's intro to 'Blasé' (Actuel 18)*
*underneath.*
*Black again. Spot up on* **Joe Shawcross** *and* **Angie** *in*
*bedroom set.*
   *Music up. A sort of abstracted fuck-ballet, the figures*
*distinct in the spot, the room barely there as yet. The*
*fuck is bad. Joe is frozen: Angie goes down with her*
*lips. He kneels for a while, inert, takes it; then*
*imperceptibly draws away from her. Music down; lights*
*up. The bedroom.*

# Act One

## SCENE ONE

*10 May 1968. Early evening.*

*Bedroom at the Shawcross house, SW7, somewhere. Big, white, sunny, rather cool. Hockneys and Botys. 7 ft. bed. Door to adjoining dressing-room. Door to landing.*

*Joe clicks off the record player, walks into the dressing-room. Angie half lies, half kneels on the bed, watching him; then stands, pulls on a pair of knickers and tights, sits smoking a cigarette, staring at nothing, deep in her own vacancy.*

*Silence. Gradually, the faintest sounds of retching from the dressing-room area. She smokes on, hardly aware of it. Finally.*

**Angie**  You all right? (*Silence.*) You all right? (*No answer.*)

*She looks round at the door, doesn't move. Joe appears. He wears a sweat shirt, underpants, sailing shoes.*

**Joe**  What?

**Angie**  I said: Are you all right.

**Joe**  (*looking around rather aimlessly*) What time are you going out?

**Angie**  Nineish. (*looking at watch, standing*) Christ.

**Joe**  Will you be late back?

**Angie**  Possibly. I'm not sure.

**Joe**  I can't find my jeans.

**Angie**  In the basket. They stink.

**Joe** (*into dressing-room*) Do they? (*back in hopping into them*) Does Milanka know you're . . .?

**Angie** Ahunh.

*He sits down, drained, on the other side of the bed, back to Angie, begins to put on canvas shoes.*

Are you all right?

**Joe** Yes. I'm fine.

**Angie** You look terrible.

**Joe** I'm fine. Jesus Christ.

*Silence. Each busy, separate.*

**Angie** How was your thing?

**Joe** What time is it?

**Angie** Ten to. (*She waits.*)

**Joe** What?

**Angie** Frau Elise?

**Joe** Fine.

**Angie** Good. (*lipstick*) And how is it?

**Joe** (*getting up, zipping trousers, fastening belt*) Addictive. I talk, she listens. What more could a man ask of a woman? (*sings, absently*) 'Freudians are forever . . .' We reached my father today. She told me to tell her the most significant fact I knew about him. So I said: 'My father takes less home in a week than I'm paying for this session.'

*He looks at Angie. She continues making up.*

And she said: 'No. Tell me something about your *father*.'

**Charlie**, *aged three or four, calls 'Mummy' several times. Angie gets up, looks round for her clothes.*

**Angie** (*with undemonstrative resignation*) All right.

*She walks into dressing-room. Joe stretches out, head propped on the bed. Charlie calls 'Mummy' once more, goes quiet. Joe smokes, vacantly.*

(*off*) Try and get rid of Sloman, will you.

**Joe** He's all right. He's lying down somewhere.

**Angie** (*off*) This will be four nights running and he's pissed the bed every night.

**Joe** I'll have a word with him.

**Angie** (*off, half irony*) What will you say?

**Joe** I'll say: Don't piss the bed so often, Malc.

**Angie** (*in, short stunning dress, boots in hand*) Ha. Ha. You want to try getting it out sometime. (*Pause.*) Is he doing something for you?

**Joe** Mmmm. A ninety. 'Play of the Month.' November.

**Angie** Will he sober up in time?

**Joe** Don't worry about Malc.

**Angie** I'll try not to. If he wrote like he drank, he'd really be something.

**Joe** He's something already. Drink helps him believe otherwise.

**Angie** (*not understanding*) What?

**Joe** Nothing.

*She persists silently.*

He . . . can't bear the thought of himself as . . . successful . . . in a society he longs to destroy.

*Long silence.*

**Angie** I see. (*Pause.*) Is that why he drinks?

**Joe** I don't know. (*He begins rubbing the webs of his right foot through his socks.*)

**Angie** (*inspecting herself in the wall mirror; casually*) Is that what's wrong with you, Joe?

**Joe** No. It's athlete's foot actually.

*She stares hard at him.*

Tinea pedis.

*Silence.*

Don't be simple, Angie.

**Angie** Can't you answer simple questions?

**Joe** (*up*) No.

**Angie** I meant: Is it getting . . . better?

**Joe** No. But as Harold Wilson might put it, it's getting worse more slowly. We have it in hand.

**Angie** Do you want to talk?

**Joe** I thought you were going out.

**Angie** I am but . . .

**Joe** Well then. Go. I'm surviving.

**Angie** Tell me . . .

**Joe** Don't go on about it, eh.

*He walks into the dressing-room. She hunts for a pair of cotton gloves in a chest of drawers.*

**Angie** (*calling*) If I don't see your brother before he leaves . . . say good-bye for me, won't you.

**Joe** (*in, struggling into another tee-shirt*) Yeah.

**Angie** Will he get the job?

**Joe** I don't know. I hope not.

**Angie** Oh? He seemed to think it was worth having.

**Joe** There's nothing for our kid down here.

**Angie** Have you told him that?

**Joe** No.

**Angie** He wouldn't thank you. What have *you* got on?

**Joe** I've got a meeting. Just a few people.

**Angie** Here?

**Joe** Mmmmmmmmmm.

**Angie** Anyone I know?

**Joe** No, I don't think so.

**Angie** Is *he* coming?

**Joe** Who?

**Angie** John whatsisname. You know.

**Joe** You make him sound like Moloch. 'Is *he* coming?'
Jesus.

**Angie** Is he?

**Joe** Yes.

**Angie** He gives me the creeps.

**Joe** You've only met him once.

**Angie** Once was all I needed.

**Joe** I thought he was very civil.

**Angie** Yes. Civil. Like a hangman's civil.

**Joe** Don't be so . . . bourgeois.

**Angie** (*displaying herself*) What do you suggest I be? Proletarian?

*He looks at her in silence.*

When are we going to talk?

**Joe** I don't know. Not now, eh.

**Angie** No. Not now. Of course. (*She's ready to leave. Gives herself a final look in the long mirror.*) I'll call in and see Charlie on the way out. Shall I tell him you'll be coming?

**Joe** Sure. Take care. (*He blows her a toy kiss.*)

**Angie** Don't make plans for tomorrow night. We're going to the Aldwych with the Carters.

**Joe** All right.

**Angie** I want *you*, Joe.

*She leaves abruptly. He sits for a moment, looking at the door, then crosses to the record player, places a record on the turntable, selects a track with care, returns to the bed, slowly kneels on it to face the wall-length mirror, takes out his penis, fists it, begins to beckon it to life. Fade in Archie Shepp/Jeanne Lee: 'Blasé'. Room lights down. Joe and his reflection remain lit.*

Blasé
Ain't you darlin
You
Who shot your sperm into me
But never set me free
This ain't a hate thing
It's a love thing
If lovers ever really love that way

The way they say.
I give you a lump of sugar
You fill my womb till it runs
All of Ethiopia awaits you
My prodigal son.

*A burst of mute film from the preparations for the night*
*of the barricades. Pics, fast, like identiscan:*
*Cohn-Bendit.*
*Alain Geismar.*
*Jacques Sauvageot.*
*Yves Niaudet.*
*Jean Labib.*
*Alain Krivine.*
*Henri Weber.*
*Caption: 'Nous Sommes un Groupuscule.'*
*Take out Joe light. Black.*
*Caption: 'L'anarchie c'est moi.'*
*Black.*

## SCENE TWO

*Music: 'Street Fighting Man' (Stones). Slow single spots*
*light first a wall picture of Lenin, then, after some*
*moments, a balancing shot of Trotsky (Army). They're*
*joined by a fun pop print, sexual in content and blatant in*
*feel. The images hold, disembodied, without context. A*
*sudden surge of intense white light drowns the stage,*
*washing out not only these images but the set as well. A*
*gradual correction establishes the Shawcross living-room.*

*Same evening, moments later. Late light filters through*
*the french windows. There is a suggestion of covered patio*
*and lawn beyond.*

*The room is mainly white walls and black leather. The*
*furniture is expensive, tasteful and tentative: Chesterfield,*

*two big chairs, stools, rugs, huge floor cushions, white
carpets, extensive Bang and Olufsen hi-fi, early colour TV
(like a Wurlitzer), $\frac{1}{2}$ in. VTR and monitor; mirror,
paintings, prints, decorative plants and fronds, shelves of
hardbacks, two shelves of LPs. There are a dozen or so
slung or standing spots to light the room. The impression
is of purpose narrowly triumphing over comfort; of rich
ease scored by persisting puritan principle.*

*A warm Friday evening, after a hot friendly day. The
windows are open wide. The TV screen to the room is on;
a news bulletin (9 o'clock) is almost at an end. We listen to
it in the empty set for some moments, before* **Eddie
Shawcross** *enters from the hall. He's about medium height,
stocky, dark, balding slightly; uncomfortable in this room,
this house. The unaccustomed dark suit, collar and tie
don't help. He watches the set for some little while, then
has a wander. Touches things tentatively, not caring to
leave marks.*

**Newsreader** . . . In all, more than 150,000 people will
have visited Danish Fortnight when it closes at the end of
this week. In the local borough elections, Conservative
Central Office is now claiming 571 gains to 13 losses. The
gains include 16 London boroughs and 25 key towns,
(*Eddie in*) many of them thought to be impregnable
Labour strongholds until now. Our political
correspondent, Hardiman Scott, reports:

**Scott** A black day for Labour. A swingeing defeat at the
hands of the Tories in the local elections, coupled with an
unprecedented personal attack on Mr Wilson by the editor
of the *Daily Mirror*, will give Transport House much food
for thought over the summer months. Continued silence
from prominent Labour leaders – not least, Mr Wilson
himself – has given rise to some speculation on the
possibility of radical changes in policy, harnessed to a
thorough-going Cabinet reshuffle. But it should be

remembered that this defeat was expected by the Labour camp and that, paradoxically, the fact that it wasn't even more substantial may be read by the Prime Minister and by his colleagues as a qualified endorsement of government policies to date.

*Eddie grins a little, turns away to perch on a stool and study his* Evening Standard.

**Newsreader** The new 50 penny piece was announced today.

*Eddie perches on a stool, watching the set.*

It has, as you can see, a seven-sided design and will replace the 10 shilling note by February 1971, when the conversion to decimal coinage is expected to be completed.

*Joe in.*

**Joe** Hi, kid.

**Eddie** Hi.

*Joe watches the set.*

**Newsreader** Finally, back to Paris and those students, reports are still reaching us of a massive build-up in the Left Bank area of Paris. Some 15,000 demonstrators have already begun their anti-government march, and informed sources claim double or even treble that number will be in action before midnight. Student leader Daniel Cohn-Bendit has called for the immediate withdrawal of French police from the Latin Quarter and the Sorbonne, which the students regard as their 'rightful home'. According to our Paris correspondent, it will be a miracle if large-scale clashes can be averted in the hours of darkness later tonight. (*Pause for the smile.*)

*Joe winks at Eddie, who smiles back at him.*

That's all from the newsroom. Late news at 10.45. And now a look at the weather.

**Joe** Are you watching?

**Eddie** No.

*Joe switches it off.*

**Joe** So, how'd it go?

**Eddie** (*head in racing results*) Bloody Europeana let us down for a tenner at Beverley. I don't know why I back that N. MacIntosh, I don't.

**Joe** What about the *job*?

**Eddie** Yeah. They said I could have it. Foreman cutter.

**Joe** Yeah? How do you feel about that?

**Eddie** All right. They showed me the bandknives. Honest, they looked like someat out of a ship's engine. Hundred dozen at a time they cut. It's not a cutter they want, it's a Chief Engineer.

> **Milanka**, *the au pair, in, carrying a guinea pig. She's Czech, the first fruits of the Cernik accession: eighteen, between high school and university; tall; hefty but lithe, wears a blue and white tracksuit with a Czech national badge across the back.*

**Milanka** I put Novotny back, Mr Shawcross.

**Joe** Yeah, that's fine, Milanka.

> *She crosses to the french windows, goes out on to the terrace. The pig squeals, high and grating.*

**Eddie** Big girl.

**Joe** Yes.

**Milanka** (*off*) All right, Novotny. All you do is squealing.

You had good time, remember.

**Joe** So. Do you take it or what?

**Eddie** I might. I'll have to talk to *her* first. She won't like it down here.

**Joe** Will you?

**Eddie** I dunno. It'll be better than rowing third oar on a slave ship. Marginally.

   *They grin at their old joke. Milanka in.*

**Milanka** Novotny is to bed. He said good night to Charlie.

**Joe** That's nice. And I read him a story.

**Milanka** Good. Now I sing him asleep with my Czech song.

**Joe** He'll like that.

**Milanka** Tonight I have training. (*Pause.*) I spoke with Mrs Shawcross. (*Pause.*) She said I should speak with you.

**Joe** (*uneasy, fast*) Yes, sure, all right, Milanka, that's fine.

**Milanka** Thank you. I'm not late. Tomorrow I sing for *you*. 'Ej od Buchlova' perhaps.

**Joe** Thanks.

   *She goes. Joe grins at Eddie.*

**Eddie** I wouldn't mind a song meself. Don't you get tempted, our kid?

**Joe** I don't have time.

   *Pause.*

**Eddie** I thought I might go out. It's too late to go back.

**Joe** Yeah. Have a night on the town, eh. Are you all right for . . .? (*Hand at back pocket.*)

**Eddie** I'm fine. They coughed up. Expenses.

*Milanka back in, duffel bag over shoulder.*

**Milanka** Some men brought food on wooden trays. In kitchen.

**Joe** Good. Thanks.

**Milanka** And . . . the man with the beard is lost. Mister . . .

**Joe** How do you mean, lost?

**Milanka** He was here in house. Now no longer.

**Joe** Maybe he's just . . . gone. All right, I'll see to it, you get off.

*She leaves, smiling.*

**Eddie** Is that that . . . Malc?

**Joe** Yes.

**Eddie** Is he still here?

**Joe** There seems some doubt about it. He was an hour ago. I saw him.

**Eddie** He's all right him, inne?

**Joe** Yeah. Good bloke.

**Eddie** Can't half shift some stuff. He's from up our way, inne?

**Joe** Salford. Used to play for United Colts.

**Eddie** Gerrout. Him?

**Joe** S'right. Left-back.

**Eddie** Christ. I bet they were bloody terrible. What'd's'e do?

**Joe** He's a writer.

**Eddie** Oh.

*Silence.*

Me mam said when're you coming down to see 'em.

**Joe** I'll come up in the summer, tell her. August, p'raps.

**Eddie** She thought you might manage Wakes.

**Joe** When's that?

**Eddie** *Wakes.*

**Joe** Yes. No, I don't think so. I'm going to France. To see some films . . .

**Eddie** I'll tell her August then.

*Silence.*

You don't fancy a night out, do you?

**Joe** (*uneasyish*) No . . . I'm babysitting. I've got some people coming round anyway.

**Eddie** (*tentative*) Have you thought any more about the 300 quid?

**Joe** (*uneasier still*) Shit. No I haven't. I meant to mention it to Angie before she went out. Never mind, I'll have a word with her before you leave.

**Eddie** I should've set up on me own years ago really. All I need's a coupla rooms, coupla machines, a buttonholer and a bandknife, piece of cake. I'll show you the shop I've got in mind. Market Street. It's a blinder. I could do all me own stuff.

*Phone rings. Joe looks at it, leaves it down.*

**Eddie**  I'll push then.

**Joe**  Stay if you want.

**Eddie**  No. I fancy going out. See you later on?

**Joe**  Yeah. Sure. Got your key?

*Eddie nods.*

Go easy.

*They exchange grins.*

**Eddie**  Oh yeah. (*He leaves.*)

**Joe**  (*to phone*) Hello? John. Uhuuh. Of course. What time is it now? (*checking watch*) No, that'll be fine. Well, we'll manage. Nobody yet, but it's early. Fine. It'll be on the latch. See you then.

*A loud groaning bellow from the region of the floor cushions by the wall.*

Sorry, I missed that.

*Another groan. The cushions move, rise. Joe watches.*

Got it. I'll expect you then. Take care.

*Phone down. The cushions erupt like lava and* **Sloman** *appears, on his knees. He is in some disarray. He is jacketless; his shirt is open to the waist; his shoes are tied neatly around his neck. He is pushing forty, gross, bearded, puffy with booze, yet powerful still. His eyes are closed. He moans, as though crying. Opens his eyes. Sees Joe.*

**Sloman**  Joe.

**Joe**  Hello, Malc.

**Sloman** I'll have to stop this, Joe.

**Joe** So you keep saying.

*Sloman stands slowly, crosses to the drinks alcove.*

**Sloman** (*examining bottles, smelling glasses*) I've forgot what I were on.

*He holds a bottle up to Joe, who shakes head.*

No? (*Pours large Scotch.*) How was your meeting?

**Joe** It hasn't happened yet.

**Sloman** Really? (*He almost retches at the first sip of the Scotch.*)

Oh. (*Pause.*)

**Joe** What're you going to do, Malc?

**Sloman** I've decided to dedicate the remainder of my life to subtlety, sexuality, ambivalence and malice. Anything Pinter can't quite say, I can't quite say better, as it were. How do you mean?

**Joe** I mean, are you staying for the meeting?

**Sloman** That too. Yes.

**Joe** Fine. (*He begins redistributing cushions, rearranging chairs etc. for the meeting. It takes a little time and continues through the chat that follows. He ends by adjusting the ceiling and wall spots by means of a dimmer control switch by the doorway.*) The *News* rang again. Twice.

**Sloman** Lovely people.

**Joe** Why don't you *tell* them?

**Sloman** I've told 'em. They can stick their best play award up their managing editor's capacious and much-lipped rectum. Why should I tell 'em anything? (*finger on nose*) Tell 'em nowt. Have a drink.

**Joe** (*busy*) No. Not just yet.

*Sloman pours himself another, kills the bottle, holds it to his cheek, mock-lovingly.*

**Sloman** Poor bugger. You're empty, son. They'll stop pestering you now, you see. (*He returns to the centre of the room, shoes and socks still round his neck.*) How's things, flower?

**Joe** (*smiling*) Fine.

**Sloman** (*acute*) Are they? (*Pause.*) Still with the Kraut?

*Joe nods.*

I've finished with her. I reckon two years is long enough with any analyst. The minute they start getting interested – I mean, *actually interested* in your life and that – it's time to flit, find yourself another cold sod with fish eyes and a new line in polyvinyl platitudes. The minute I walk out of that room I want to be forgotten. Zam. Door slams. 'Who? Malcolm Who? No, I don't think so.' Know what I mean? I can't be doing with the idea of actually forming the object of somebody's . . . conjectures and . . . musings, later on. It's undignified.

**Joe** I find her pretty professional.

**Sloman** Yeah? The last time I went, she smiled as I walked in and said: 'Take a seat won't you, Mr Sloman,' without looking at the file once. I don't have to take that sort of thing from an analyst. I'd have her struck off if I had my way. Failure to expunge all memory of client the moment he clears field of vision. She's probably a liberal. Probably can't help it.

*Joe begins adjusting the lighting. Sloman falls silent,*

*watches him, absorbed.*

I think you want to take down . . . er . . . (*pointing*) six, is it? . . . about two points. And four could go up a point or two: what've you got four at?

**Joe** (*grinning*) Piss off.

**Sloman** Bloody hell. This TV lark's going to your head, old son. I remember you when you were nobbut a scruffy little actor touting for walk-ons at the Court.

**Joe** Aye. And I remember you when you used to write the Bedsit Cookery Column in the *Mirror*, so don't start that game.

**Sloman** Ah. A thousand ways to make New Zealand lamb taste like meat. Halcyon days!

**Joe** (*surveying the room*) Right. I'll have a drink. (*He crosses, pours himself a small red wine.*) Will you have another, Malc?

**Sloman** It's dead. I can't find another.

*Joe stoops, opens cupboard, surveys stack of bottles.*

**Joe** I've no blended. Could you drink a malt?

**Sloman** I suppose I'll have to, if you've nowt else.

*Joe pours him a long malt, hands it to him.*

**Joe** Cheers, Malc.

**Sloman** Cheers, flower.

*He drinks, pulls a face, shudders a little, sits down. Joe sits opposite him. Silence.*

Liked your kid.

**Joe** Yeah, he's all right.

**Sloman** We had a few pints in The Anchor, last night was it, yeah I think it was last night.

**Joe** He said.

**Sloman** He was going for a job or someat. How did he go on?

**Joe** They've offered, I think.

**Sloman** Good.

**Joe** He's started getting ambitious.

**Sloman** How'd'you mean?

**Joe** He wants to set up on his own.

**Sloman** Uhunh.

**Joe** Wants me to stake him.

**Sloman** Mmmm? And will you?

**Joe** I don't know.

**Sloman** Is it a lot?

**Joe** No. It's nothing. Couple of hundred.

**Sloman** So what's the problem?

**Joe** There's no problem. It just makes one feel . . . uneasy.

**Sloman** Yeah? Why?

**Joe** It seems illogical to use my surpluses to help set up a capitalist enterprise, that's all.

**Sloman** A what?

**Joe** That's what it'll be, Malc. Our kid being the boss doesn't make it different or special. There'll be people working for him and he'll be making a profit on their labour, just as in any other capitalist enterprise. I ask myself: If this were someone else – not my brother – asking me to help him set up a shirt factory, what would I say? No, wouldn't I? And that fast too.

**Sloman** So why the unease now, mmm? If it's that clearcut, say no and have done with it.

*Pause. Joe looks away.*

Unless there's something else.

*Silence.*

P'raps you need a brother . . . down there . . . with the workers, eh?

**Joe** It's not that.

**Sloman** No? Perhaps not.

*Silence.*

**Joe** (*checking watch*) Do you want to talk about the ninety?

**Sloman** (*reclining, eyes closed*) Jesus Christ, Joe, I sometimes wonder if there exists a background you couldn't adapt to. It's a play, Joe. Somehow or other, when it's written, it will be squeezed and tugged and shunted and fattened and primped until it finally slurps and slithers into the ninety minute . . . hole . . . your masters have graciously reserved for it. (*Pause.*) It's a *play*, Joe.

*Pause.*

**Joe** Do you want to talk about the *play* then?

**Sloman** No. (*He gets up, crosses to the cabinet; he's fairly sodden.*) How's the wife, as they say.

**Joe** She's fine. She's out.

**Sloman** Tell me something. (*Pours with exaggerated care.*)

Why do your wives always hate me so. (*He smiles sweetly in Joe's direction, takes a testing sip from the glass he's just filled with Glenmorangie.*)

**Joe** Do they?

**Sloman** Kara was the same. Reviled the ground I trod on.

**Joe** Your taste for melodrama is virtually bottomless, Mr Sloman. Neither Angie nor Kara hate you. They simply find you mildly detestable. Nothing singular in that: it's a finding they share with just about the whole of your social network.

**Sloman** Ah, well, that's er obviously a matter of nuance, Mr Shawcross. The . . . detestation with which most of those I know greet and treat me you very properly characterize as mild; whereas what I sense emanates from your erstwhile wife and her enviably beautiful successor is of such virulence and extent that not even my deep sentimental attachment to your good self can serve to persuade me from my original and persistent contention; namely, that both the bitches fucking well hate me. When did we learn to talk like puffs, Joe? Cheers.

**Joe** You sneer more than you used to.

**Sloman** I know. I lack love.

*Joe leaves the room, headed for the kitchen. Sloman stands, has a little sodden wander barefooted round the room. He reaches the door Joe has gone through.*

What're you doing?

**Joe** Fetching the food.

**Sloman** What food?

*Joe appears with a trolley laden with chicken pieces, cole slaw, french rolls, etc.*

**Joe** *The* food. (*He places the trolley carefully by the drinks cabinet, looks around the room.*)

**Sloman** You don't need a wife, Joe. You need a husband.

*Joe ignores him, breaks open a 200 packet of Senior Service.*

Who've you got coming then?

**Joe** Hard to say. Ford, do you know Andrew Ford? *Review*? He said he'd be here.

**Sloman** Not the Gower Street Terror, Flash Ford, the New Left's answer to Joseph Stalin!

**Joe** Ford's OK. I've asked him to have something ready, in case we need it. General background, that kind of thing . . .

**Sloman** Oh. Terrific. Who else?

**Joe** Somebody from Agitprop. Ball, I think he's called. Doing good stuff in the factories.

**Sloman** Women. What about women?

**Joe** Kara. My erstwhile etc.

**Sloman** Oh Jesus. *Women* I said. I think you've forgotten what they are! Kara's not a woman, she's a political position. (*Pause.*) And like I said, she hates the sight of me. (*He grins.*) It's a cunt, innit!

**Joe** I asked a couple of girls from I.S.

**Sloman** Ah. Thank God for I.S. Who else?

**Joe** Jeremy Hayes.

**Sloman** Oh Christ. Worse and worse. Listen, it's bad enough I have to see my agent on business. You're not serious.

**Joe** Why not? He's starting a weekly paper soon. He's raised the *bread*, Malc. You know? While others sit and sneer at the playboy literary agent with a penchant for left-wing politics, he's raised two and a half grand and the paper is going to happen.

**Sloman** Well, Joe, old flower, when you've seen a copy or two, mebbe you'll have cause to change your opinion. What's he going to call it? The *Opportunist*? Who else?

**Joe** John Tagg.

*Silence. Sloman puts his glass down.*

**Sloman** John Tagg?

**Joe** That's right.

**Sloman** You always had a touch of the marriage feast at Cana in you, Joe. S'what makes you a good producer, I suppose. How come?

**Joe** Simple. He asked me to call the meeting.

**Sloman** Asked you. Why you? I don't get the connection.

**Joe** I met one or two of his people at the union branch. They seemed to talk a lot of sense.

**Sloman** They do, they do.

**Joe** So, I er . . . went down to Battersea and met . . . Tagg and one or two others. And er . . . he said he was keen to get some sort of dialogue going on the left. So I offered my place for a meeting.

**Sloman** Nice of you. (*Pause.*) Is that what he said: Dialogue?

**Joe** Ahuuh.

**Sloman** A dialogue with the Trots. That should be worth trying to stay sober for.

**Joe** Perhaps I should've told you earlier then.

**Sloman** Don't worry about me, old son. I'll make out.

*The doorbell rings twice.*

Ah. Ladies first, I trust.

**Joe** (*at doorway*) Are you er . . .?

*He points to his neck and chest. Sloman blinks at his shoes, the socks half hanging from them.*

**Sloman** I lose 'em else, Joe. Yeah sure.

*Joe leaves. Sloman stands unsteadily, tries to undo the knot at the back of his neck; can't.* **Susie** *and* **Kate** *in (the two I.S. people) early twenties, attractive in an earnest sort of way.*

**Susie** Hello. I'm Susie Plaistow.

**Sloman** (*blinking, smiling a broad silly smile*) Welcome Susie. You look like an International Socialist to me.

**Susie** That's right, how did you know.

**Sloman** (*tapping it*) The nose knows, Susie. Trust it always. Malcolm Sloman.

**Kate** '24 Hours'.

**Sloman** (*looking at watch, frowning*) What?

**Susie** '24 Hours' is on in three minutes. We want to see what's happening in Paris.

**Sloman** That's no problem. (*He switches the set on.*) Come round here then where it's warm.

**Kate** (*crossing*) Kate Stead. How do you do.

*She shakes his hand firmly. Sloman has his hand shaken. They stand in front of him staring at the box. It's amateur boxing. Sloman peers from Susie to Kate and back again, over their shoulders. It's a thorough inspection.*

**Kate** It's late.

**Susie** Mmmmm.

**Sloman** (*tentatively*) On your own, are you then, Susie?

*The door opens and* **Louis Preece,** *black, big, American, mid twenties, enters, followed by* **Richard Maine,** *younger, I.S., into student politics at LSE.*

**Susie** S'all right, you've missed nothing, it hasn't started yet.

**Maine** Fat lot you care. Why can't you park your own car?

**Susie** (*to Sloman*) Sorry, what did you say?

**Sloman** (*sad*) Nothing. I didn't say a thing, love.

**Kate** Shh. It's on.

*'24 Hours' music. Louis turns the sound up. Sloman picks up his drink, walks slowly out through the french windows unobserved, shoes still around his neck. Joe ushers in* **'Grease' Ball,** *a burly north London anarchist working in street theatre.*

**Joe** Make yourself at home, Grease. I'll do the introductions when *that* ends.

**Grease** Ta.

*Grease sniffs round the room, pecks a smile or two at the watching others as he catches an eye, settles finally in front of the set.*

**Joe** There's food on the trolley, if anyone's interested. Booze over there. Give a shout if you want anything else.

I'm expecting others . . . so . . . p'raps we should watch
this for a bit anyway.

*Mostly he's ignored. Louis gives him a bland wink but
no smile and returns to the screen. Close but not vital
attention at this stage, as Robert McKenzie gives a
studio background to the present discontent. Suddenly
they move by satellite to Paris itself and the scene of the
student demonstration. Louis turns up the volume, the
atmosphere becomes immediately more charged and
sparky. Fade lights; bring up the bulletin they're
watching on the wall screen behind them. The grand
march to the Sorbonne has begun. Torches flare, there is
much banter, humour and resolution. Caped police and
CRS line routes and hold strategic points along it. A
rather breathless English commentary tries to account
for what we see.*

*Fade everything to black.*

*Fade up again. TV, wall screen pic, followed by room
lights. People still stand or sit, rather stunned and
excited. On the screen, Harry Carpenter is sunnily
welcoming us back to the ringside at the Albert Hall,
where England are matched with Poland.*

**Louis** Right on! Doesn't that blow your mind though?
Jesus Christ, I need a j. (*He fiddles in his pocket for grass
and papers.*)

**Susie** (*crossing to switch set off*) What're we doing here,
for Christ's sake! It's started, man.

*Animated chat develops among those who know each
other. Wall pic disappears. Room back to full light.
Others have arrived during the programme:* **Katra
Massingham**, *early thirties, attractively mannish, in light
blue suede trousers and matching suede tasselled
waistcoat, and* **Jeremy Hayes**, *late thirties, suave,
attractive, a trace of south London still there beneath*

*the Kensington charm.*

**Grease** (*at the food trolley*) All right if I help myself, is it?

**Joe** Sure thing. Please do. Drink over there. (*generally*) Listen. P'raps it'd be better if we said who we were as and when. I'm Joe Shawcross.

*For the next several minutes people settle in, grab food, help each other to drink etc.*

**Louis** (*licking paper delicately*) Louis Preece. I'm with Kate. Hi.

**Maine** Richard Maine. LSE.

**Joe** Hello.

**Susie** Is that all right?

**Joe** Of course. This is er . . . Ed, is it?

**Grease** (*chicken in each fist*) Someat like that. Grease'll do. Howdy.

**Joe** Grease is in street theatre. Erm. Kara Massingham . . . works for the *Guardian.*

*Kara smiles.*

And Jeremy Hayes.

**Hayes** Hi.

**Joe** (*to Kara*) Did you see Malcolm Sloman anywhere?

**Kara** What, here? No.

**Susie** (*pointing to window*) Through there.

*Doorbell rings.*

**Joe** (*turning to Kara*) Watch out for him if he comes back. (*He swivels an imaginary glass.*)

**Kara** No! Really?

*Joe gets the door. Louis hands the joint to Susie.*

**Kate** (*mock-northern, at the splendid room*) Not short of a bob or two, are we!

**Louis** Don't be small town, chickie. Some of my best friends are rich Liberals.

**Kate** I bet.

**Susie** Stop bitching, for Christ's sake.

**Maine** (*serious, taking joint*) That's right. Where should he live, a hovel?

**Grease** Why not? That's where most of us live.

**Maine** Speak for yourself.

**Grease** (*mildly*) I do, brother.

**Louis** (*to Kate*) Hey, hey, hey, hey. Time enough for squabbles *after* the revolution. It's a nice pad. OK. Finish.

*Hayes and Kara look at each other frowningly. They feel themselves no longer this juvenile. Joe in with* **Andrew Ford,** *around thirty, tallish, blond, pale skinned, rather beautiful in the face. He's a lecturer in sociology; sharp, articulate, arrogant beneath the slight charm.*

**Susie** Hello. How are you?

**Ford** (*cool*) Fine. How're you?

**Susie** OK.

**Joe** Erm . . . Andrew Ford, LSE, etc., etc. Erm . . . well, I guess you'll find who everybody else is by closing time. Food (*pointing*), booze (*looking round*). Right. I suppose I ought to try and set things rolling.

*People settle down a little. Ford helps himself to food and drink. Sloman in from terrace. He carries an empty Scotch bottle. He taps on the window.*

**Sloman** (*boy's voice*) Excuse me, is this where they're going to have the revolution?

**Joe** Come on, Malc . . .

**Sloman** (*in*) Hello, Susie. How you doing, chick? Oh, and beautiful Kara, up to her delectable directories in theory. What a lovely surprise. It must be Ex-Wives' Night. I hope to Christ mine don't show.

**Kara** (*to Susie*) It's all right. He has to rattle his balls from time to time, to make sure they're still there.

**Sloman** (*to Susie*) Inspection's in an hour, love, if you're interested. Actually I'm looking for a small drink of thingie, you know. (*seeing Hayes*) Something for you, Jeremy? Small hemlock, maybe?

**Hayes** I'm fine, Malcolm.

**Sloman** Good. That good. (*He wanders over to the drinks, where Ford stands.*) Hello, Flash, how's it been then? Still sorting Cuba out are we?

**Ford** (*cool*) Hello, Sloman.

**Sloman** (*over shoulder, to Joe*) Where's Tagg, then, Shawkie? He'd be late for his own insurrection would that one.

**Joe** Get your drink and sit down, Malc.

**Sloman** Aye aye, sir. (*He carries a bottle over towards the windows, lies flat on the floor, the bottle on his chest. Muttering*) God help you, that's all. All of you.

**Ford** Did he say Tagg?

**Joe**  Yes, I was trying to explain.

**Sloman**  (*muttering*) I bet.

**Joe**  This is one of a series of small, private meetings that the Revolutionary Socialist Party's organizing, both here in London and er . . . throughout the country generally. Now, I'm not a member of the Party, but I'm convinced that what the left in Britain needs now more than ever is a united and coherent focus for its efforts. But above all, we need theory. Not necessarily the RSP's but a genuine socialist analysis of our situation that will give us a rational basis for political action beyond the single-issue activities that have kept us fragmented and . . . impotent . . . in the past.

**Kara**  But why Tagg?

**Louis**  Who's Tagg, for Christ's sake?

**Sloman**  Who's Mighty Joe Young!

**Joe**  John Tagg is the National Organiser of the RSP and an executive member of the reconstituted Fourth International. Why Tagg? Why not? At least he's clear about what he wants. He has an organization. And above all he wants to talk. He wants a dialogue.

**Kara**  He's after money. I know Tagg.

**Joe**  (*calmly*) Put it to him. He'll be here directly.

**Grease**  You mean we gotta sit around waiting for him?

**Joe**  No, no. Not at all. You got something to say, you say it.

**Grease**  I mean, it's just bleeding pointless sitting here getting pissed, I can do that at home.

**Ford**  What does he aim to do when he does come?

**Joe** I don't know. Talk, I suppose.

**Sloman** (*from floor*) You bet.

**Kara** He won't do much listening, that's for sure. P'raps he'll organize a séance. The last meeting of his I went to he called up the ghost of Lev Davidovitch from a bound copy of the *Transitional Programme*. It was amazing.

**Ford** Tagg's all right. He can be handled.

**Sloman** (*muttering but clear enough*) Cream bun, I've seen him eat bigger fellers than you with a pint of Guinness and a pickle on a plate. You'd do better sticking to your (*lies down again*) Late Night Line-Up.

**Kate** (*bored*) Meantime . . .

**Sloman** How about a sing song?

**Ford** Who was it said Personality is the gonorrohea of the left? Would anybody mind if we talked politics? Mmmm? I don't mind kicking off, if there are no objections.

*Silence of assent.*

OK.

*He looks at the students; he's assured, confident, pleased to be in charge; already rejecting the notes in his brief-case.*

Joe asked me to make a few notes on general background theory, but it's pretty obvious where the body of our interest lies. So I suggest we put the notes away. (*He puts the case down and gets started.*)

*The door opens and* **Tagg** *walks in. He's short, stocky, very powerful, about sixty, Scots, from Glasgow. He wears an old-fashioned double-breasted suit, tie slack at open-collared neck; neck bursting to be free. His face is cragged, expressionless. He carries a small flat pigskin* *document case in his right hand.*

**Tagg** (*mildly*) Good evening. Sorry I'm late.

*Silence. Even Sloman sits up, relishing the moment.*

**Joe** John. Good to see you. Come in, come in. We were just getting underway. Eats and drinks over there, let me get you something.

**Tagg** (*advancing into room*) No, I'm fine thanks. Why don't you just carry on and I'll sit and listen for a while?

**Joe** Do you want me to introduce you . . .?

**Tagg** No no. (*to room*) My name's John Tagg, for what it's worth. That'll do for now.

**Joe** Fine. Andrew?

*Ford deliberates for a moment, not sure whether to cede the floor at once; or perhaps unconsciously modifying his presentation now that Tagg's arrived.*

**Ford** Well. It seems there are a number of options open to us. Quite frankly, I'm more interested in talking about France – or Paris, to be more precise – than about general Marxist theory. On the other hand, perhaps it would do no harm to try and tease out some basic agreement on . . . well, terminology, for example.

**Sloman** (*muttering, on back*) Oh yeah, I think we should tease that out. Definitely.

**Ford** (*to Tagg*) What do *you* think?

**Tagg** (*simply*) I leave it to you.

**Ford** I mean, I'm perfectly happy to hand over to you right now, if you'd prefer it.

**Tagg** No no. You go ahead.

**Grease** I don't wanna talk about terminology. Jesus Christ, what is this!

**Joe** Well, what's the general feeling then? Mmmmm?

**Kate** Let him speak.

**Louis** (*rolling joint*) Right on.

**Maine** Right.

**Joe** Kara? Jeremy?

*They nod.*

**Susie** Some on, come on. There's twenty thousand people contesting state power in Paris and we can't even decide what to talk about! (*to Ford*) *Say* something eh!

**Ford** Right. (*Brief-case back in hand and opened. Seminar voice developing – as he pushes at once into his favourite game of political theory.*) Let me try to offer a relatively unexceptional account of the basic Marxian analysis; and then suggest a few (*glance at Tagg*) . . . revisions of my own. (*Pause.*) It's in *Economic and Philosophical Manuscripts*, written in 1844, that we receive our first authoritative definitions. Communism, says the young Marx, is the positive abolition of private property, of human self-alienation and thus the real appropriation of human nature, through and for man. It is therefore the return of man himself as a *social*, that is, really human being, a complete and conscious return which assimilates all the wealth of previous development. He elaborates the point later on thus: Communism is the *definitive* resolution of the antagonism between man and nature, and between man and man. It is the true solution of the conflict between existence and essence, between objectification and self-affirmation, between freedom and necessity, between individual and species. It is the solution of the riddle of History and knows itself to be this solution. Now I think we have there a crucial locus, both moral and scientific, for almost everything we say and do as socialists now. We have, there, at once a vision of future societies in which the social, that's to say, fully *human* aspects of mankind will flourish; and in addition, some indication of its historical inevitability. As Marx has it: 'Communism as a complete naturalism is humanism, and as a complete humanism is naturalism.' The task Marx and the nineteenth-century Marxists set themselves was to chart, precisely and empirically, the way in which these future societies would form or be formed. Part of that . . . description concerned itself with the nature of social classes; in particular, with the three major classes in post-feudal society: bourgeoisie, peasantry, proletariat. The precondition for the domination of society in general by a single class is, according to Marx, that that class should identify itself with the society, and will be felt and recognized as the general representative of that society. Its aims and interests must genuinely be the aims and interests of society itself, of which it becomes, in Marx's phrase, the 'social head and heart'. But even that's not enough. For one class to represent the whole of society, another class must concentrate in itself all the evils of society and embody and represent a general obstacle and limitation. In his words: 'For one class to be the liberating class *par excellence*, it is essential that another class should be openly the oppressing class.' But notice: it is never enough that these competing classes should merely co-exist at a particular historical conjunction. Classes that wish to become liberating classes must possess, as it were, self-consciousness sufficient to enable them to organize their victory. Logic, insight, courage and clarity – these are the social qualities that would-be liberating classes must possess if they are to realize their full historical potential. I dwell on this part of the model, because it represents a most interesting duality or conjunction, between material inevitability on the one hand, and human agency on the other. A thumbnail sketch of Marxist praxis in the nineteenth century would show, I think, an increasing and debilitating emphasis on inevitability and a critical undermining of the role of agency. Hence the Second International, with its over-mechanistic view of what constituted the 'proper' historical-material conditions for a genuine proletarian revolution; and, in particular, a slavish adherence to the Marxian tenet that a proletarian revolution was impossible in societies that had not first undergone a bourgeois revolution. It was the unique and deeply original contribution of Lenin – a poor Marxist, in the academic sense of the term – that he redressed this balance; that he reintroduced human will and agency to the Marxist discourse. Stressing organization, ruthless discipline and the central role of the party, he pretty nearly singlehandedly forced through a working-class revolution in what was, by any standards, a materially underdeveloped, still largely feudal society. In other words, he showed that it was possible to tear down the inflexible historical model and fashion history, to some extent at least, in the image of his own Bolshevik party. (*Pause.*) Of course, what I'm suggesting here is that . . . 'revisionism' has a thoroughly . . . revolutionary . . . antecedence: the late Marx revised the early Marx, Engels revised the late Marx, Lenin revised the lot of them. (*Pause.*) Well, a few modest revisions of my own . . . It seems to me that, from Lenin on, the older model has grown increasingly more irrelevant, for a number of reasons. I mean, one look at France or Britain today is enough to make the point, I think. The world we now inhabit and hope to act upon is a vastly different one from that on which Marx made his largely empirical calculations and observations. The Russian revolution is a fact. Its development – in a single country, with all the distortions that have inevitably occurred as a result – is a fact. The post-Second World

War Soviet camp in Europe, modelled on those precise deformations of Russian socialism, is a fact. Equally, the nature of capitalism – particularly its deep technical and bureaucratic self-transformations and adaptations – national to multinational via multicorporative – is an empirical fact that in a sense leaves the classical nineteenth-century Marxian analysis behind. So that we must increasingly come to regard the history of twentieth-century Europe as a history of vacuums: no German revolution; no French revolution; no Italian revolution; no British revolution. Instead, the gradual absorption, the slow assimilation of European proletariats into the institutions of the reformed and superadaptive bourgeois state. And if we accept the model so far we cannot avoid taking some account of the what? – hegemonic mechanisms – through which that . . . inhibition of revolutionary potential was achieved. Because one of the first things those states have sought to do is to mediate, to obscure, to mystify their own class nature, by securing unto themselves a vastly more powerful and pervasive system of propaganda; by which I mean, of course, educational institutions, art forms, newspapers, television, and all the many large- and small-scale means of communications existing in contemporary post-industrial societies. In 1968, European proletariats can no longer be said to be a subversive force inside capitalism, because European proletariats no longer feel themselves faced by a European bourgeoisie that concentrates in itself, to return to Marx; 'All the evils of society, embodying and representing a general obstacle and limitation.'

*He pauses, enjoying himself more than he dare show. In his proper element. Varieties of reaction: Tagg impassive. Finally.*

**Sloman** You don't say.

**Ford** (*ignoring him*) So, we need a new model, perhaps a new concept. The Marxian notion of a revolution carried by the majority of the exploited masses, culminating in the seizure of power and in the setting up of a proletarian dictatorship which initiates socialization, is overtaken by historical development. I would even argue that Marx himself would now see that that analysis pertains to a stage of capitalist productivity and organization which has been overtaken; it does not project the higher stage of capitalist productivity self-evidently achieved in the last half-century, including the productivity of destruction and the terrifying concentration of the instruments of annihilation and of indoctrination in the hands of the state or its class representatives. Nor does that analysis take account of the machinery of what Marcuse calls the 'repressive tolerance' of neocapitalist societies, of which, if I may say so, we are all living, breathing examples. The very fact of our being tolerated tends to render us impotent. (*Pause. Another pan round the listening group*) The element so far omitted, of course, is what has been termed the Third World. China, Cuba, Vietnam: these are the new centres of the world revolutionary struggle. The national liberation movements in the colonial enclave are probably the sole and certainly the principal revolutionary forces at work in the world today. The capitalist heartland is no longer London, or Paris, or Turin: it is Saigon, it is Angola, it is Mozambique. The 'weak link' in the capitalist chain is now at the periphery, and it is there, if anywhere, that the chain will be induced to snap. We move from centre to epicentre, which becomes the new centre. Our function, in the old centres, is to assist, however we may, the final victory of these anti-capitalist, revolutionary movements. Whether we are blacks in Detroit or white proletarians in Manchester, that is our sole remaining revolutionary purpose and duty. And, a last note of direct application here, I think, we must not seek to impose upon these movements the theoretical and organizational patterns elaborated for and applied to the strategy of metropolitan areas; such as city-based leaderships, centralized party control, and all the dead wood of European practice. (*Pause. To Joe*) I'll stop there, if that's all right.

**Joe** Sure, sure. Thanks very much.

**Ford** (*coolly*) I don't want to steal anybody else's thunder.

*An awkward silence develops. The students look at each other, pulling faces.*

**Joe** Well . . .

**Grease** It's just books. What's the point, I mean!

**Hayes** I found it useful. But I thought you could've found a spot for students as a sub-class in your model. Bearing in mind what's been happening in Europe and America, I mean. You know, I think the Rudi Dutschke shooting and what's happening in Paris really do need some serious analysis.

**Louis** Students! How about *blacks*, for Christ's sake! Holy Jesus!! Forty-six American cities under black siege this year and we haven't even started the summer yet. That's where the future lies, man. That's the only revolution that's gonna matter, believe it.

*Some expostulation, counter-argument etc.*

**Ford** Blacks and students, sure. Nobody's denying their importance. All I've tried to do is give a general theoretical framework into which they can fit . . .

**Kara** And women?

**Sloman** (*sitting up*) Where, where?

**Ford** Yes, but which women? Are they all equally

oppressed? All potentially revolutionary?

**Maine** (*pompous*) I missed any telling reference to social democracy and its relation to capitalist structures.

*Silence greets this. He grows uneasy.*

I think . . . a socialist analysis should . . . have something to say about . . . the Wilson government . . . and its record.

*Sloman gets up and walks to the drinks cabinet, saying 'Ehhhhhhh' as he goes.*

**Grease** It doesn't matter, any of it. It's not bloody *relevant.* None of it answers the question: What are we going to *do?* I've *been* to extra-mural classes . . . That's why I'm here now.

**Sloman** (*pouring drinks*) Why don't we form an International Brigade to keep the Spanish off Gibraltar!

**Ford** (*to Joe*) Oh Jesus, is he going to go on all night with this puerile patter?

**Joe** (*low*) No, it's all right, he'll . . . er . . . settle down.

*The lack of direction is showing. Still Tagg sits tight, a hard and impassive Buddha. A few glance towards him, frustrated, a trifle angry at the fragmented nature of the meeting so far. Sloman ambles back to around centre, stops, chicken leg in one hand, Scotch in other, stares very deliberately at Ford.*

**Sloman** (*swaying very slightly*) I've heard better warm-ups at a funeral. (*He sniffs, drinks, tries to think. To Tagg*) How about it, John? Are you going to tell us about how, if the earth hadn't been created flat, man would have had to flatten it? I like that one. I think it's your best one, I do.

*Silence. Sloman's smile hardens the offence.*

**Tagg** (*mild but deliberate*) Sloman. I'm not here to talk salon rubbish with a drunk. It that all right?

**Joe** Why don't you go out for a bit, Malc?

**Sloman** (*bullish*) I don't want to go out!

**Kara** Well, shut up, will you. You're a bloody nuisance!

**Sloman** (*to Joe*) See! See! Don't tell me nothing. The bitch hates me!

**Hayes** Rubbish, Malcolm. We all love you dearly.

**Sloman** Oh yes. And you've twenty grand in the bank to prove it, agent.

**Tagg** (*to Joe principally*) Did you agree a form?

**Joe** I'm sorry?

**Tagg** A form. For the meeting.

**Joe** Erm, well no, not really, no. Do you have something in mind?

**Grease** What's wrong with just talking?

**Tagg** Free for all is free for nobody. I'm not interested in conversation. I'm here for discussion. Structured. With a shape and an end.

**Grease** You want us to number from the left or something?

**Tagg** No. But we could have a chair.

**Grease** What do we want a chair for? Jesus Christ. There's *ten* of us, man. Suddenly we need a bureaucracy.

**Joe** Well, I don't know. What does anybody think?

**Hayes** Doesn't bother me either way. If it makes Mr Tagg feel happier, we'll have a chair.

**Kara** The hell we will. He's right. Talk at will.

**Louis** Jesus, elections! We haven't even got a platform!

**Kate** That's right. (*She takes Louis's joint.*)

**Joe** Andrew?

**Ford** I've no objections to a chair. I don't even object to an elected executive that meets in the garden to draw up an agenda. I simply object to the tactic.

**Joe** What does that mean?

**Ford** It's all boringly familiar, Joe. Do we have a form, let's get ourselves organized. I've heard it all before. What's important is to stifle spontaneity. (*ironic*) By all means, let's have a chair.

   *Silence.*

**Tagg** (*mildly*) All right. No chair. It doesn't matter.

**Sloman** (*by window now*) You should take that back, playboy.

**Tagg** Why don't you go somewhere else, Sloman?

**Sloman** (*raging suddenly*) Because I don't fucking well WANT to Tagg. Don't come your God the Father bit with me, right?

**Joe** Easy, Malc.

**Sloman** (*blowing*) FUCK OFF. I don't need your . . . protection you creeping get. Just get off my back.

   *He lurches, kicks a bottle and some glasses over, clutches at a chair as he loses balance, drags it down to the floor with him, struggles to get up again, turns another chair over. People clear a circle for his mad sprawl. He stands at last, a bottle in his hand.*

**Joe** (*through this*) Malc, for Christ's sake take it EASY will you, man, will you?

**Sloman** Fuck off. (*swallowing, puffing, searching for control*) What do you lot *know*, eh. Any of you? Preening. Preening. On the scene. It doesn't *hurt*, does it? Any of it. (*at the main group*) Does it!!

*He swings round suddenly to hurl his bottle through a window. Glass cascades on to the floor. Joe closes.*

**Joe** Come on, Malc, let's have you. Come on.

*Joe goes to put his arms round Sloman, is hurled backwards by a tremendous thrash of arms and shoulders.*

**Sloman** Get off me. Just get off. Just get your hands off me. I'm not a bloody *plaything*. (*He blinks and scowls, drunk, dangerous, in pain.*) I just want to say something. You see, if you could understand it, we could . . . get somewhere. If you could feel it, I mean. (*quoting, searching for the words*) 'As long as I breathe I shall fight for the future, that . . . radiant future, in which man, strong and beautiful, will become master of the drifting stream of his own history . . .'

*He stands a little dazed and hypnotized, not sure where he is or why. One or two Jesuses from Kate and Kara. Everyone still apprehensive. Tagg gets up slowly and walks towards Sloman.*

**Tagg** 'I can see the bright green . . . strip of grass beneath the wall and the clear blue sky above the wall, and sunlight everywhere. Life . . . is beautiful. Let the future generations cleanse it . . . of all evil . . . oppression, and violence, and enjoy it to the full.'

*Sloman is quiet and close to tears. The tears are only half self-pitying, he is truly moved by the words and the delivery.* (*gently*) Have a sleep.

**Sloman** You're . . . old, John.

**Tagg** Have a sleep.

*Sloman looks around the room, at the broken window, then lurches out into the garden. The guinea pig sets up a whining squeal as he bangs against the cage.*

**Sloman** (*off*) Go thou! I'll fetch some flax and whites of egg, to apply to his bleeding face.

**Ford** (*scathing*) What a wreck!

*The pig's squeals get louder. Charlie begins to cry upstairs. Milanka in from training, bag on shoulder.*

**Milanka** I'll see to him. (*She leaves.*)

*Muttering and staring, Tagg looks round the room, as the squeals tail off and Charlie's crying is muted by Milanka's indistinct soothings.*

**Tagg** (*finally*) Will we make a start?

*Black.*
   *Black stage. 'The Red Flag', in French, vibrant, full-lunged, it fades. Lights up front left; a segment of terrace, hint of long, controlled lawn and gardens. A swing, a kid's bike, a climbing frame, canvas chairs, plants in tubs, the pig hutch, knocked askew on its supporting brick stacks, the wall of the house. Joe carries a bulky flash-light with a flashing red top, scores the lawn area (out front, that is) with it. He stops to right the hutch, strokes the wires gently with his finger, returns to his search eventually. Upstairs, Milanka has been singing 'Ej Od Buchlova' to Charlie.*

**Joe** Malc. Malc. Come on in.

*The singing stops. An upstairs window opens.*

**Milanka** (*from window, soft, into the darkness*) He is quiet.

**Joe** (*whispering*) Fine. Thanks.

**Milanka** I make coffee?

**Joe** Thanks. Big pot.

**Milanka** How is Novotny?

**Joe** Indestructible.

**Milanka** I make the coffee.

*She withdraws. Joe turns into the garden again.*

**Joe** Malc.

*A crashing sound somewhere in the dark. The pig shrieks once.*

Malc. It's Joe. Come on in.

*No answer. Joe stands for a long time staring out, immobile, inert. He is without energy or direction. Kara appears behind him; watches him for several moments without speaking. She shivers a little in the cool night air.*

**Kara** (*finally*) Leave him. He'll be all right.

**Joe** He's there somewhere. (*Pause.*) He's hurt.

**Kara** He's just drunk.

*Pause. Kara lights a Gauloise.*

**Joe** What's happening . . .?

**Kara** Someone's cleaning up the mess.

**Joe** Yeah?

*They both laugh, though tentatively.*

**Kara** And then Tagg brings down the tablets.

*Pause.*

**Joe** You with Hayes?

**Kara** Sort of.

**Joe** Uhunh. What about Margaret?

**Kara** He's left her. There was nothing there.

**Joe** Oh.

**Kara** Is that all right?

**Joe** Sorry. (*Pause.*) So, what're you doing with yourself?

**Kara** Oh, surviving, as they say. Jeremy's trying to get this paper out.

**Joe** I heard about it. Sounds good. Are you involved?

**Kara** Yes. Sort of. We've formed a collective to run it. Seven of us.

**Joe** Do you have a line?

**Kara** Several. About seven.

**Joe** Sounds familiar.

*Pause.*

**Kara** How about you?

**Joe** Yeah I'm fine.

**Kara** Angie?

**Joe** Yes. She's fine too. She's out.

**Kara** I noticed. (*Pause.*) Do you want to talk?

**Joe** No. I'm fine. Really.

**Kara** Why don't you give me a call at the office, we'll have a drink sometime.

**Joe** I will. D'be nice.

**Kara** You've stopped talking, haven't you?

**Joe** Howd'you mean?

**Kara** You don't say anything. I watched you in there. You have . . . no opinions. You have no . . . energy.

**Joe** They also serve who only keep their lips buttoned.

**Kara** Don't go under, Joe.

**Joe** D'you remember the Fields Season at the NFT? (*He flicks an imaginary cigar, perfect Fields voice.*) 'Never drink water. Fish make love in it.' (*own voice*) I just stopped drinking water.

*Silence.*

**Kara** Drink water.

**Joe** I'm sick of . . . opinions.

**Kara** Oh yes?

**Joe** No, it's . . . tones of voice I'm sick of. (*He points at the house.*) We do this like we do everything else. It's a game. It's an intellectual pursuit. Or something worse. It's part of being . . . bourgeois. Peel the onion: find the nuance beneath the hint, the insight in the discrimination, the complexity below the conceit. I'm sick of metaphors. They induce only inertia. (*Pause.*) We've got upper second souls. Do you know?

**Kara** Mmmm. Well, at least you're drinking water again.

**Joe** (*smiling*) Sipping.

**Kara** We fucked out here once. Do you remember?

**Joe** Yes.

**Kara** It was good then.

**Joe**  Was it?

**Kara**  Only from here. (*She turns to go in. Turns back.*) What's your connection with Tagg?

**Joe**  Why?

**Kara**  I think he's poisonous. Don't let him bite you.

**Joe**  No. He doesn't play our sort of game, that's all.

**Kara**  Come on, Joe. You're not falling for all that sentimental working-man crap, are you. (*Pause.*) Think of your father. Eh?

**Joe**  Is it likely? I never fell for anything in my life. Perhaps that's why I'm such a sodding shambles.

**Kara**  He'll leach you dry. I'm telling you. I know Tagg. And he's irrelevant. You can drive a coach-and-four through his analysis. He's a brutal shite underneath with a fist where his mind used to be. Now I'm telling you.

*Silence.*

**Joe**  (*very quiet*) Yeah.

**Kara**  You coming in?

**Joe**  Sure. In a minute.

*She wavers, finally leaves. Joe stands looking out into the garden, sweeps the darkness once, twice, with the torch, switches to red alarm signal, places the torch on the ground, walks slowly in. It flashes throughout the remainder of the Scene.*

*Living-room lights up, as Joe re-enters. Kara has rejoined Hayes. People sit or lie. Lights lower than before, no longer quite natural. Tagg roughly centred, marginally better lit, perches on a stool, not at home in this room. The mess has cleared. Milanka carries out the last of the glass in a dustpan.*

**Tagg** (*to Joe*) OK?

**Joe** (*shutting french windows*) Yes, of course.

**Tagg** I'll erm . . . take issue with our comrade's er . . . analysis and model presently. I'd like to start by explaining why I'm here. It's very simple really. I'm National Organizer and Executive Council Member of the RSP, which is the British branch of the reconstituted Fourth International, and bases itself on the *Transitional Programme* drawn up by Trotsky some years before his death. I spend most of my time with workers – dockers, miners, engineers, car-workers, bricklayers, seamen. And as I'll try to explain later, a revolutionary party or faction that fails to establish itself in the working class, to base itself upon it, can lay no claim whatsoever to serious attention. (*Pause.*) But a revolutionary Marxist who has lived in Europe, America, or almost anywhere else, for that matter, during the last three or four years, would have to be blind and deaf not to have noticed a considerable . . . revolutionary potential, shall we call it? growing among sections of the population whose relation to the working class is either nonexistent, or extremely tenuous, or positively antagonistic. I'm thinking of such categories as students, blacks, intellectuals, social deviants of one sort or another, women, and so on. And so we've decided to begin a general campaign of political education – including *self*-education, I should add – that might result in a broader and more experienced base for all our efforts. (*Pause.*) It's not a sudden accession of humility, I should point out. It's not a drive for membership. It's not a fund-raising effort. It's not a search for ideological compromise and political blandness. If our analysis is correct, we're entering a new phase in the revolutionary struggle against the forces and the structures of capitalism. The disaffection is widespread: in London, in Paris, in Berlin, in the American cities; wherever you care to look, bourgeois

institutions are under sustained and often violent attack.
New forces are rising up to throw themselves into the fray.
The question is: How may they be brought to help the
revolution? Or are they simply doomed forever to be
merely 'protests' that the 'repressive tolerance' of 'late
capitalist' societies will absorb and render impotent?
(*Pause.*) We shall need some theory, to answer questions
like those. But I suspect the theory will not be entirely in
accord with that which we have heard expounded by our
comrade here tonight. (*Pause.*) There's something
profoundly saddening about that analysis. And, if I might
be permitted a small digression, it seems to reflect a basic
sadness and pessimism in you yourselves. You're
intellectuals. You're frustrated by the ineffectual character
of your opposition to the things you loathe. Your main
weapon is the word. Your protest is verbal – it has to be: it
wears itself out by repetition and leads you nowhere.
Somehow you sense – and properly so – that for a protest
to be effective, it must be rooted in the realities of social
life, in the productive processes of a nation or a society. In
1919 London dockers went on strike and refused to load
munitions for the White armies fighting against the
Russian revolution. In 1944 dockers in Amsterdam refused
to help the Nazis transport Jews to concentration camps.
What can *you* do? You can't strike and refuse to handle
American cargoes until they get out of Vietnam. You're
outside the productive process. You have only the word.
And you cannot make it become the deed. And because
the people who have the power seem uneager to use it, you
develop this . . . cynicism . . . this contempt. You say: The
working class has been assimilated, corrupted,
demoralized. You point to his car and his house and his
pension scheme and his respectability, and you write him
off. You build a whole theory around it and you fill it with
grandiloquent phrases like 'epicentres' and
'neocolonialism'. But basically what you do is you find

some scapegoat for your own frustration and misery and then you start backing the field: blacks, students, homosexuals, terrorist groupings, Mao, Che Guevara, anybody, just so long as they represent some repressed minority still capable of anger and the need for self-assertion. (*Pause.*) Well. Which workers have you spoken with recently? And for how long? How do you know they're not as frustrated as you are? Especially the young ones, who take the cars and the crumbs from the table for granted? If they don't satisfy *you*, why should they satisfy the people who actually create the wealth in the first place? You start from the presumption that only you are intelligent and sensitive enough to see how bad capitalist society is. Do you really think the young man who spends his whole life in monotonous and dehumanizing work doesn't see it too? And in a way more deeply, more woundingly? (*Pause.*) Suddenly you lose contact – not with ideas, not with abstractions, concepts, because they're after all your stock-in-trade. You lose contact with the moral tap-roots of socialism. In an objective sense, you actually stop believing in a revolutionary perspective, in the possibility of a socialist society and the creation of socialist man. You see the difficulties, you see the complexities and contradictions, and you settle for those as a sort of game you can play with each other. Finally, you learn to enjoy your pain; to need it, so that you have nothing to offer your bourgeois peers but a sort of moral exhaustion. You can't build socialism on fatigue, comrades. Shelley dreamed of man 'sceptreless, free, uncircumscribed, equal, classless, tribeless and nationless, exempt from all worship and awe'. Trotsky foresaw the ordinary socialist man on a par with an Aristotle, a Goethe, a Marx, with still new peaks rising above those heights. Have you any image at all to offer? The question embarrasses you. You've contracted the disease you're trying to cure. (*Pause.*) I called this a digression, but in a

way it describes very accurately the difficulty I experience
when I try to deal with our comrade's . . . analysis.
Comrade Sloman was right, under it all. Theory isn't
abstract; it isn't words on a page; it isn't . . . aesthetically
pleasing patterns of ideas and evidence. Theory is
concrete. It's distilled practice. Above all, theory is felt, in
the veins, in the muscles, in the sweat on your forehead. In
that sense, it's moral . . . and binding. It's the essential
connective imperative between past and future. (*Pause.*)
Now when I look for any of this in our comrade's account,
I can't find it; it isn't there. It's simply part of an elaborate
game he enjoys playing and plays well.

**Ford** (*angry but cool*) Do I get a chance to answer this?

**Tagg** I hope you will. But let me finish first. (*Pause.*) I
don't propose a catalogue of counter-assertions to refute
the major points made, because I think we can use our
time more profitably doing something else. And my text
for tonight is really the role of the party in the formulation
of revolutionary theory and the building of the socialist
revolution. But I'll need to offer a vastly different political
conspectus before I can do that. (*Pause.*) Comrade Ford
describes the history of the twentieth century as a history
of vacuums. That's to say, no proletarian revolutions in the
heartland of world capitalism; initially Europe,
increasingly, thereafter, America. Well, I felt he ran just a
little fast through the actual events, you know. I mean,
Germany 1919–20; Italy in the same period; Hungary;
Bulgaria? Spain in '36. France in the same year, the year of
the great General Strike, five million workers raising the
question of state power. Greece in '44. The absence of
revolution is not final evidence of the elimination of
revolutionary potential. But how does he account for this
loss of revolutionary direction in Europe? Via Marcuse,
we learn that the proletariats of advanced societies have
been 'absorbed' into the value systems of the capitalist

states, that they are now junior partners in capitalism with a stake in its future and the deepest resistance to anything that would upset the *status quo* of collective bargaining in a property-owning democracy. And this, in itself, is the final refutation of Marx's contention that capitalist societies were class societies whose inherent tensions and contradictions necessarily result in their supercession by social ownership of the already socialized productive forces of those same societies. All right, let's grant, descriptively, at least, an extraordinary low level of revolutionary militancy in metropolitan proletariats. What we have to decide, on the evidence, within the theory, is how this has come about and how it can be changed. Unless, of course, we slip the question altogether, by arguing that the revolutionary moment has gone floating off somewhere else and now rests with the peasant of Asia or Africa or South America, who presumably now must face not only the combined weight of imperialist expansion, massing behind the most sophisticated technology of destruction yet devised by man, but also the active opposition of bourgeoisified proletariats eager to defend their share of the cake against all comers, however oppressed and miserable they may be. (*Pause.*) What's missing is any genuine grasp of the dialectic, of the relationship between the class struggle *inside* the capitalist state and the extruded version of it being waged outwith. The fact is: the two are inextricably linked. There will be no victory in one without victory in both. But it must be the victory of the metropolitan proletariats that will herald the end of imperialist oppression. It is genuinely inconceivable that it could happen the other way round – think of it, think of it. Of course, the colonial struggle will go on, but does anyone really believe that America and Britain and France and Germany – mature capitalist states, at their level of technological development, with their economic resources and degree of destructive potential –

will allow significant reversals to occur in their economic expansion without doing something about it? It's unthinkable. (*Pause*.) So we must answer the questions: How is it that metropolitan proletariats lack revolutionary potential; and how might this be changed? Because if we don't answer them, we might as well take up chess or billiards, because there will be no way in which we can effect the transition we've been talking about and trying to work towards. (*Pause*.) The European and American proletariats appear to have settled for the *status quo*, in my opinion, because they have been consistently and systematically betrayed by their leaders; and particularly by the Communist parties of the various European countries. A simple historical fact that finds no place in Comrade Ford's analysis: Stalinism. Socialism in one country meant the damping down of revolutionary ardour everywhere, even where the flame of revolution was breaking through every crevice of capitalist society. By 1933 the German Communist party, the strongest in Europe outside Russia, had delivered the German working classes to Hitler on a plate. The French General Strike of 1936, which was undoubtedly based on a spontaneous proletarian desire to contest state power, i.e. a genuine revolutionary situation, was cynically reined back by the Stalinist hacks who led the PCF and turned quite deliberately into a struggle for wage increases. Wage increases! At Stalin's behest. The working class throughout Western Europe is even now, in most places, the prisoner of those miserable, anti-revolutionary leaderships, where they are not the dupes of the forces of social democracy. (*Pause*.) If we are to change all this, if we are to put proletarian revolution back on the agenda of European history, we are going to have to replace those defunct and corrupt leaderships with vital and revolutionary ones. (*Pause*.) But those leaderships will emerge not as loose coalitions or spontaneous coalescings, but as a result of patient organization and disciplined effort. That's to say, those leaderships will develop from new revolutionary *parties* which in turn will base themselves in and on the class they seek to lead. There is only one slogan worth mouthing at this particular historical conjunction. It is: 'Build the Revolutionary Party'. There is no other slogan that can possibly take precedence.

*He stops, mops his wet face and neck. Nobody speaks. Buttocks are shifted, feet wriggle, a match flares and sputters.*

**Ford** (*finally*) Finished?

**Tagg** Almost. (*Pause.*) The party means discipline. It means self-scrutiny, criticism, responsibility, it means a great many things that run counter to the traditions and values of Western bourgeois intellectuals. It means being bound in and by a common purpose. But above all, it means deliberately severing yourself from the prior claims on your time and moral commitment of personal relationships, career, advancement, reputation and prestige. And from my limited acquaintance with the intellectual stratum in Britain, I'd say that was the greatest hurdle of all to cross. Imagine a life without the approval of your peers. Imagine a life without *success*. The intellectual's problem is not vision, it's commitment. You enjoy biting the hand that feeds you, but you'll never bite it off. So those brave and foolish youths in Paris now will hold their heads out for the baton and shout their crazy slogans for the night. But it won't stop them from graduating and taking up their positions in the centres of ruling class power and privilege later on.

*Milanka in, with coffee etc, on trolley.*

**Milanka** Some coffee?

*Some release of tension. Buzz, hum.*

**Tagg** Why not?

*On the fade, the film screen bursts into life, CRS and students bloodily locked around the Sorbonne, the volume massively up, the red alarm light still flashes on the terrace.*

*Blackout.*

# Act Two

*Living-room. 2 a.m., Saturday, 11 May.*
*The meeting has broken. Louis, Maine and Kate have already left. Hayes is on the terrace looking for Sloman. Grease, crash-helmet on knee, leathers half buttoned, is listening to a record on expensive cans. Susie sits on a Chesterfield, thumbing quickly through a vast mound of papers and journals accreted over the week. Tagg is at the telephone, his back very much to the room, holding.*

**Joe** (*to Susie*) Any luck?

**Susie** No. I thought it was the *Telegraph*, but there's no sign of it.

**Joe** Never mind. There's a cuttings service provided. I'll get it sometime. Probably round about the third repeat.

**Susie** Anyway, it implied the Drama Department was in the hands of communists and troublemakers and was clearly bent on subverting the democratic process and leading the country to the dogs.

**Joe** Yeah? Things are looking up. I wish I knew who they were. I spend some lonely days in the East Tower, I can tell you.

**Tagg** (*to phone*) Hello. Hello.

*Ford, car keys in hand. Sound of lavatory flushing down the hall.*

**Ford** (*to Susie*) OK?

**Susie** Sure.

157

**Ford** Are you still at Wandsworth?

**Susie** Yes.

**Ford** OK. (*to Joe*) Thanks, Joe. Nice evening. I'm not sure what we achieved, but still . . .

**Joe** Thanks for coming, Andrew. As long as you didn't find it a complete waste of time . . .

**Ford** No, no. You know me. As the man said, words are our stock-in-trade . . .

*A silence. Grease uncans, the record over.*

**Joe** Well. Good luck with the Cuba book.

**Ford** Oh Jesus, don't remind me. There'll have been a counter-revolution before they've even got it in galleys. Thanks anyway.

**Grease** (*joining them*) It's all right. Lead guitar a bit flashy, but it's . . . funky. I like it. (*looking round*) Right then. Back to the pit.

**Ford** Are you all right?

**Grease** (*helmet up*) Yeah. There's 120 ccs of concentrated Lambretta waiting out there for me. With the right conditions prevailing I could be in Camden by noon.

**Tagg** (*on phone*) Hello. Hello. (*turning*) I think this thing's gone dead, Joe.

**Joe** With you in a tick, John.

*Tagg turns his back again, pushes rest up and down.*

**Ford** Right. We'll go. (*to Susie*) OK?

**Susie** (*to Joe*) Thank you for the . . . I enjoyed it. It was different anyway.

**Joe** (*takes her hand*) Good-bye.

**Ford** 'Bye.

*They leave.*

**Grease** Keep at it then.

**Joe** Mmm. And you. Let me know what you're doing . . .
We might be able to put something on the box.

**Grease** That'll be the day. (*to Tagg's back*) Good-bye.

**Tagg** (*turning slowly*) Aye.

*Grease leaves. Joe crosses to the phone, takes it from
Tagg, listens.*

**Joe** Hello. Hello. Oh hello. (*He listens, finally*) She's trying
the number now. She's been waiting for lines. (*He hands
the receiver back to Tagg.*) It takes a while.

*He leaves Tagg again, mooches a moment, switches off
the player. Hayes in from the garden, nearly ready for
off.*

**Hayes** No sign of him. If it weren't Malcolm I'd begin to
show signs of concern. He does happen to constitute a
substantial part of my daily bread, you know. (*looking
round*) Kara?

**Joe** She's er . . . looking at my kid. She won't be long.

*Hayes nods, wanders over to the bookshelves.*

**Tagg** (*phone*) What? Oh Christ. Well will you keep
trying? Ahuuh. 589 6129. That's it. Ta. (*He bangs the
phone down.*) No answer. She's trying again.

**Hayes** (*ironic*) Maybe the Paris exchange has fallen. De
Gaulle too. They've probably already set up a provisional
government under the leadership of an eleven-year-old
grammar-school boy. (*turning*) Funnier things have
happened. Not many though.

**Tagg** (*to Joe*) Any sign of Sloman?

*Joe shakes his head. Tagg crosses to the windows, peers out into the darkness.*

**Hayes** He'll be all right.

**Tagg** (*deliberately*) Will he? How do you know?

**Hayes** I'm his agent. I have to know these things.

**Tagg** Do you know why he's always drunk?

**Hayes** I said I was his agent. Not his wife.

**Tagg** That must make him feel good.

*Phone rings sharply. Tagg crosses at once to answer. Hayes pulls a mock injured face at Joe, sits down on the Chesterfield.*

Hello. Hello. Yeah, hello. Thank Christ, I've been holding for hours. What? No, it's all right, I'm with Shawcross, Joe Shawcross? Aye. Go on then.

*He listens for a long time. We never lose this call through what follows, though Tagg says very little for the rest of it, beyond reacting, prodding, asking for description, qualification and expansion.*

**Hayes** He has his own sort of charm, doesn't he?

**Joe** *We've* got charm, Jeremy. Look at us.

*Kara in from hallway. Hayes stands, ready to go.*

**Hayes** OK?

**Kara** Why don't you get the car?

*Pause.*

**Hayes** (*finally*) All right. Cheers, Joe. (*ironic*) Nice party.

**Joe** Yeah.

**Hayes** Any word on the Godard deal?

**Joe** No. Frank's there now. He'll ring tomorrow. (*Looks at watch.*) Today.

**Hayes** When are you going to Cannes, by the way?

**Joe** I don't know. Saturday, I think. I don't think Julie's booked it yet.

**Hayes** Tell her to give Biddy a ring, we'll go together.

**Joe** Fine.

**Hayes** Say goodnight to our . . . friend, won't you. And if you do manage to find Malcolm, pour him into a cab and send him home before he does any actual damage.

**Joe** Will do. See you.

*Hayes looks at Kara: leaves. Kara comes into the room.*

**Kara** Do you have a cigarette?

**Joe** There's some around somewhere.

*Kara searches mantelpiece, finds an open pack, lights one. She then turns to look at Joe. Tagg's call grows momentarily distinct, in the silence.*

**Tagg** Who did? Mandel! Mandel did! (*hard laugh*) Who else! (*Pause.*) So they marched back . . . ahunh . . . No. No . . . they were perfectly right, I'd say . . . Ahunh. (*He begins listening again, making the odd note on a pad in front of him.*)

**Kara** He's lovely. (*Joe looks at her.*) Charlie.

**Joe** Oh. Yes, he's a nice enough little bugger. He's got fallen arches. Like me. And he pees the bed.

**Kara** Like Malcolm.

**Joe** What?

**Kara** Nothing. You always said you didn't want kids.
They'd get in the way, you said.

**Joe** Yes. (*Pause. Smiles.*) Embourgeoisement. Build the
Family.

**Kara** I don't know how you can sustain . . . that amount
of self-loathing, Joe.

**Joe** (*ironic*) I know. It's quite a struggle, I can tell you.

**Kara** Christ. (*Pause.*) You're . . . terrified aren't you?

**Joe** A bit. Mostly I'm numb. *That's* fairly terrifying.

*She gets up, stubs the cigarette.*

**Kara** I'd better go. (*She crosses, kisses him softly on the
cheek. Indicating Tagg*) Watch this one. He's the one
who's playing games. He'll suck you dry if you give him
half a chance. Listen. You've got a talent . . . and a life to
lead. So lead it. (*Pause.*) Make the revolution *there* where
you *are*. Not in somebody else's *head*.

**Joe** Sure thing.

**Kara** I wish I'd been better for you.

**Joe** (*softly*) Get stuffed.

**Kara** Take it easy.

*She looks hard at Tagg's back: leaves. Joe follows, when
she's gone, as far as the doorway, as though to watch
her.*
*Tagg finishes the call, looks around the room, crosses
to the windows, still pondering the conversation he's
just had. He draws a few deep lungfuls of air.*
*Joe plays with the lights, tries different combinations,
using the dimmer, finally settles for the cluster of spots
that pool the two leather armchairs, and leave the rest
of the room dark. He sits down, gaunt and tired, in one.*

**Tagg** (*at window*) Frank.

**Joe** Frank.

**Tagg** In the thick, by the din.

**Joe** Frank *Hetherley*?

**Tagg** That's right.

**Joe** I don't understand. He's supposed to be doing a deal with Godard for me. For ITV.

**Tagg** He said he'd speak to you in the morning.

*Silence.*

**Joe** Is Frank . . . with you?

**Tagg** Mmmm.

**Joe** I didn't know. (*Pause.*) So what's happening?

**Tagg** The riot police have attacked the students. The students are . . . defending themselves.

**Joe** With what?

**Tagg** Barricades.

*A long silence. Tagg crosses, sits opposite Joe.*

The police are using gas and detonator caps. He could hardly speak, he was so hoarse. (*Pause.*) The students are tearing up the pavements and setting fire to cars.

*Silence again.*

**Joe** Christ.

**Tagg** We have a section there. (*Pause.*) The question is: Who will control the movement. As of now, it appears to be leaderless. (*Pause.*) But the opportunists are already thicker than maggots in a bone yard. Mandel for example. Mandel?

*Joe nods.*

Apparently Mandel had his car burned. The story is he stood on a barricade to watch it, shouting, 'Ah! Comme c'est beau! C'est la Revolution!' (*Pause. No irony*) A revisionist to the end.

**Joe** Is Frank involved? I mean, is he actually fighting . . . with your section?

**Tagg** (*quietly, simply*) Our section is not fighting.

*Pause.*

**Joe** Not?

**Tagg** Not. (*Pause.*) A revolutionary faction cannot afford to be romantic. Because of the *folie de grandeur* of a handful of petty bourgeois anarchists who're making the running, hundreds upon hundreds of brave young men and women are having their bodies mangled right now by the armed might of the bourgeois state. It is true that without insurrection there is no revolution. But unless there is a party with the correct line to organize and lead it, insurrection is simply another term for suicide. (*Pause.*) How often must it be said before the truth is clearly seen? Revolution is not a speculative gamble, a flutter devised by casino playboys. Revolution is the implacable conjunction of objective material forces and human organization, discipline, courage and will. (*Pause.*) Our section walked away from the barricades before the major confrontations occurred. In my view, they took the correct decision. Because such a confrontation could only result in defeat, even rout. It lacks revolutionary perspective, and those who promoted it . . . Mandel and his cronies . . . are, in the objective sense, enemies of the working-class revolution in France.

*Long silence. Tagg closes his eyes, appears to sleep. Joe is frozen, unable to comprehend what he has just heard.*

**Joe** Is that how you see it ending then?

**Tagg** How else can it end? When the workers replace the students, and when the revolutionary party leads the workers, we will have a revolution. (*Pause.*) What . . . terrifies me now is that the working class may well declare its solidarity with the students against the brutalities they have witnessed.

**Joe** But . . . isn't that what's wanted?

**Tagg** (*banging chair arm suddenly*) No! Anything but! Who do you think will lead the workers, if they do decide to involve themselves? Us? It'll be the CP, through the CGT. So that, however it begins, whatever the spirit and resolution the workers evince, slowly the movement will be bled dry of genuine revolutionary content, until Waldeck-Rochet and his Stalinist henchmen can do a secret deal with De Gaulle and get the workers off the streets and back to their benches. Can't you see it? It's a nightmare. It'll be a massive defeat for the revolutionary spirit. It will make our task more difficult.

  *Silence.*

**Joe** I'm sorry the meeting . . . wasn't better.

**Tagg** It's a start. (*Pause. Tagg sinks into himself.*)

**Joe** Don't you have . . . doubts?

**Tagg** Doubts?

**Joe** I've been trying to figure out what makes you different. It's not your analysis. It's not your style either. I think it's . . . there's no . . . scepticism in you. I can find no trace of what my psychology tutor used to call 'the civilized worm' in you, gently insisting on the possibility of error. (*Pause.*) Perhaps it's just that you have no way of being wrong.

**Tagg** (*softly*) Do *you* have a way of being right?

**Joe** No. I don't.

**Tagg** I'm not afraid of being wrong. As long as I'm right just once. That's all it'll take.

*Silence.*

(*smiling briefly*) I'm proletarian. I killed the worm before it turned. (*He takes in the room, piece by piece, then back to Joe.*) Mebbe you should've done the same.

**Joe** Me? I'm just a . . . producer. I don't actually *do* anything? I just . . . set up the shows.

*Silence again.*

**Tagg** I met Trotsky, you know. Just the once. In a pension in southern France. '36. '36 I think it was. He was trying to set up the Fourth International to counter the obscenities of Stalin's Third. There were about fifty of us, from all over: France, Italy, Switzerland, Belgium, Holland, Germany, Sweden, Denmark . . . Poland . . . Australia . . . America. And me, from Glasgow. Just thirty. (*Pause.*) He spoke mainly in French. I barely understood a word. But I watched him. Watched him. His big head. His eyes behind the spectacles. (*Pause.*) Authentic. This voice, speaking a language I didna comprehend, was the sole remaining authentic voice of the Russian revolution. While just about everything else was being expunged by Stalin or just . . . papered over by the Wilsons of their day . . . this one burning intelligence sat there refusing to be quenched, to be put out. (*Long pause.*) It's helped, that. Of course, it's no substitute for analysis and argument, for *theory*. But it helps a wee bit when the nights start getting longer. (*Pause.*) He said one thing I did understand. He said: 'We only die when we fail to take root in others.'

*Silence for a long time.*

I'm trying to take root, Joe. (*Pause.*) I'll be dead by the end of the year. (*Pause.*) I have this tumour. (*He holds his stomach.*) They've been trying to treat it for a while now, you know. But it's . . . spread just the same. I was there tonight. That's why I was late.

**Joe** I'm sorry . . .

**Tagg** (*completely naturally*) Ach, it's nothing. It's just such a bloody waste. I was banking on ten more good years to build the party.

**Joe** Are there . . . dependants?

**Tagg** No. (*He stands up suddenly, a hard, stern lump.*) We'll meet again, eh?

**Joe** (*standing too*) Yes.

*Tagg holds his hand out. Joe takes it.*

Let me call a cab.

**Tagg** Not at all. It's only a couple of miles. The walk'll do me good.

*He leaves, Joe in his wake to the front door. Joe in again, crosses to windows, draws curtains, returns to chair, checks time on watch, settles back as though to sleep.*
*Fade.*
*Black. Lutoslawski's Funeral Music.*
*Screen. Mute film. Dawn in Paris. Cars smoulder, barricades burn, char. Police poke in and out, like carrion. Silent, still. Fade slowly.*
*Fade up on scene as before. Dawn or just before. Joe asleep across two chairs. Sound of dawn chorus starting up.*
*A fumbling at the french window. Sloman in, draws curtains half back, to half light the room. He is grey,*

*dirty, dishevelled. His shoes are, as before, in a neat
knot round his neck.*

*Joe stirs as the light halves the darkness. Sloman
watches him until he subsides, then moves towards the
drinks shelves, stands a long time looking, finally selects
a can of beer, punctures it, takes a big, rinsing mouthful,
swallows, closes eyes, rubs the cool can across his
forehead. He looks round the room, leaves for the
kitchen, returns a moment later, carrying an open can of
frankfurters. He tries one experimentally; another; is
marginally impressed.*

*Joe wakens without moving. Stares at Sloman.*

**Sloman** Fancy one?

**Joe** No. What are they?

**Sloman** (*reads from the can, in perfect Hitler rally style*)
Neu! Jedes Wurstchen dieser Dose ist mit einer besonderen
Folie umgeben. Alle guten Eigenschaften, die man an
feinen Wurstchen Schatzt, bleiben durch diese Folie voll
erhalten – sie sind daher immer kostlick frisch, besonders
zart im Biss und noch feiner im Geschmack. (*Pause.*)
Frankfurters.

*Joe turns back to his litter.*

What's the matter, frightened to wake?

**Joe** (*sitting up slowly*) As you to sleep, happen.

**Sloman** Happen. What time is it?

**Joe** (*checking*) Five o'clock.

**Sloman** Is it? Listen them bloody birds. Aren't they
incredible. They have an order, you know, for starting up.
Finches, lapwings, first; larks; sparrows, last. Lazy little
buggers. (*Pause.*) I was reading somewhere, it takes two
hours, north to south, right down the country. So the

finches here probably get their alarm call every morning from the sparrows of . . . Bedfordshire or somewhere.

**Joe** Christ. It's five o'clock, Malc.

**Sloman** That's what I'm telling you.

**Joe** Have you thought of going home?

**Sloman** Not recently. (*He removes the mound of journals etc. from the settee, lies down on it, takes a drink from the can of beer, fishes out another cold frankfurter.*) Which *home* did you have in mind anyway? The thin bitch in Salford with the kids packed in around her like forwards wheeling for the line? Or Sally Svelte from sw7 with the manicured mind and a We Never Closed sign in neon at the top of her legs? Home. Home. 'He that diggeth a pit shall fall into it.' Ecclesiastes.

*Joe gets up, ignoring him: shivers a little.*

Go on.

**Joe** (*thinking*) 'Pride goeth before destruction, and an haughty spirit before a fall.' Proverbs.

**Sloman** Good. Yes, Erm. 'They were as fed horses in the morning; everyone neighed after his neighbour's wife.' Jeremiah?

**Joe** 'Saying peace, peace, when there is no peace.' Yes.

**Sloman** 'Is there no balm in Gilead; is there no physician there?

**Joe** 'Write the vision, and make it plain upon tables, that he may run that readeth it.'

**Sloman** Habukkuk! (*They both laugh.*) Cunt! 'His head and his hairs were white like wool, as white as snow; and his eyes were something . . . as the flame of fire.'

**Joe** 'His voice as the sound of many waters.'

**Sloman** 'I am he that liveth and was dead.'

**Joe** 'Be then faithful unto death, and I will give thee a crown of life.'

**Sloman** 'But he shall rule thee with a rod of iron.'

**Joe** 'And because thou art lukewarm, and neither cold nor hot, I will spue thee out of my mouth.'

**Sloman** 'And behold, a pale horse, and his name that sat on him was Death.' (*Long silence. Sloman finishes his can, swills a little of it over head and face, rubs it around.*) The Revelation of St. John. Apt enough for five o'clock of a Sat'day morning. (*Pause.*) There's nowt'll replace the formative intellectual matrices of a really well-run Sunday school. By Christ.

*Joe crosses to the french windows, draws the remaining curtain, and begins to examine the glass still remaining in the broken pane. He goes into the kitchen, returns with a mallet, chisel, gloves, etc. He examines the job carefully, kneeling to get a better look.*

**Joe** Pass me a couple of those, will you. (*He points to the mound of papers on the floor by Sloman's hand.*)

**Sloman** (*rummaging*) *Financial Times? New Statesman?* How big a job is it?

**Joe** Just pass 'em, will you.

*Sloman chucks two* Times *towards the window. Joe spreads them by the foot of the window to catch any glass falling inwards, puts on the gloves, begins tapping glass carefully with mallet. Sloman evinces pretty nearly total disinterest, his attention, such as it is, now stuck on the pile of papers. He riffles through it, sampling for dates from top to bottom.*

**Sloman** Jesus God, that's a week's worth!

**Joe** What?

**Sloman** You're so bloody *earnest*, Joe. I mean, I look at that lot. The *Economist*. The *Daily Telegraph*! The *Listener*? I mean, it's harmful.

*Joe goes on with his job. Sloman begins to work his way down the pile.*

(*A voice for each paper or item.*) 'Dockers Once More Support Powell on Issue of Immigration. Clashes with students averted.' (*on*) 'The centrepiece of the Cecil Beaton exhibition of theatre designs is a scale model of his principal sets for *My Fairy Lady*, which he . . .' (*He studies the page more closely, blinks, coughs, picks up another paper.*) 'The *Sunday Telegraph* is pleased to announce that as from this Sunday its Drama Critic will be the distinguished playwright Frank Marcus.' (*Pause.*) 'It is understood from reliable sources that Mr Marcus is considering an appeal.' (*on. New paper*) 'Russian Troop Movements on Czech-Polish Border Seen As Hint of Pressure on Dubček and Svoboda.' 'Professor Herbert Marcuse, the eminent Marxist philosopher and father of the so-called New Left, arrived in Paris late this evening for the centenary celebrations of the death of Karl Marx arranged by . . . UNESCO?'

*He looks at Joe, who works on.*

(*new paper*) 'Welwyn Garden City – the drug-tormented town in Hertfordshire where, I can disclose today, at least three teenagers in every hundred are using the killer drug heroin.' (*He throws the* People *down, picks up another.*) '"France: Stable, Prosperous and Infuriating" by Patrick Brogan.' Ha. (*He flings* The Times *away and picks up another.*) 'In a survey conducted last month, in Bucharest, 25 per cent of the sample identified General de Gaulle as

the First Secretary of the French Communist Party.'
(*Pause.*) 'President de Gaulle leaves for his state visit of
Roumania later this week. In a statement issued by an aide
last night, it was learnt that the French Communist party
would be led, in his absence, by M. Waldeck-Rochet (107)
of 13 Tuileries Gardens, Paris 8. (*Pause.*) 'It is understood
from reliable sources that M. Waldeck-Rochet is
considering an appeal.'

**Joe** (*almost finished*) What are you on about?

**Sloman** (*copy of* Evening Standard) Hang on. 'If there are
no deaths tonight, I'll turn in my badge,' said a French
police officer this afternoon. What?

> *Joe wraps the glass fragments in the newspaper, carries*
> *them out on to the terrace, picks up the pieces on the*
> *other side, dumps them carefully, returns. Sloman sits*
> *up.*

**Joe** What about the play?

**Sloman** What about it?

**Joe** When do you reckon you might have something for
me to look at?

**Sloman** What is it now?

**Joe** (*looking at watch*) The 11th. May.

**Sloman** I don't know.

**Joe** It doesn't matter. I just thought you might be able to
give me some idea.

**Sloman** How does Monday sound?

**Joe** What?

**Sloman** Monday. About six in the evening?

**Joe** Come on Malc, what?

**Sloman** I could put in a hard day tomorrow.

**Joe** Malc, we're talking about a ninety-minute play.

**Sloman** You're right. Tuesday then.

*Joe turns away, unwilling to be drawn further.*

(*quietly*) It's a sort of . . . presumption you have that you're different, Joe. That's all. Nothing else. And you're not. There is nothing . . . objectively . . . to distinguish you from all the rest . . . Shaun and Gerry and Cedric and . . . Irene . . . mmm? You occupy the same relationship to the means of production as every other . . . producer in that golden hutch at Would Not Lane you call the Centre. Socialist? A socialist producer? What's that? It's irrelevant.

**Joe** You're preaching, Malc. (*Pause.*) Fake it if you like.

**Sloman** Wrong. I'm not asking your *permission*, I'm *telling* you, Joe, you have no right to expect anything other than a fake. Any more than the rest have. The pimps. The gold lamé boys. The shredders. The suckers-in. The apologies for the system. The machine's maintenance men.

**Joe** Jesus, not *now*, Malc. It's five o'clock.

**Sloman** Sure. Sure.

*Silence.*

**Joe** So what are you going to do?

**Sloman** Fuck knows.

**Joe** Great. (*Pause.*) Look, I need a good piece. Right? Don't piss on me, Malc.

**Sloman** It doesn't make any *difference*.

**Joe** Malc . . .

**Sloman** It *doesn't*. The only thing you're allowed to put in
to the system is that which can be assimilated and
absorbed by it. Joe, this is a society that has 'matured' on
descriptions of its inequity and injustice. Poverty is one of
its best favoured *spectacles*. Bad housing, class-divisive
schools, plight of the sick and the aged, the alienating
indignities of work, the fatuous vacuities of 'leisure' –
Jesus God, man, we can't get enough of it. It's what makes
us so 'humane', seeing all that, week in, week out. We've
had centuries of it, man. I give you Wordsworth. Half a
dozen years after the Revolution in France that . . .
implosive moment not yet completed, not yet in the past –
our English Willie was arguing for the unhampered
ubiquity of beggars . . . beggars, Joe . . . as a way of
increasing the yield of virtue in society as a whole:
'While from door to door
This old man creeps, the villagers in him
Behold a record which together binds
Past deeds and offices of charity
Else unremembered, and so keeps alive
The kindly mood in hearts which lapse of years
And that half-wisdom half experience gives
Make slow to feel, and by sure steps resign
To selfishness and cold oblivious cares.
Among the farms and solitary huts,
Hamlets and thinly scattered villages
Where'er the aged Beggar takes his rounds,
The mild necessity of use compels
To acts of love; and habit does the work
Of reason; yet prepares that after joy
Which reason cherishes. And thus the soul,
By that sweet taste of pleasure unpursued,
Doth find herself insensibly disposed
To virtue and true goodness.'
Wednesday Plays? It's the Liberal heartland, Joe. Every
half-grown, second rate, soft-bowelled pupa in grub street

is in there fighting with you. It's the consensus. It's the condition of our time. Impetigo. Pink. Itchy. Mildly catching.

*Joe picks up some dead glasses, cans, etc., walks with them towards the kitchen, talking as he does so.*

**Joe** I know all this, Malc. (*Pause.*) I'd just sooner do a play by you than . . . you know. You know? (*His voice lifted from outside.*)

**Sloman** (*lifting too*) Yeah, I'd sooner play chess than draughts. So what?

*Joe back in for more pots.*

**Joe** (*quietly, gathering*) I just once . . . want to say yes to something.

**Sloman** Yeah. It'll pass.

**Joe** Yes. (*He continues his cleaning, leaves the room with another handful calling as he does so.*) Did you ever go to Chick's? Chick Hibbert's? Openshaw Palais?

**Sloman** Oh aye. Couple of times. Birrofa dump.

**Joe** (*off*) Mmm. I went every week, with our kid. Fighting. Fucking. Trying to. I had my first woman there. Met her there anyway. Beryl. In the back of a mate's Bedford, him in the front with his. And we kissed for a bit, and touched, and then I took it out and pushed it between her legs and held it there and waited . . . silent . . . it was there, you know . . . all but there. All it needed was a yes. And I could hear a voice in my head saying: If I were thee I'd say no. And then she rolled on her back, up and out went her thighs and I sank, a foot, a yard, a mile into her yes. (*He's back in the doorway.*) It seemed – seems still – an act of absolute courage.

**Sloman** Or absolute folly.

*Silence. Joe collects more glasses etc., leaves for the
kitchen. Sloman takes his shoes from round his neck,
begins to put them on. Sounds of dishwasher distantly
starting up. Angie in. Quiet, tired. Stands inside the
doorway, leaning against wall. Sloman is down with his
shoelaces.*

(*Calling, abstractedly*) I knew a Beryl once. From
Wythenshawe. She had huge calves. Her dad was a
rozzer.

*No sound from the kitchen. Sloman looks up, sees
Angie. Normal voice, to her.*

*She* showed a lot of courage.

**Angie** Did she?

**Sloman** Yes. I decorated her personally. Several times.

**Angie** Where's Joe?

**Sloman** Kitchen. Mopping up.

**Angie** Why don't you send over for some things? You
could move in.

**Sloman** (*straight*) No, no. I wouldn't want to come
between you.

**Angie** Stay with comedy, whatever you do.

*Pause.*

**Sloman** Been slagging?

**Angie** Don't you ever get tired?

**Sloman** I can remember you when you weren't a bitch.
You were nice then.

**Angie** Oh yes. That was when there was still a chance I
might be induced to become common property . . . To

each according to his need, wasn't it. Like dogs around a lamppost.

*Sound of dishwasher closing down; odd clank of pots. Birds again.*

**Sloman** It's the new sexual imperialism. Technologically necessary. Corporate cunt. It has nothing to do with the *Communist Manifesto*. Ask Kara. She knows.

**Angie** Kara?

**Sloman** She was here. To the meeting.

**Angie** (*turning, leaving*) Go home, will you. (*She's gone.*)

**Sloman** (*standing*) 'I will show unto thee the judgement of the great whore that sitteth upon many waters.' (*He crosses to the drinks shelves, punctures another can, takes an extravagant swig at it, is slightly sprayed by the contents.*)

*Joe in, two mugs of coffee, on a tray, and a large carrot.*

(*taking his, draining can*) Ta. What's that?

**Joe** For the pig.

**Sloman** (*half turning to windows*) Oh yes. He's a fearsome bugger.

**Joe** Yes. He nearly had you.

**Sloman** Your wife's back. Upstairs.

**Joe** Uhunh.

**Sloman** She looked tired.

**Joe** Yes?

**Sloman** Mmm.

*Long silence.*

Joe. I'm sorry about last night.

**Joe** (*softly*) Get stuffed.

**Sloman** The poor old sod.

**Joe** Who?

**Sloman** Tagg. Who do you think!

**Joe** How do you mean?

**Sloman** I don't know. He makes me want to cry. Every time I see him. (*Pause.*) He's a walking fetish. The 'Revolutionary Party' is a fetish. 'Build the "Revolutionary Party",' it's all he's ever said, over and over, all his bloody life. An absolute injunction. Timeless. No matter what the objective conditions, the other supervening historical processes, build the bleeding party.

**Joe** While you get slewed out of your head . . . and I . . . wallow in my impotence.

**Sloman** Maybe. I can't speak for you, old love, but sometimes *I'm* actually sober. You know? It doesn't matter where you meet Tagg, he'll be building the party. There's nothing else. There couldn't be. He'd have to tear it down and start again, if it ever did get built. (*deliberately*) Listen. I spent a year in that lot. Yes. On the rebound from the CP. And let me tell you, they make the Bolsheviks look like TOC-H. It's rigid. It doesn't bend for anything, least of all events. If reality doesn't come up to scratch, it's rejected, sent back down the line; expunged. (*Pause.*) The function of a party member is to carry out his orders, faithfully and without question. (*looking at wall pics*) 'Comrades, none of us wishes or is able to be right against his party. The party in the last analysis is *always* right, because the party is the sole historical instrument given to the proletariat for the solution of its basic problems. I know that one cannot be right against the party. It is only possible to be right with the party and through the party, for history has not created other ways for the realization of what is right.' (*Raises coffee mug*) Right, Lev Davidovitch? You didn't wait till '38 to snivel that out, did you? 1924, you coined that little gem. 13th Party Congress. He could've been Bukharin's scriptwriter.

*Joe turns away. Sloman turns to look at him.*

There won't be a revolution because John Tagg forms a tiny Bolshevik party in South London. There'll be a revolution, and another, and another, because the capacity for 'adjustment' and 'adaptation' within capitalism is not, contrary to popular belief, infinite. And when *masses* of people, masses mind, decide to take on the state and the ruling class, they won't wait for the word from the 'authentic voice of Trotsky' or anyone else. They'll be too busy 'practising the revolution'. And the class will throw up its own leaders and its own structures of leadership and responsibility. And they'll find the 'germ' from inside the class, not from 'outwith'. Because the germ's there, the virus is there, and however many generations of workers are pumped full of antibiotics or the pink placebos of late capitalism, it will persist, the virus, under the skin, waiting. I remember me dad. A model worker. A perfect working man. Chapel every Sunday: blue serge suit, white shirt, tie. Shiny pointed shoes. Hair parted; watered. Thirty-nine years for the same firm. Maintenance sparks. And when he was fifty-five they gave him a fortnight's notice, declared him redundant. He had a gold watch for long service, stuff like that. I remember him, he came home the night they told him they were putting him down the road, and he sat in his chair for about an hour and he didn't speak. Just looked into the fire. Then he sniffed and spat. He said: 'I could kill the bastards.' I only ever heard him swear once before. That was when me mam got her foot caught down a grid on the front at Blackpool and an illuminated tram nearly cut her in half.

**Joe**  And meanwhile?

*Sloman walking to the doorway, holds arms out. The front door bangs.*

**Sloman**  Precisely. I think I'll go home. Joe. Beware the last revelation. 'I am Alpha and Omega, the beginning and the end, the first and the last.'

*He leaves. Some slight greeting and banter in the hall. Joe stands for a moment longer, then takes the carrot out on to the terrace.*
*Eddie in. Tie off, jacket off shoulder. He's drawn, looks old. He looks around, flops into a chair, draws a crumpled* Sun *from his jacket pocket, begins to check a bet against a piece of paper he fumbles out of his wallet.*
*Joe in.*

**Eddie**  Hello.

**Joe**  Hello, Ed. How was it?

**Eddie**  Great. I had a good time.

**Joe**  (*looks at watch*) Musta bin.

**Eddie**  What time is it?

**Joe**  S'nearly six.

**Eddie**  Bloodyell. Eh, don't tell our Jean. She'd have a fit.

**Joe**  I bet.

*Eddie back to the bet.*

Fancy a coffee?

**Eddie**  I wouldn't mind a tea.

**Joe**  Right.

*He leaves. Eddie takes a pen out, begins making out a new bet.*

(*off*) How many sugars?

**Eddie**  Cup or a mug?

**Joe**  (*off*) Cup.

**Eddie**  Three then.

*Joe back in with cup on saucer.*

Ta, kid. (*Drinks.*) By gum, that's welcome, it is an all. (*Becomes aware of Joe's stare.*) Owt up?

**Joe**  No. Just the way you said that. Me dad used to say it.

**Eddie**  Did he? He liked his pot of tea, the old man. (*to paper*) Fancy a bet? Piggot's got five mounts at Leicester. He's flying back from France, so I reckon he's a good thing.

**Joe**  Do you ever win?

**Eddie**  Win? Course I win. How'd you mean?

*Pause.*

**Joe**  Have you thought any more about the job?

**Eddie**  No, not a lot. I'd take it, if there were just me. I suppose I could get used to watching Arsenal.

**Joe**  What would it . . . mean to you?

**Eddie**  Five quid a week, better hours, bit of free time.

**Joe**  Is that enough?

**Eddie**  What's 'enough'? It'll do to be going on with. (*Pause.*) You don't want me to take it, do you?

**Joe**  I didn't say that Eddie . . .

**Eddie**  You don't. I can tell. (*Pause.*) Why not?

**Joe**  I . . . don't know whether it's right for you . . . down here.

**Eddie**  How do you mean, down here? It's no different from Manchester, int this. There's factories and people work in 'em, there's houses and people live in 'em, there's dogtracks and racecourses and boozers and bingo halls, they have the same newspapers (*Sun*) and telly, that fat little get from Huddersfield tells *them* what to do just like us. It's just down the road. (*Pause.*) I don't know what you mean, down here. (*Pause.*) I wouldn't bother you.

**Joe**  Eddie.

**Eddie**  I wouldn't. They said there might be a house in Islington if I wanted. I went to have a look last night. It's far enough.

**Joe**  Eddie, you're being . . . daft.

**Eddie**  Maybe. I just thought I'd say it. (*gently*) All right?

*Joe nods. A silence.*

Does that mean you've decided not to lend us the three hundred?

**Joe**  Is that what you want, your own place?

**Eddie**  Yeah. Don't you?

**Joe**  All right. I'll send a cheque on Monday.

**Eddie**  Do you mean that?

**Joe**  Yes, I mean it.

**Eddie**  Thanks. (*Pause.*) I knew you would, our kid.

*Silence.*

I picked a bird up last night.

**Joe** Did you?

**Eddie** Aye. She were all right too. (*Pause.*) Took me back to her flat and everything.

**Joe** Great.

**Eddie** Yeah. She was all right. She wasn't a slag.

**Joe** Not lost your touch then.

**Eddie** Aye. Don't let the hair fool you.

**Joe** Are you still playing?

**Eddie** Nah. Sundays. British Legion.

**Joe** Scrubbers.

**Eddie** It's a game. Gerra good thirst up for Sunday lunch. Wharrabout you?

**Joe** No. Not kicked a ball in years.

**Eddie** (*getting up*) Ah, the loss to the game! (*Pause.*) Are they gonna win today?

**Joe** Who?

**Eddie** City! They're at Newcastle. Need both points for t'league.

**Joe** Yes?

**Eddie** They'll get 'em too! (*a touch inward, yet ironic*) I suppose I'd better get a new suit. Now I'm gonna be Mr Dynamic. (*turning back*) I can get a tube to Euston, can't I?

**Joe** Change at Leicester Square.

**Eddie** I'll do that then.

**Joe** Go easy.

**Eddie** Yea. And you. (*He stands in the doorway.*) Come and see ma. She's allus talking about you.

**Joe** Yeah.

*Pause.*

**Eddie** It *was* a slag. Cost us four quid.

*He leaves. Joe turns, surveys his room. Eyes objects, takes in spaces, between, around his objects. The guinea pig shrieks. Joe is rooted, frozen. Angie in, short bathrobe, naked underneath. Joe remains with his back to her.*

**Angie** Do you want anything?

**Joe** No.

**Angie** Come to bed, Joe.

**Joe** Frank's ringing sometime.

**Angie** Not at six o'clock.

**Joe** (*turning*) He's going to say whether we become a company or not.

**Angie** Is he back from Paris?

**Joe** No, I don't think so. He'll call from there. If Godard will play.

*Angie crosses to the window, inspects the neat gap.*

**Angie** Is it what you want?

**Joe** (*numbly*) Is it what I want. I don't know how to answer that.

**Angie** It seems the logical step.

*He watches her. She continues to inspect the window.*

Looks as if you had fun. (*She stands. Looks at him.*

184

*Crosses to the door to the hall.*) Do you want to share my bath?

**Joe** How's David?

**Angie** (*deliberately*) I thought I'd take Charlie over to mother's this afternoon. She's talking of taking him to the Danish Fortnight at Earl's Court. I can't think why. I thought if I took your car and you took a cab over this evening, we could go straight on to the Aldwych from mother's and leave Charlie there. Or you could take a cab to the Aldwych if you prefer. (*Pause.*) You've remembered the Aldwych?

*He nods.*

Good. (*Long pause.*) David's fine. He sends his regards. Would you remind Milanka to clean the hutch? It's started to stink again.

*She goes.*
*Joe stands; dead.*
*He crosses to the hi-fi. Brings up Jeanne Lee/Archie Shepp – 'Gilead'. She sings.*

'There is a balm in Gilead
To make the wounded whole
There is a balm in Gilead
To heal the sin-sick soul.'

*He goes out on to the terrace. Returns with the pig. He stands centre, pig in hand. Lights fade until he is in spot. As spot begins to fade, he appears, pig in hand, on the wall screen behind him.*

# COMEDIANS

# Characters

Caretaker
Gethin Price
Phil Murray
George McBrain
Sammy Samuels
Mick Connor
Eddie Waters
Ged Murray
Mr Patel
Bert Challenor
Club Secretary

**Comedians** was first performed in Great Britain at the Nottingham Playhouse on 20th February 1975. The cast was as follows:

**Caretaker**  Richard Simpson
**Gethin Price**  Jonathan Pryce
**Phil Murray**  James Warrior
**George McBrain**  Stephen Rea
**Sammy Samuels**  Louis Raynes
**Mick Connor**  Tom Wilkinson
**Eddie Waters**  Jimmy Jewel
**Ged Murray**  Dave Hill
**Mr Patel**  Talat Hussain
**Bert Challenor**  Ralph Nossek
**Club Secretary**  John Joyce

*Directed by*  Richard Eyre
*Designed by*  John Gunter

# Act One

*A classroom in a secondary school in Manchester, about
three miles east of the centre, on the way to Ashton-under-
Lyne and the hills of east Lancashire. Built 1947 in the
now disappearing but still familiar two-storey style, the
school doubles as evening centre for the area, and will
half-fill, as the evening progresses, with the followers of
yoga, karate, cordon bleu cookery, 'O' level English,
secretarial prelims, do-it-yourself, small investments and
antique furniture. Adults will return to school and the
school will do its sullen best to accommodate them.*

*This room, on the ground floor, is smallish, about a
dozen chipped and fraying desks, two dozen chairs set out
in rows facing the small dais on which stands the teacher's
desk, with green blackboard unwiped from the day's last
stand beyond. Two starkish lights, on the window side of
the room, are on, flintily, lighting about a third of it. A
clock (real: keeping real time for the evening) over the
board says 7.27. Cupboards of haphazard heights and
styles line the walls, above which the dogged maps, charts,
tables, illustrations and notices warp, fray, tear, curl and
droop their way to limbo. Windows on the left wall show
the night dark and wet.*

*The* **School Caretaker**, *old, gnarled, tiny, is trying to
sponge recent graffiti from the blackboard, in the lit
segment of the room. He has done away with the 'F' fairly
successfully and now begins on the 'U'. C,K,O,F,F,N,O,B,
H,O,L,E stretch out before him. He mutters 'Dirty
bastards, filthy fuckers' as he sponges.*

**Gethin Price** *arrives, in wet raincoat, carrying a long
canvas bag and a pint of hot water. He puts down bag and*

*mug by a desk, removes coat and shirt, takes shaving
tackle from the bag and sits, in his greying vest, to shave in
the tiny mirror he has propped before him. Price wears a
flat Lenin-like cloth or denim hat, which he leaves on.*

*Corridor sounds, as people hurry for their classes. Price
shaves with deft precision, surprisingly dainty-handed.*

*The Caretaker finishes, descends, catches sight of Price,
almost falls the final step to the floor.*

**Caretaker**  Are you in here?

*Price looks round, behind, about, with strange clown-
like timing, the foam gleaming like a mask, brush
poised.*

**Price**  (*finally*) Yeah.

*The Caretaker sniffs, looks for his clipboard and list of
classes; scans it.*

**Caretaker**  I don't see it.

**Price**  Been here since January. (*Pause.*) Mr Waters . . .

**Caretaker**  Waters. Oh, him. (*studying Price at his
ablutions*) What is it, Gents' Hairdressing?

**Price**  Yeah. Some'at like that.

**Caretaker**  I thought you practised on balloons. I saw it
once in a film . . .

*Caretaker stumps out, dragging his waste bag, pins **Phil
Murray** to the door as they pass. Murray in. Stops in
doorway as he sees Price's foaming white face.*

**Phil**  (*sour, his dominant note*) Jesus, is it Christmas
already.

*Price shaves on, smiling briefly. Murray carries his two
suitcases to a desk and deposits them tidily before sitting
down. He's twenty-nine, small, dapper, an insurance*

194

*agent in thick-fitting dark three-piece suit.*

Christ, what a flap. God knows where that bloody idiot of a brother of mine's got to. (*He checks his watch against the clock.*) He's probably forgot, the stupid mare. Be having a game o'bones in the New Inn. (*across to Price*) Are you ready then?

*Price grunts yes or no, it makes no matter.*

*I* am. By God, I am. I've worked meself puce for tonight. I have. I have that. And if that dozy prick . . .

*He leaves it hanging, minatory.* **George McBrain** *in, straight from work. He's a docker, big, beefy, wears an old parka, jeans, boots, shock of black hair, extrovert Ulsterman in his late thirties.*

**McBrain** (*arms wide in doorway*) De Da!

*Nothing. He looks from Murray to Price.*

Well, I found the stones, now all I've gotta do is find the classroom. (*advancing, bag in hand*) Are we all ready then? Tonight you will see . . . something! Overtime every night this week but am I worried? Not a bit of it. Because I have what it takes. And when you have it . . . (*He produces a can of Worthington 'E' from his bag on the desk.*) . . . by God you have it!

**Phil** (*to Price*) He sounds as if he's had it for a while too.

**McBrain** Mock on, brother. I can forgive your jealousy.

**Phil** You get more like that Paisley every day, George –

**McBrain** (*Paisley at once*) Mock not the reverend doctor, Mr Murray. There's not many left of us can walk on water.

*Price finishes, replaces shaving tackle, begins to dress.*

How's it going then, Geth?

**Price**  OK.

*He picks up the mug. Leaves the room. McBrain slowly follows him half-way, stops, looks at Phil.*

**McBrain**  Feeling the strain, doubtless.

**Phil**  (*trying a shiny pair of black pointed shoes on*) Teacher's pet? He's just a moody bugger.

**McBrain**  Where's your kid, then? And where's the bloody rest of 'em? Look at the time . . .

**Phil**  Don't ask me about our kid. It's bad enough I have to work with him. I was picking him up on Market Street wasn't I, seven o'clock. *I* was there. Parked on a double yellow line wasn't I? If he'd been there, there'd've been two of us.

**Sammy Samuels** *and* **Mick Connor** *in. Samuels, forty-one, fat, Manchester Jewish, cigar, heavy finely cut black overcoat, homburg, white silk scarf, black attaché case, first in.*

**McBrain**  (*Stan Laurel voice*) Hi, Olly.

**Samuels**  (*evenly*) Piss off.

*He crosses to a desk, carefully removes hat, coat (which he shakes), scarf, and adjusts his shirt cuffs so that the diamond cufflinks do their work below the sleeve of his good wool suit. Connor stands in the doorway, rain dripping from his donkey jacket, beneath which we glimpse hired evening dress and crumpled buttonhole.*

**McBrain**  Oh, Christ.

**Connor**  Almost, my son. Try again.

**McBrain**  You're drowned. What've you come in your gear for?

**Connor** Laid off again. Thought I'd get it done with. Bloody weather. No pigging buses.

**Phil** You'll look like a dog's dinner.

**McBrain** (*an explosion*) The Kennomeat Kid. Ha! That's good that! I like that! (*Frank Carson voice*) It's the way I tell 'em.

*The groans of the others increase his glee.*

**Samuels** (*strong Manchester accent, occasional Jewish nasality*) These pipes are hot, Mick. Get over here and dry out.

*Connor crosses to the pipes. We see 'Wimpey' on the PVC patch on the back of the jacket as he removes it.*

(*seeing the suit jacket*) Hey, that's not a bad fit. Where'd you gerrit, Woolworth's?

**Connor** S'matter of fact belonged to a feller I know passed on.

**Samuels** Not surprised wearing a suit like that.

**Connor** What's wrong with the suit? It's a bit wet . . .

**Samuels** S'hard to put your finger on . . .

**McBrain** . . . as the actress said to the bishop . . .

*Groan.*

**Samuels** (*studiously contemptuous of the interruption*) It's the sort of suit you walk into a tailor's in and ask for the cheapest suit in the shop and he says you're wearing it.

*Groan.*

Don't groan, you scum, learn.

**Connor** (*studying the suit*) S'been a good suit.

**Samuels** It was doomed the moment it left the animal. Believe me, I know about these things.

**Phil** Christ, he's doing half his bloody act . . .

**Samuels** Don't worry about me, old son. Plenty more where that came from.

**McBrain** Right. Why should Ken Dodd worry about some obscure Manchester Jew nicking his lines? Ha!

*Samuels smiles, a little frost around the teeth, at McBrain.*

**Samuels** Why indeed. Why indeed.

**Connor** (*aware of that faint crackle*) Sure it's a detail. A detail it is.

**McBrain** (*in Waters's exact voice, assuming his manner*) Ah, but detail, friend, is all. Think on now.

*Eddie Waters in, quick, purposeful, behind Samuels's back.*

**Samuels** Where *is* His Grace, by the way . . .?

**Waters** He's here.

*There's a small but discernible reaction in the others, a regression to childhood responses.*

(*Already within reach of his desk*) Sorry it's late. I had to check the equipment down at the club. No piano.

*'Bloody hell's of concern.*

It's all right, they've had one sent down from Edge Lane. (*Pause.*) Right, let's get cracking, we haven't got all night. (*He's deposited his gear around the desk, papers, books, a stop watch, other materials and equipment.*) Get the tables sorted and settle down while I take a leak . . .

*He's on his way to the door. The others break and begin
drawing the desks and chairs into roughly parallel sides
of a hollow square. In the doorway he meets Price,
returning. Price has removed his hat to reveal an almost
wholly shaven skull, the hair dense and metallic on the
scalp.*

(*stopping, staring*) Mr Price. (*over shoulder, very dry*) Less
noise if you would, gentlemen. There may be people trying
to sleep in other classrooms. (*Back to Price now, staring at
head.*) All . . . ready?

**Price** Yeah. Just about, Mr Waters.

**Waters** (*the head incomprehensible yet unmentionable*)
Still finishing on the song . . .?

**Price** I'm not doing a song.

**Waters** How d'you mean? How're you gonna get off?

**Price** (*evasive, stubborn*) I've er . . . I've bin working on
some'at else.

**Waters** (*some faint concern*) Since when?

**Price** Oh, last week. I dint like the act. I found some'at in
the book you lent us.

**Waters** Yes, but you've not changed the basic . . . I mean a
week . . .

**Price** (*breaking deliberately into the room*) It'll be all
right, Mr Waters.

*He takes a desk end with Phil. Waters watches him,
leaves.*

**McBrain** (*to Price*) Hey.

*Price looks at him over his shoulder.*

Love the hairdo.

**Price** (*evenly*) Nice, innit.

**Samuels** Reminds me of a girl I used to know. (*reflective*) I've known some funny women.

**McBrain** Reminds me of the wife. After the operation.

**Connor** She's had it as well has she?

**McBrain** Ey, eh . . .

*They square up to each other in mock battle stances.*

**Phil** Are you shifting these desks or what?

**McBrain** I heard the Church had granted the Pope a special dispensation . . . to become a nun.

*Beat.*

**Connor** That's right. Only on Fridays though.

*They grin, begin humping a desk.*

**Phil** Look at the bloody time. I'll cut his legs off.

**Samuels** And he'll still be bigger than you.

*Price has taken a tiny violin and large bow from his bag, begins to tune it quietly.*

**McBrain** (*miming M.C. in the cleared central area between the desks*) Ladies and gentlemen, welcome to the Factory Street Copacabana, where a feast of comedy talent on tonight's bill, includes Mr Sammy Samuels, the Golda Meir of Gagland hot from his recent sizzling successes in the Gaza Hilton, not forgetting, of course, the Telly Savalas of Comedy, author of the highly acclaimed *The Naked Jape*, Mr Gethin – what the *hell's* that thing?

**Price** (*as to a child, slowly*) This? It's a . . . very, very small . . . violin. Vi. O. Lin. Try it. Vio. Lin.

**McBrain** Vio. Nil. Vay. Lone. Velo. Line. No. Velo. No . . .

**Price** Vio. Lin. Keep practising. It'll come.

*MacBrain stands blinking, trying to say the word.*

**Samuels** Hey. Vic Oliver. You're never Jewish.

**Price** (*perfect Manchester Jewish*) You wanna make some kind of a bet, Moses?

**McBrain** (*elated*) Violin! Got it! Vaseline, shit!

*Waters back in. They sit down at their desks with a muffled clatter and scrape.*

**Waters** Right, let's see who's here . . . Jack Thomas is out. Tonsillitis.

**McBrain** Tough. Poor old Jack.

**Waters** What about your brother, Mr Murray?

**Phil** (*nervous*) He'll be here, Mr Waters. He's probably been held up somewhere.

**Samuels** Likely he got a bit behind with his milk-round.

**Connor** I've heard tell it's more than behind these milkmen are after getting. Sure my wife's the only woman in the street ours hasn't parked his float in.

*Beat.*

**Connor**
**McBrain** } The stuck-up bitch!
**Samuels**

*Laughter.*

**Waters** (*dry*) Oh, we're working tonight, gentlemen. How can they say Music Hall is dead when jokes like that survive . . . down the ages? Right, settle down, we'll make a start. (*looking at clock*) Now, we're down at Grey Mare Lane at eight thirty-five or so for a nine o'clock start. That gives us till about twenty-five past. And remember we come back here as soon as it's finished, just to round things off and er . . . listen to the verdict. Which brings me to the man they're sending. (*taking opened envelope from inside pocket, taking letter out*) His name's . . . Bert Challenor . . . some of you may have heard of him . . . he worked Number Ones a fair while way back, before he took up . . . talent-spotting. He'll be here back side of eight, so you'll get a chance to weigh him up before the off. (*Pause. Scanning them*) I don't want to say much about him. He's an agents' man. Which means he has power. I'd better say this, though: I've never rated him. And he doesn't reckon much to me either.

**Connor** Sounds a nice chap.

**Waters** Now I'm not saying any of this is going to count against you. But we . . . have our differences. I'd hoped for someone else, to tell the truth.

*Puzzled looks, faint consternation.*

**Samuels** How do you mean, differences?

**Waters** I don't wanna spend all night on it . . . I never joined his . . . Comedy Artists and Managers Federation, for a kick-off. They took it bad, for some reason. I didn't like what they stood for. I've been a union man all my life, it wasn't that . . . They wanted the market . . . They wanted to control entry into the game. I told 'em no comedian (*odd, particular emphasis*) worth his salt could ever 'federate' with a manager. (*Pause, sniff.*) And as far as I'm concerned no comedian ever did . . .

**Price** (*very distinctly*) You think he'd . . . fail us . . . just for that, Mr Waters, do you?

**Waters**  That's not what I said . . .

**McBrain**  Nobody'll fail me. I'm unfailable.

**Connor**  Hark at the Pope, now.

**Price**  (*piercing, within the control*) Well, what then?

**Waters**  Well, put baldly, if I've done a job with you lot, he'll see it, and he won't like it. That's all.

*They look at each other, a trifle more concerned.*

**McBrain**  (*reassuring*) What does it matter, a comic's a comic.

**Samuels**  Not in Rabbi Challenor's book he ain't.

**Waters**  (*deliberate*) Not in Eddie Water's book either.

*Silence. Some sniffs.*

I probably overstate the problem. You're all good enough . . . now . . . to force his hand, without playing down . . .

**McBrain**  Crème de la crème.

**Samuels**  A little clotted here and there perhaps.

**McBrain**  More there than here, Isaac.

**Price**  Why don't we start?

*Others repeat 'Why don't we start? Why don't we start?' rather crazily to each other, begin to discuss it.*

**Connor**  What an excellent suggestion, give that man a balaclava for his pains.

**Waters**  All right. In the time remaining I thought we might just run through a few exercises to get the blood running . . .

**Ged Murray** *half backs into the room, soaked through. He's large, gentle, direct, open, very far from stupid.*

*Pale, with bad teeth and balding. He wears a milkman's brown coat and hat. He continues, a line at a time, as he makes his way into the room, greets people with winks or smiles, finds his chair, adjusts it, sits down, apparently wholly unaware of the interruption of process he represents. A brilliant comic performance, in other words.*

**Ged** (*taking coat off, shaking it, adjusting himself*) Sorry I'm late. It's bloody pissing down out there. I fell asleep on the settee watching *Crossroads*. So I had to nip down t'depot and borrow a float to get here. And t'bloody battery were flat. Got stuck on the Old Road. Walked the last sodding mile. Evening, Mr Waters. (*He hits his seat next to brother Phil.*) Evening, all. (*A big friendly grin.*)

**All** (*in chorus*) Good evening, Mr Woodentop.

*Waters waits, a little impatient, for quiet.*

**Phil** (*hoarse, hostile*) I waited ten minutes on a double yellow line . . .

**Ged** (*easily*) Don't worry, I'm here now.

**Phil** Couldn't you have put some'at else on?

**Ged** What's wrong with this?

**Phil** What you watching *Crossroads* for?

**Ged** It helps me sleep.

*Waters taps the desk with a piece of chalk.*

**Waters** If you've nearly finished . . .?

**Ged** Sorry, Mr Waters.

**Phil** (*suppressed mutter*) So you bloody should be . . .

**Connor** How's the wife then, Ged?

**Ged** (*simply*) All right.

**Waters** Bloody hell, what is this? We'll do sewing if you like . . .

   *Some laughter. Ged indicates his apology facially.*

Right, let's get you warm. (*Points to McBrain, immediately to his right.*) Character. Stupid.

**McBrain** (*fast, in character*) Excuse me, miss, where do I put this thing? (*Long pause.*) Oh . . .

**Waters** (*to Samuels, next*) Ancient.

**Samuels** (*fast, in character*) Course I remember Moses. Little feller . . . (*musing*) . . . bad teeth, oy that breath . . .

**Waters** (*to Connor, on end*) Silly.

**Connor** Erm . . . (*furtive*) I'll take a pound of the sausages. With the leaves left on.

   *Waters snorts, sustaining the speeded rhythms of the exercise.*

**Waters** (*to Price, end of left desk*) Feminine.

**Price** (*fast, perfect*) Four quid, dearie.

   *Waters thrown a little, perhaps by the unexpected harshness.*

**Waters** Try another.

**Price** (*same voice*) . . . All I said was, all I *said was* . . . four quid doesn't cover sheets . . . Just take your shoes off, is that a lot to ask?

**Waters** (*to Ged, next*) Posh.

**Ged** (*almost own voice, a strange modification, after thought*) Could you get me some clean bread for this dip, miss . . .?

**Waters** Nice. (*to Phil*) Absent-minded.

**Phil** (*bad Robb Wilton*) Al never forget –

**Connor** (*distinct whisper*) Whatsisname.

**Phil** Whatsisname. Look, piss off will you, Mick . . .?

**Waters** OK. Coming. It's speed . . . and it's detail. It's the detail inside the speed that makes the difference. A bit sluggish. We'll send it the other way. (*to Phil*) Willy.

**Phil** Willy Nilly.

**Ged** Willy Won'ty.

**Price** Willy Nocomebackagain.

**Connor** Willy Ell.

**Samuels** (*pulling face*) God Villy . . .

**McBrain** (*same face*) Willy Nands.

**Waters** God. (*to McBrain*) Sammy.

**McBrain** Sammy . . .?

**Waters** Yes, yes . . .

**McBrain** (*desperate*) Sammy Circle.

**Waters** (*urgent*) Right, come on.

**Samuels** (*very Yiddish*) Sammyterwidyu?

**Connor** (*Italian*) 'Sa me you wants see? Why dincha say so?

**Price** Sammykazi. (*Pause.*) The Suicidal Shithouse.

**Ged** (*singing*) Sammy, Sammy, you aren't half jammy . . .

**Phil** Sammy Professional.

**McBrain** Did someone call? I thought I heard my name.

**Waters** Not bad. Let's stretch it a bit. (*stopwatch, tape-recorder*) Let's see if you can handle a cough. Off you go.

*They enter the half circle to play the coughing tape-recorder.*

**McBrain** (*fluent*) By, she's coughing well tonight. What've you been doing to her, eh? Dirty thing, you.

**Samuels** There's an old Indian remedy for coughing in women, you know. Full of spices and herbs and other Asian comestibles. Do you like that? Grub. It's a sort of curry linctus . . .

*Groans all round.*

They say it's very good . . .

**Price** (*perfectly acted*) Do you realize, we're all sharing the same air with that man. Just listen to him. (*Waits.*) Every time he does that there's a million infectious droplets joins the pool. He's emptying his lungs over everyone here. Go on, empty away, son, we don't mind . . .

**Connor** I tell you what, why don't you come up here and cough and we'll all sit down there and laugh at you . . .

**McBrain** Mek a change for *your* act, Mick.

**Ged** I think she's trying to tell me something.

**Phil** Yeah, you're rubbish.

**Ged** Oh you speak the language do you? That's nice.

**Phil** Yes, I learnt it at school.

**Ged** Oh they dint teach us out like that. They taught us spittin'. And peein' up walls . . .

**Phil** Ay well, that's the secondary modern system for you init. S'just a bad system.

**McBrain** Cough and the world coughs with you. Fart and you stand alone.

**Waters** (*tough*) All right . . .

*Price is already climbing up on to his desk.*

**Price** There was a young lady called Pratt . . .

**McBrain** Yes, yes . . .

**Price** Who would hang from the light by her hat . . .

**Connor** No, no.

**Price** With a frightening cough . . .

**Samuels** Yes.

**Price** She would jerk herself off . . .

**McBrain** Ah . . .

**Price** (*vicious but quiet*) By sinking her teeth in her twat.

**All** Olé!

*Waters stares at him. The others laugh, puzzled yet amused.*

**Caretaker** (*from doorway*) Smoking is not allowed on these premises. Thank you. (*He turns again.*) Or standing on desks. Or anything else like that.

*He leaves with dignity. Price gets down, white, impassive, avoiding Waters's eyes, which follow him, close and tense as he resumes his seat.*

**Waters** (*quiet, still*) Is somebody trying to tell me something? (*Pause.*) Mmm?

*No answer. Price twangs a tiny violin string, once, twice, three times. Slight sense of discomfiture as they try to locate his meaning.*

The traitor distrusts truth.

*They look at him.*

The traitor distrusts truth. Tongue twisters. Shall we twist tongues, gentlemen?

*They take it up in turn.*

(*he calls*) Faster.

*The phrase gradually loses its shape and meaning in the struggle for facility. Waters sends it down McBrain's line first, then Phil Murray's, so that we end on Price.*

**Price** (*effortlessly, at speed*) The traitor distrusts truth. The traitor distrusts truth. The traitor distrusts truth. The traitor distrusts truth. The traitor distrusts truth. The traitor distrusts truth. The traitor distrusts truth . . . (*Long pause. Very levelly, measuredly, at Waters*) The traitor distrusts truth.

**Waters** (*finally, mild, matter-of-fact*) I've never liked the Irish, you know. Dr Johnson said they were a very truthful race, they never spoke well of each other, but then how could they have?

*They look around, faintly puzzled, amused.*

Big, thick, stupid heads, large cabbage ears, hairy nostrils, daft eyes, fat, flapping hands, stinking of soil and Guinness. The niggers of Europe. Huge, uncontrollable wangers, spawning their degenerate kind wherever they're allowed to settle. I'd stop them settling here if I had my way. Send 'em back to the primordial bog they came from. Potato heads.

*Pause. McBrain clenches and unclenches his fists on the desk, watches them carefully.*

**Connor** (*slowly*) Would that be Southern Irish or
Northern Irish, Mr Waters?

**Waters** (*mildly on*) Or Jews, for that matter.

**Samuels** What you staring at me for?

*Uneasy laughter, dying fast.*

**Waters** (*still very matter-of-fact*) They have this *greasy*
quality, do Jews. Stick to their own. Grafters. Fixers.
Money. Always money. Say Jew, say gold. Moneylenders,
pawn-brokers, usurers. They have the nose for it, you
might say. Hitler put it more bluntly: 'If we do not take
steps to maintain the purity of blood, the Jew will destroy
civilization by poisoning us all.' The effluent of history.
Scarcely human. Grubs.

**Samuels** (*unfunnily*) He must've met the wife's family.

**Waters** Negroes. Cripples. Defectives. The mad. Women.
(*turning deliberately to Murray's row*) Workers. Dirty.
Unschooled. Shifty. Grabbing all they can get. Putting coal
in the bath. Chips with everything. Chips and beer. Trade
Unions dedicated to maximizing wages and minimizing
work. Strikes for the idle. Their greed. And their
bottomless stupidity. Like children, unfit to look after
themselves. Breeding like rabbits, sex-mad. And their
mean vicious womenfolk, driving them on. Animals, to be
fed slops and fastened up at night. (*Long pause.*) The
traitor destroys the truth.

*Silence. Coughing. Shuffling of feet.*

**Price** Gone very dark in here all of a sudden.

**McBrain** Fancy a hand of crib?

*Silence again. Waters looks down at his desk. They
exchange inquiring looks across his space.*

**Ged** (*finally*) I don't get that. (*Pause.*) Were it some kind of a joke, Mr Waters?

**Waters**  Not exactly a joke, Mr Murray.

**Ged**  I mean. There's good and bad in everyone.

**Waters**  Is there now?

**Connor**  Didn't you say so yourself?

**Waters**  Did I?

**Samuels**  You're always saying it. 'A comedian draws pictures of the world. The closer you look, the better you'll draw.'

*In the silence that follows, a penny begins to drop.*

**Price** (*laconic, drawn out*) Lesson Three: 'Stereotypes'.

*Some faint embarrassment, the sense, however obscure, of having let Waters down.*

**Samuels**  You were having us on. That's a relief. I was beginning to get worried.

*Some relaxation, smiles, off the hook.*

**Waters** (*driving home*) If I've told you once I've told you a thousand times. We work *through* laughter, not *for* it. If all you're about is raising a laugh, OK, get on with it, good luck to you, but don't waste my time. There's plenty others as'll tek your money and do the necessary. Not Eddie Waters.

**McBrain** (*conciliatory, apologetic*) So, a few crappy jokes, Mr Waters . . .

**Waters**  It's not the jokes. It's not the jokes. It's what lies behind 'em. It's the attitude. A real comedian – that's a daring man. He *dares* to see what his listeners shy away from, fear to express. And what he sees is a sort of truth, about people, about their situation, about what hurts or terrifies them, about what's hard, above all, about what they *want*. A joke releases the tension, says the unsayable, any joke pretty well. But a true joke, a comedian's joke, has to do more than release tension, it has to *liberate* the will and the desire, it has to *change the situation*. (*Pause*.) There's very little won't take a joke. But when a joke bases itself upon a distortion – (*at Price, deliberately*) – a 'stereotype' perhaps – and gives the lie to the truth so as to win a laugh and stay in favour, we've moved away from a comic art and into the world of 'entertainment' and slick success. (*Pause*.) You're better than that, damn you. And even if you're not, you should bloody well want to be.

**Connor**  I want to be famous. I want to be rich and famous. What's wrong with that, Mr Waters?

**Waters**  More than you want to be good?

**McBrain**  What's wrong with being all three?

**Waters**  Nothing. So long as you're good *first*. Because you'll never be good later.

**Price** (*suddenly*) Was it my limerick?

**Waters**  I don't want to personalize this discussion . . .

**Price**  Oh, I see. You think talking to the six of us makes it impersonal, do you . . .?

**Phil**  Oh, come on, Pricey, don't argue . . .

**Price**  Why not? He's accusing us . . . me . . . of doing some'at . . . immoral, I want to know what he means, it's pretty important to me . . .

**Samuels**  Look, we don't want a scene . . .

**Price**  Who wants a scene? I put a simple question. I'm just looking for a 'truth' . . . Was it my limerick he took objection to? (*Pause.*) Because if it was, I'd like to know what his objections are, that's all.

**Samuels**  Well just don't push your luck, OK?

**Ged**  (*gentle but firm*) It's not up to you, Sammy.

**Waters**  All right. Let's hear it again, Mr Price.

**Price**  What?

**Waters**  Will you recite it for us?

**Price**  What for?

**Waters**  Give us a chance to look it over, see what we're dealing with.

**Price**  It was it then, was it?

**Waters**  *You* think it was.

**Samuels**  Let's hear it then.

**Phil**  Yeah, let's hear it.

>   *Pause. Price bites his lip, sullen, moody. Waters waits.*

**Price**  (*slowly*) All right.
There was a young lady called Pratt
Who would hang from the light by her hat
With a frightening cough
She would jerk herself off
By sinking her teeth in her twat.

>   *Silence.*

**Waters**  It's clever. Is it your own?

**Price**  You could say that.

**Waters**  How do you mean?

**Price**  I made it up. Just then.

**Waters** It's very clever.

**Ged** (*marvelling*) You never made it up, did you?

**Price** Look, Mr Waters, I don't want compliments, just say what you don't like and we can get on . . .

**Waters** What do you think it says?

**Price** I don't know. You tell me. I felt like saying it.

**Waters** (*crossing to board, chalking up key words one beneath another, fast monotone*) Pratt. Pratt says twat. Lady, twat. Twat, bad word, unsayable. I've said it, will say it, might say it, *hat*, fooled you, build the suspense, cough, cough, jerked herself off, women masturbate, naughty, must say it now, dadadadadadada *twat. There!*

**Price** So?

**Waters** It's a joke that hates women, Gethin.

**Price** How come?

**McBrain** Ha ha. (*He shuts up quickly.*)

**Waters** It's a joke that hates women *and* sex. Do I go on?

**Price** (*cool*) Why not?

**Waters** In the Middle Ages men called the woman's sexual organ the devil's mark. According to Freud, men still see them as shark's mouths, in dreams. When you walk into that arena with a joke, you've gotta know why you're there.

**Price** Maybe I'm just frightened.

**Waters** Maybe. But who do you blame, with your joke? Your lady 'jerks' herself off. Is she a man?

**Price** It rhymes with cough.

**Waters** *Off* rhymes with cough. What do you *think* of your lady?

**Price** Not a lot.

**Waters** Acrobatic but nasty? Sex-starved? Sex-mad? A nympho. Sexually insatiable.

**McBrain** Can I say something?

**Waters** By all means.

**McBrain** I mean, I do take your point and that, but doesn't his rhyme do just what you said you wanted? If fellers fear women and sex and that the way you say . . . doesn't that wee rhyme kind of . . . liberate the fear, sort of?

**Waters** I don't think it does. I think it recognizes it and *traps* it. Leaves it exactly where it is. Doesn't help it on. Doesn't do anything to *change* it. (*to everyone*) Look, this is probably the last chance I'll get, and I want to state it as simply as I can.

> *The door opens and an* **Asian** *enters, soaked and gleaming, small, slim, dark, delicate, a large muslin-wrapped something under his arm. He stops, smiles, shyly wavers. They turn to look at him. He leaves, closing the door behind him. Waters crosses to the door after a moment, looks out down the corridor.*

**Samuels** (*sotto voce*) If that's Challenor, we're all done for.

**Phil** Blacked up for the evening.

> *Waters returns to his desk.*

**Waters** A joke that feeds on ignorance starves its audience. We have the choice. We can say something or we can say nothing. Not everything true is funny, and not everything funny is true. Most comics *feed* prejudice and fear and blinkered vision, but the best ones, the best ones . . . illuminate them, make them clearer to see, easier to deal with. We've got to make people laugh till they cry.

Cry. Till they find their pain and their beauty. Comedy is medicine. Not coloured sweeties to rot their teeth with.

*The Asian reappears in the doorway.*

Can I help you?

**Asian** Please, Learning to Read?

**Waters** No . . .

**Asian** Please.

*He puts down his parcel, fishes a leaflet from his sodden overcoat, hands it to Waters. Waters studies it, turns it over to read the other side.*

Learning to Read.

**Waters** (*reading*) 'Reading to Learn'.

**Asian** No. Learning to Read.

**Waters** No, it says Reading to Learn. (*He shows him.*) Reading. To. Learn.

*The Asian is perplexed.*

It says it's a class in literary appreciation for intending students of the Open University. BBC. I'm no wiser than you, really . . .

**Asian** A man gave it to me in the library . . .

**Waters** Aye, well he probably had a sense of humour.

**Asian** Perhaps somewhere else . . .?

**Waters** (*glancing at clock*) Look. I'll take you up to the Principal, he'll sort you out . . . (*He leads him towards door.*) I won't be a minute. Try and sort the order out while I'm away, will you, George. Look at you, you're soaked, man, how far've you come . . .?

*They leave.*

**Samuels** (*standing, lighting cigarette*) What a fuck up *this* is! (*at Price*) Why don't you keep your bloody trap shut, eh?

**McBrain** Come on, Sammy.

**Samuels** Fuck off. I want to think about me act, not arse the night away on . . . philosophy! Especially after he tells us we've got a bent adjudicator.

**Phil** Me too.

**Connor** I thought you said you couldn't care less whether you did well or not tonight.

**Samuels** (*terse*) Well I do.

**Connor** With having your own club and that up Moston way.

**Ged** Yeah. You said you could always employ yourself.

**Samuels** Listen, cretin, do you wanna know something, I wouldn't be seen dead working a club like mine, I want the tops, I want TV, I want the Palladium. You can work my club, I'll book you as soon as you're ready, you're just what they need. As for that little git . . .

*Points at Price, turns away angrily. Price moves, with some menace, towards him. McBrain gently interposes himself.*

**McBrain** There was this poacher, see. And he shoots this deer. Big 'un. Hatstands in its head an' that. And he puts it over his back – like that – and he's hunking it off when this gamekeeper catches him and says, Hey, you're poaching, and your man says, How do you mean? and he says, You've got a deer on your back, and he looks over his shoulder and he says, Get off.

217

*They laugh, more at the telling than the tale. Price gets up, steps onto the rostrum, becoming, in the moment, uncannily, the seventy-year-old Waters.*

**Price** Now, Mr McBrain, you must see that that joke is totally supportive of all forms of blood sports. Besides which it undoubtedly hints at the dark secret of animal buggery or, at the very least, the stealthy buggering of men by beasts of the field and forest. A *comedian*, George, would have carried all this out into the open where we could all see it . . . (*He looks for it.*) . . . so that we'd all come to realize what should've been obvious from the start, or the Middle Ages, whichever you prefer: namely, deep down we all want fucking up the arse by antlered beasties. (*Pause.*) It's a joke that hates *deer*, George.

*McBrain, Connor and Phil Murray laugh. Samuels scowls a bit in his corner.*

**Ged** (*serious*) That's not so funny.

**Price** (*sombre*) No. I suppose it isn't.

**McBrain** Why've you got it in for him then?

**Connor** Yeah, what's that about? His favourite an' all. I thought you rated him.

**Price** I don't want telling what to think. That's all. I don't want telling what to feel.

**Samuels** You'd've felt my bleeding boot up your hole if you'd talked that way to me. Look at the fucking time . . .

**Price** ( *quiet, with great, inquiring grace*) I didn't know you was Irish, Sammy . . .

*Samuels laughs, a little slow splutter in spite of himself.*

**Samuels** You're a slippy fucker. Do you know that?

**Price** (*rolling eyes*) Yes, baas. I know that, baas. Yessuh baas. Whup ma hahd an cawl me kinky.

**McBrain** Answer the question. Why're you so bent on riling the old man? *He's* no different.

**Price** So maybe I am. (*He strokes his cropped head, an unconscious gesture.*)

**Connor** Yeah. Maybe it's more than your hairs you've been losing.

*Price turns away, smiling.*

I'll tell you some'at. He's a good old man. And he's a comic to his toenails. He doesn't *need* to do this for peanuts, you know, every Friday night, *here*, on two quid an hour or whatever it is. He could take a room in a pub and charge a fortune and he'd get it too. So that he can teach pricks like us he does it. (*Pause.*) And if I get out of the building game and earn a living doing what I want to do more than anything else, always have done, I'll have him to thank and no one else. (*deliberately*) And that goes for everyone here, whether they know it or not.

**Ged** It goes for me.

**McBrain** Yeah.

**Phil** All right, he's a genius, what is this, Gala Night at the City Varieties?

**Ged** *We* knew less than nowt.

**Phil** Speak for yourself. I'd done clubs . . .

**Ged** Two. Ardwick and Oldham. One of 'em withheld your money. The other called you a taxi to drive you off to safety.

**Phil** Like the bloody wild west, both of 'em. There was nothing wrong with *me*. My troubles started when I took you on, believe me.

**Ged** (*quiet, toughly serious*) When you are gonna face it:
you're not funny. You're a straight. You can't work on
your own. (*Pause.*) But I can.

**Phil** Try it.

**Ged** Maybe I will.

**McBrain** Frying tonight, by God! Jees, listen to 'em go.
All of 'em. Those poor bloody guinea pigs of an audience
at this club'll know the meaning of tears tonight, by
Christ, won't they just. Come on, let's get the order
decided, who wants to go first? Sammy? How about you?

**Samuels** No thanks.

**McBrain** Anyone? (*Nobody.*) OK. (*Takes pack of cards
from his pocket, cuts it twice.*) Lowest loses, aces high. (*He
deals five cards in sequence to correspond to the five turns.
They peer at the cards.*)

**Connor** Shit!

**McBrain** You Mick! Tough.

**Connor** Ah well. At least they'll be awake.

**Samuels** You'll no doubt manage to do something about it
though . . .

**McBrain** Second, Sammy?

**Samuels** All right.

**McBrain** Ged? Phil?

**Ged** OK.

**McBrain** (*looking at Price*) How do you feel about last?

**Price** All the same to me.

**McBrain** Right. Top of the bill, kidda. Will they be
waiting for you! Now, who wants music? (*They show,*

*McBrain writes it down.*) Gethin, you have music don't you?

**Price** No.

**McBrain** I thought you got off with that song. What was it . . .?

**Price** No, I've changed it. No music.

**Samuels** You're a cool sod, I'll give you that. The bleeding nerve of it, working up an act for three months and then altering it half an hour before he goes on. You'll come a right cropper one day, you will. I can feel it in me water.

**Price** (*deliberately*) Well, piss over somebody else for a change, Sammy.

**McBrain** Hey, hey, hey, any more of that and you'll go in the book . . . (*He brandishes a book in his right hand, a referee.*)

*Waters in, followed by the Asian. Waters carries a tray with eight teas in plastic cups, spoons, sugar.*

**Waters** I got the teas in.

*They move towards the tray.*

Gentlemen, this is Mr Patel.

**Ged** Hello, Mr Patel.

*A few more grunts of acknowledgement.*

**McBrain** Hey, if you've got any good jokes, I'll have a word with you before you go . . .

**Patel** *smiles innocently.*

**Waters** Mr Patel is going to stay with us a little while, I've promised him a lift into town on the way down to the Club. He's, erm . . . he's been sent on a wild goose chase

. . . and the monsoon is still with us, as you'll no doubt have observed for yourselves. Sit there if you would, Mr Patel, by the pipes. Take your coat off if you like.

**Patel** (*sitting*) Thank you no, sir. I'm very comfortable, please . . .

*Waters resumes the desk, picks up McBrain's list.*

**McBrain** That's the order.

**Waters** Fine. And the asterisks are music, yes?

**McBrain** Ahunh.

**Waters** (*at clock*) Right. I don't want anything from your acts from now on, all right. Just let them lie and get yourselves limber. OK. Close your eyes. Come on, close your eyes.

*They close their eyes, frowning or amused.*

Now think. Think about yourselves. What you've been, what you've done, what you are, what you want. All right? Keep thinking. Now, take one incident, anything, any little thing, that means something to you, maybe something that embarrasses you or haunts you or still makes you frightened, something you still can't deal with maybe, all right? Now think about it. It may be some'at very gentle, very tender, some'at you said, some'at you did, wanted to do . . . All right. Open up.

*They blink at each other.*

**Ged** Bloody hellfire, I were just gettin' into that.

**Waters** Let's hear it then, Mr Murray.

**Ged** (*and others*). What?

**Waters** I want you to tell it. Any way you like, in your own time. (*Pause.*) But make it funny.

**Ged** Jesus wept!

**Samuels** He'd been watching your act.

**Ged** I were thinking about wife.

**McBrain** Haha. Very good, very good. It's the way he tells 'em you know.

**Waters** (*softly*) You're next, George. (*to Ged*) So tell us about it. Be funny. Try.

**Ged** She went in hospital, have the nipper. Ancoats. Bout two in the morning. He musta lay there best part of a year, all snug like, planning it. I rang up from Beswick depot next morning about half-five. Nothing. Seven, nothing. Half-nine. Half-ten. I musta bin nervous, I found mesel smoking me own fags. I went to our mother's dinnertime, for company I suppose. (*difficult now*) Me dad'd been off work for a while, Clayton Aniline . . . he'd had a sorta breakdown . . . (*He touches his head*.) . . . gone a bit queer in the head . . .

**Phil** Bloody hell, what you talkin' about that for . . .?

**Ged** Anyroad, I rang again and they said she'd had it so I got a bus and went down. (*Pause*.) When I got to the ward, I couldn't go in.

**Connor** The door was locked.

**Ged** I suddenly thought, what if it runs in the family.

**McBrain** Like crabs, you mean.

**Ged** I thought, what if there's some'at wrong with it.

*Silence now, the story rivets.*

She were holding it in her arm. I saw it ten beds away. Black hair. Red face. Little fists banging away on wife's face. (*Pause*.) He were bloody perfect. He were bloody perfect.

*He looks around, unembarrassed, largely unaware of
his effect. Some coughs, stirrings, sniffs.*

**Phil** (*mutter*) What you talkin' about that for?

**Ged** (*simply*) I were thinkin' about it.

**Phil** You were thinking about it. Jesus wept.

**McBrain** I'm not following that, Mr Waters. No thanks.

**Price** I went nutty once.

**Samuels** (*queer*) Well, you do surprise me, Gethin.

**Waters** Is that what you were thinking about?

**Price** Sort of.

**Waters** Go on.

**Price** I thumped a teacher.

**Connor** Oh the hard bastard of a thing you are.

**Price** (*simply*) Not really. Were a woman. She called us a
guttersnipe. In music. I clocked her one. It seemed the only
thing I could do. She went white. Whiter than me even.
Then she cried. Little tears. They sent me to a
psychologist. Thirteen. Me I mean, *he* were a bit older.
Though not much. We developed a sort of tolerant hatred
of each other. He kept insisting on treating me as an equal,
you know. Patronizing me. The last time I saw him he gave
me this long piece and he said, 'You see, Gethin, basically
all any of us want is to be loved.' And I said, 'If you know
so much, how come you wear a Crown Topper?' (*Pause.*)
That's when I decided I'd be a comedian. (*He sniffs,
twangs the violin string.*)

**Ged** That's about as funny as mine.

**Phil** Yeah, laugh a minute.

**Waters** It's hard isn't it. Not exactly queuing up to go, are we, gentlemen? (*He scans McBrain's row, then stares at Phil Murray.*) Why *is* that, do you think? It wouldn't have been *all* waste, Mr Murray, if your child had been born defective, would it? I mean, it would at least have afforded us a worthy subject for the comic's wit. (*Pause.*) Do we fear . . . other people . . . so much that we must mark *their* pain with laughter, our own with tears? People deserve respect because they are people, not because they are known to us. Hate your audience and you'll end up hating yourself. All right. We'll stop that there . . . (*Looks at clock: about 8.20.*) Any final queries about your spots? George? Sammy?

*Both give negatives.*

Mick?

**Connor** (*fiddling*) Y'aven't a dickie have you, this keeps fallin' off . . .?

**Waters** I'll have a look at it in the van going down. Gethin?

*Price shakes his head.*

Sure?

*Price nods.*

What about you two?

**Phil** We're fine, Mr Waters.

**Waters** (*to everyone*) I want to wish you luck. You worked hard, you've sweated, you've been honester than most. I'll be pulling for you all tonight. And you'll *know* if you're good. You'll not need tellin'.

**Challenor** *knocks, enters on the knock. He's maybe five years younger than Waters, rather waxen, discreetly*

*dressed, with a homburg, and umbrella, which he
shakes. His self-regard is almost a mannerism, though
he retains a residual lithe charm.*

**Challenor** Evening, Eddie. I'll never understand why they
don't run boats to Manchester.

**Waters** We're waiting on London to give the word. Hello,
Bert.

**Challenor** Spry as ever. Eddie Waters, the Lancashire Lad.

**Waters** Relax. You'll see forty, don't you fret.

**Challenor** I thought you'd have taken the bungalow at
Southport by now, Eddie.

**Waters** Nay. I'm a Manchester man. I'd miss the rain.

*The relaxed yet glinting spat ends.*

**Challenor** These your lads, then?

**Waters** Aye. Mr Challenor of the C.A.M.F., Phil and Ged
Murray, Gethin Price, Mick Connor, Sammy Samuels,
George McBrain.

**Challenor** How do you do. (*He's looking in Patel's
direction, inquiringly.*)

**Waters** He's not part of the class.

**Challenor** No? There's one or two about, you know.
Midland clubs. Awful lot of people, of course . . .

**Waters** Is there anything you want to say before we get
down there?

**Challenor** (*checking watch*) I wouldn't mind a word or
two, Eddie. Is it far?

**Waters** No. No. Ten minutes.

*The Caretaker comes in. He carries a shattered lectern.*

**Caretaker** (*to Waters*) I told the Principal you were looking for him. (*He points in Patel's direction*) He's back now. He had to go down to the other centre in Beswick. (*He makes a drinking sign with his right hand.*)

**Waters** Thank you, I think we can manage now . . .

**Caretaker** I told him you were looking. He's in his office. Waiting.

**Waters** It's very good of you.

**Caretaker** (*looking at lectern*) They've gone bloody *mad* down there, that Karate lot. (*He leaves.*)

*Challenor looks at Waters.*

**Challenor** Don't mind me, Eddie.

*Waters doesn't want to leave, can't show it.*

**Waters** We'll go and see the Principal, Mr Patel, just to make sure you're in the wrong place.

*Patel crosses behind him to the door.*

(*to class*) I'll be back . . .

*They leave. Challenor mounts the dais carefully, stands at the tall, sloping desk, places his black attaché case on the ledge.*

**Challenor** Going to give me a good show then?

**McBrain** That we are. Crème de la crème. You'll laugh tonight, Mr Challenor, that you will.

**Challenor** That's good news, brother. It's been a particularly unfunny day.

**Samuels** Your worries are over, Mr Challenor, mark my words. Five of the finest comedy acts west of Royton. I'm *very* funny.

**Challenor** I'll watch out for you.

**Samuels** Trap three. It'll guide in.

**Phil** I saw you at the Hulme Hippodrome just after the war, about 1951. Frank Randle top of the bill. Bert Challenor, the Cockney Character.

**Challenor** Right. Played Number Ones for twenty years, right through to the end. History to you lot . . .

**Price** Did you really play with Frank Randle?

**Challenor** I did.

**Price** What were he like? Were he one of the best?

**Challenor** Best of his kind, I suppose.

**Price** How do you mean, of his kind?

**Challenor** He was *local*, wasn't he? South of Birmingham he was nothing. A whole set of 'em – Sandy Powell, Albert Modley, Jimmy James. George was the giant. Took the country. George was the great one. He's the one to study, if you're keen to get on.

**Price** Formby?

**Challenor** Ahunh.

**Connor** Didn't Mr Waters work with your man before the war?

**Challenor** Eddie did a lot of things before the war.

**Samuels** Was he good?

*Pause.*

**Challenor** He were brilliant.

**Samuels** Yeah? What happened then?

**Challenor** (*quietly*) He didn't . . . want enough. (*Pause.*) I

228

don't know. He just stayed up here . . .

*Pause.*

**Price** Have you seen Randle's films? I've seen 'em all. He's untouchable. (*He gets up suddenly, assumes an uncanny Frank Randle stance and gait.*) 'I'm as full of vim as a butcher's dog – I'm as lively as a cricket. Baaa, I'll sup it if it keeps me up all neet. I'll take anybody on of my age and weight, dead or alive, and I'll run 'em, walk 'em, jump 'em, fight 'em, aye, and I'll play 'em dominoes. Baaa, I've supped some stuff toneet. Listen, ony t'other day I went to a funeral, I were stood at graveside, a chap looked at me, he said, How old are yer? I said eighty-two, he said I'm eighty-four. I said, I don't think it's much use thee going home at all.'

*The group laugh. Challenor smiles thinly, undazzled.*

**Challenor** Try it in Bermondsey, sonny. Try it in Birmingham even.

**Phil** Pay him no heed, Mr Challenor.

**Samuels** He argues like other people breathe.

**Challenor** Well. Nice meeting you. Good luck for tonight. (*He dwells, enjoying the attention.*) A couple of . . . hints. Don't try to be deep. Keep it simple. I'm not looking for philosophers, I'm looking for comics. I'm looking for someone who sees what the people want and knows how to give it them. It's the people pay the bills, remember, yours, mine . . . Mr Waters's. We're servants, that's all. They demand, we supply. Any good comedian can lead an audience by the nose. But only in the direction they're going. And that direction is, quite simply . . . escape. We're not missionaries, we're suppliers of laughter. I'd like you to remember that. See you down there. Oh. A text for tonight. Perhaps we can't all be Max Bygraves. But we can try.

*He takes his leave. Silence. McBrain opens another two cans of 'E', hands one to Connor. Samuels lights a panatella. They sit looking at each other, scanning for concern or alarm.*

**Samuels** (*disgust staining his voice*) Oh, that's marvellous. That's . . . marvellous.

**Phil** (*backing his chair to the floor savagely as he stands*) What the fuck are we gonna do?

**Samuels** We're gonna get the bum's rush, that's what we're gonna do.

**McBrain** Not at all. What're you on about?

**Samuels** Look, you heard him, Seamus . . .

**McBrain** (*thinking, already doubtful*) He had to say that. He's an old enemy of the Boss's, what else could he say?

**Phil** Sod that, what're we gonna *do*?

**Ged** What's that supposed to mean? We're gonna do our act.

**Phil** He'll murder us. You've got to be joking.

**McBrain** That's very nearly funny.

**Ged** (*to Phil, standing heavily*) Look, what are you talking about?

**Price** (*piercing through the din*) He means – do you not? – how can you change your act at this short notice to suit Challenor. Isn't that what you mean?

*He takes in the whole group in the silence that follows the question. People sniff, shuffle, look at others.*

**Samuels** (*finally*) It's not such a tragedy. I can paste some'at together. Fortunately, I've managed to keep my distance . . .

**Connor** Challenor'll get the act I came with. He don't bother me.

**Samuels** OK, so be the funniest hod-carrier at Wimpey's.

**Connor** (*steely*) I don't carry a hod, Sammy.

**Ged** We've got an act . . .

**Phil** We've got several acts. What about the one we used Christmas?

**Ged** What? You heard what Mr Waters thought of that . . .

**Phil** Look, Ged, I mean, look, fuck Mr Waters, I don't intend to spend the rest of my days on the pigging knocker collecting club money. Now I don't. All right?

**Ged** (*implacable*) I don't care what you do or don't do tomorrow. Tonight, we do the act.

**Phil** Do we.

**Ged** We do.

**Phil** You're stupid.

**Ged** (*dangerous, very swift*) No, Phil. Leave it.

*Price watches them all from a distance, limbering up.*

**Samuels** What about you, George?

**McBrain** I'll think of something. Well known you know for my flexibility. In any case (*Frank Carson voice*) it's the way that I tell 'em . . .

**Phil** (*splenetic*) If you hate those bloody docks as much as you claim, you'll know what to do all right.

**Samuels** Somebody shoulda told Challenor they *do* run boats to Manchester. So that pricks like you can unload 'em.

**McBrain** (*simply*) I know what to do. Trust Georgey.

*Pause. Samuels turns to Price.*

**Samuels** Whorrabout you then?

*Price is doing left-leg squats on the dais. Stops carefully. Swivels gracefully round.*

**Price** (*innocent*) Me?

**Samuels** *You*, you slippy sod.

**Price** (*distinctly*) The traitor distrusts truth. The traitor distorts truth. The traitor destroys truth.

**Samuels** You're dafter than you think, you know.

**Price** (*inward*) I drive a van all day for British Rail. And if Challenor were on fire I wouldn't piss him out. Max Bygraves! (*The venom muscles his throat.*)

**McBrain** (*quietly*) Maybe you won't have to?

*Price's raised eyebrows ask the question.*

You've changed your act already, haven't you. Who's a clever boy then?

**Samuels** (*sourly marvelling*) Slippy.

*Silence. Ged frowns concern. Connor watches. McBrain chuckles. Samuels clicks his teeth. Phil Murray flops back in his chair. Price stands a moment longer, then moves for his gear, gathers it, turns, begins to leave.*

**Price** See you at the show, darlings . . . (*He's gone, out on amazing tiptoe, like a dancer in a minefield.*)

**Samuels** (*following slowly to door*) Waters musta mentioned Challenor, told him last week, after the lesson. They allus have a drink together in the Mare . . .

**Connor** (*far from content*) Forget it, for Christ's sake.

Who cares about bloody Challenor . . .

*He gathers his things roughly, angrily: leaves. The
others begin to gather their belongings. Waters back in.
He carries six buttonholes in plastic bags. Looks at
depleted company.*

**Waters** Ah, the others have gone on, have they . . . I
brought one of these each for you . . . Here . . . (*He hands
four out, pockets the remainder.*) Don't start boozing after
your turn. I've promised the Principal we'll be out by ten
at the latest. All set then? Let's get the van . . .

*They troop out one after the other, Waters standing in
the doorway to see them through. He gives a final
cursory look around the room and leaves, closing door
behind him.*

   *Sounds of footsteps, muffled talking. After a moment,
car and van doors being opened and closed, engines
starting up.*

   *The door opens and the Caretaker peeps in, sees the
room vacated, advances. He carries a smashed chair, the
frame in the right hand, a leg in the left.*

   *After a moment he sights Patel's muslin-covered
package. Stops, scans. Signs of slight but rising
apprehension. He reaches gingerly towards it with the
chair leg. Touches. Prods more vigorously, yet still
cringing from it, as though half-expecting an explosion.
Nothing. He drops the chair leg, opens the neck of the
bag, peers in, sniffs, sniffs again, sniffs several times, his
face crinkling with disgust. Stands. Picks up his chair.
Leaves, switching off all lights behind him.*

# Act Two

*A small club stage. A club* **Pianist** *has arrived during the interval and is just completing a medley of old favourites. The* **Concert Secretary** *arrives at his table at the side of the stage, calling, 'Yes, yes, all right Teddy. I'll see to it after the draw,' to someone off-stage and at the same time showing Challenor (Scotch in hand) to his own table stage right.*

**Concert Secretary** *(dry, tolerably sour, in charge; but real, not caricature)* Right. As announced in last week's club bulletin, there will now be a brief interval in the bingo . . .

*Groans, calls of 'No' etc.*

*a brief* interval in the bingo, to listen to some new comics setting their feet on the first rung of the ladder of fame. Now this'll last half an hour at the most and I'd like you to show these lads the traditional courtesy of the club – and then we'll get straight back to the bingo as soon as it's all over. Now . . . these are all lads who've been coached by that favourite comic of yesteryear, the Lancashire Lad himself, Mr Eddie Waters. Take a bow, Eddie.

*Waters appears and makes his way to an empty table on the other side of the stage, ignoring the Concert Secretary's urgings to say a few words, and sits down with his pint, stage left.*

So I think we're in for a treat. *(checking tatty notes)* First off, then, a young man from Ireland, now domiciled in Moss Side, your welcome please for . . . Mick . . . Connor.

*Connor appears from the wings in hired evening dress*

*and black pumps, a white carnation and black dickie.
The Pianist covers his entrance with 'If you're Irish,
come into the parlour'.*

**Connor** (*very Irish*) I told him not to say anything about
me bein' Irish. I wanted to creep up on yez, like.

*The Concert Secretary shushes the audience
authoritatively. Connor angles his head in the Concert
Secretary's direction.*

I'm talkin' as quiet as I can. (*to audience*) Good evening.
Sorry about de bingo. (*Takes mic. from stand, begins a
slow, easy walk that will take him down from the club
stage and find him sitting on the theatre stage below.*) Wuz
yez ever foreigners, any of yez? I don't mean the odd
fortnight in Brighton now, I mean like always. Jeez, it's a
funny thing . . . First day in Manchester I go lookin' for
rooms. Your woman answers the door, a neat little thing
wi' gouty eyes. I says, Do you have any low terms for
Irishmen here? She says, Yes. Piss off. Mind you that was
before the blacks came to help us out, shoulder some of
the white man's burden. Troublemakers. I never knew we
wuz troublemakers till I got to England. You don't you
know. I mean, what are you lot, eh, do you know? You
don't have to find out, do you? Just people. You'd have to
go to India or . . . Africa . . . or Ireland to find out. Mmm?
They'd tell yer right enough. Well, stick around, maybe
we'll come to you. You know, even the Catholic Church is
different here. I went to Mass at the Holy Name, like a
bloody opera. Back home in Wexford it's more like a
market. The priest charges ten per cent commission on all
transactions. And confessions . . . Jesus . . . In England
you can hear the candles melt, so you can . . . Your Irish
priest is either half deaf or half stewed. Speak up my son,
there's nothing to be ashamed of . . . so you've gotta burst
your lungs off to get absolution, safact. (*bellow*) Bless me,

Father, for I have sinned, it is six years since my last
confession . . . I have missed Mass seven hundred and
twenty three times . . . I have fornicated . . . (*own voice*)
*Then* you can hear a pin drop. I tell yer, we'd sit there by
the confession box every Sunday night . . . all the young
buckos . . . It was a great way for picking up girls for the
ceilidh. (*acting it*) Hey, dissun's a goer . . . ten times widat
Heaney feller from Ballamadurphy . . . Hey, wait while
you hear where he put his finger . . . (*He laughs.*) None of
that here, mind. Your English priest enjoys it too much . . .
Oh yes. (*English priest's voice, dripping with retracted
interest, low and breathy, close to mic*) Yes, I see, my son,
and *you* put it where? (*Self, very low, hesitant but intense*)
I put it . . . down her mouth, Father. (*Priest, slight but
controlled increase in excitement*) Did you now? Erm . . .
and why did you do that, my son? (*Self*) She 'ad dis . . .
bone stuck, Father . . . Or there's the other sort, the feller
that's gonna end up Bishop's secretary, he's very *bored*
(*Bored posh priest, testy*) All right, so you've been wearing
your sister's clothes *again*, don't you ever do anything else?
. . . Don't you fancy your mother's? . . . I mean, you're in
here every week with the same story, there's no plot,
there's no development, look, it might excite you, there's
absolutely nothing in it for me. Your penance is five Our
Fathers and five Hail Marys . . . and the next time you're
tempted to get into a frock just . . . count to ten . . . and
ask God to make you a little more inventive. (*Pause.*)
Reminds me of the old spinster lady back home confesses
fornication and the priest asks her for details . . . cause
he's interested like . . . and so he can get a good sight of
her through the grille, so she tells him about this
wonderful night of love she spent with a tinker, and the
priest says, Mary McGuire, that's the most shameful thing
you're after telling me and you a respected spinster of
seventy-three. And she says (*old maid's girlish voice*) As a
matter of fact, Father, I was thirty when it happened. I just

like talking about it. (*Pause.*) I married an English Catholic
girl you know. She's sitting on the bed, on our
honeymoon, and I see her take out these little yellow,
tablety things, I says, What's that? She says, The pill, why,
can't you take it in Ireland? And I says, Oh, I can take it
all right, it's the women that aren't allowed. I says, How
come you're on the pill? She says, Our church says we
must search our own individual consciences for the truth
and then act accordingly. (*Self*) Did you ever hear of such a
thing? Back home in Ireland them's what we call
Protestants. 'Course we had other ways. Oh yes, we were
very inventive. An uncle of mine practised coitus
interruptus all his life – till he got it right. I had lots of
cousins in Wexford . . . God . . . (*Long reflective pause.*)
He was a sad man, though. So listen anyway. Don't believe
all you hear, you know what I mean. Speak well of the
living. Especially within earshot. And the next time you
meet an Irishman, count to ten . . . and ask God to make
you a little bit more inventive. And don't keep slapping
him on the back. One day he'll stick a pack of dynamite
up his jacket and blow your bloody arm off. If he didn't
do it already. Like the IRA man who knocks at the gates of
Heaven and St Peter says, Who're you? And your man
says, I'm from the IRA. St. Peter says, Oh no, you can't
come in here, and your man says, I don't wanna come in,
I'm giving yez all three minutes to get out. Goodnight.
God bless.

*Pianist plays through Connor's applause and exit.*

**Concert Secretary** (*mic.*) A Manchester man now, from
Middleton, a warm welcome please for . . . (*reading*) . . .
Mr Sammy Samuels.

*Sammy walks on. He wears a fine-fitting white jacket,
red carnation, black bow, red satin handkerchief,
diamond cufflinks.*

**Samuels** A message for any nymphomaniacs in the audience . . . Hello. Sit down, lady, we'll have no rushing the stage. 1929 I were born. Year of the Great Crash. The sound of me father's jaw dropping. He took one look at me and said, I'm not that Jewish. Nobody's that Jewish. So, anyway, in the divorce court the judge awards me mother twenty pounds a month maintenance. And me father says, Judge, dat's very generous of you and to tell you de truth, ven business gets better I'll mebbe also help out a little. Anyway, me mother's bringing us all up like and me sister comes home from college and she says, I'm afraid I can't continue with me studies, momma. Vy? says momma. She couldn't say why. Vy. Always vy. Vy? she says. My sister says, I'm sort of . . . pregnant, momma. That did it. A chair, a seltzer, oi, oi . . . finally she says, So who's de fadder? I send you to college, I'm simple people. You got education, I don't know de proper vay to be introduced but you don't even know to ask mit whom am I having de pleasure?! Something's running down my leg; I hope it's sweat. She was some woman, momma. Bank manager rings up, he says, Mrs Samuels, you have an overdraft of fifty pounds. Is dat so? she says. So vot vos de balance last month? He looks, he says: You had a credit of twenty-two pounds. All right, says momma, and did I call you? (*He looks at the stone-faced Challenor, wipes his hands on the handkerchief.*) OK, forget the Jews. Everybody else did. Here, there was this poacher, see. Poacher? And he catches this deer. And he slings it over his shoulder and he's humping it through the forest and a gamekeeper catches him and he says, Hey you, you're poaching. And the guy says, How do you mean? And the gamekeeper says, You've got a deer on your back. And the guy goes . . . (*Looks over his shoulder and screams.*) Heard about the Irish lamp post? Pissed on a dog. Hear about the Irish cargo ship carrying yoyos? Sank forty-four times. The Irish waterpolo team. Drowned twelve horses.

This secretary runs into the boss's office and says, Can I
use your dictaphone? He says, No, use your finger like
everyone else! There's this West Indian tries to get a
labouring job on a building site. Foreman says, No chance,
I know you lot. I give one of you a job, you turn up the
next day with a gang of your friends. He begs and pleads
and finally he gets the job. Next day he turns up with a
pigmy. (*indicating*) Pigmy. Down there. The foreman said,
What did I tell you, no friends! He says, That's not my
friend, that's my lunch. What do you think of this
Women's Lib, then? Burnt your bras have you? Did you
sir, how interesting. I burnt the wife's. She went bloody
mad, she was still in it. I'm in a pub downtown and this
liberated woman person collars me, she says, You're a
brutal, loud-mouthed, sadistic, irrational, sexist, male
chauvinist pig. I said, I suppose a quick screw is out of the
question? . . . So later in bed, I'm giving her one and she
says, You're marvellous, you're marvellous. No one has
ever made love to me like that before. But, I'm sort of
kinky. Would you mind biting my ears while you're doing
it? Sure. On the lobes, gentle like. (*He mimes the delicate
lobe bites, quite slowly.*) Now, she says, can you kiss my
bust, real quick. (*He repeats lobes slowly, then adds rapid
bust kisses.*) Now, she says, can you put your hands round
the back here and pull the cheeks . . . Certainly. (*He starts
the mime at the top, adding the buttock-tugging, returns to
the lobes again.*) She says, You've slipped out! I said, No
bloody wonder, I've forgotten what I was doing! I was at
the bar there earlier and I thought I'd take a leak while it
was slack. A big black bugger rushes in. Aaaah, he says.
Just made it! I took a look, I said, There's no chance of
making one in white for me is there? I'd like to thank the
pianist. (*fast*) Thanks. Actually he's a brilliant pianist, this
man. He has a lovely touch. Actually, he got that touch off
Liberace. (*to pianist*) Am I right? And that other thing you
got off Liberace . . . has it cleared up? OK, take care of

yourselves, and if any of you ladies are accosted on your way out by a dark, handsome fellow in a white jacket and a red carnation, just remember, it's for your own good. I leave you with this thought: impotence is just nature's way of saying, Forget it. But remember . . . Maestro – (*to Pianist. Sings, 'When You're Smiling.' Bows, takes applause, leaves with mic., returns mic. to Concert Secretary, exits.*)

**Concert Secretary** (*slowly returning mic. to stand*) Two lads now from Blackley . . . a double act . . . Phil and Ged Murray . . . who call themselves . . . (*checking scrap of paper, nose wrinkling*) . . . Night and Day.

> *Pianist plays 'Night and Day' to cover the entrance. Phil Murray, in black dinner jacket and bow tie, pulls on a huge wicker basket, gestures to the deeply reluctant Concert Secretary to help him lift it onto the club stage. When he's got it set, he takes from it a small girl dummy, shy, long blonde hair, party dress.*

**Phil** (*a good 'best' voice*) Good evening ladies and gentlemen. Say good evening, Sophie.

**Doll** (*eyelashes demure*) Good evening.

**Price** Are you ready to sing your song then, Sophie?

**Ged** (*strangulated, from box: minimal but effective dummy voice*) Hey.

**Phil** (*ignoring him*) What's it going to be then, Sophie?

**Ged** (*louder*) Hey, I'm talking to you.

**Phil** (*side of mouth*) Shut up. Sophie?

**Ged** Listen, I'm not lying here all bloody night. Have you got that stupid stick-doll in 'ere?

**Phil** Be quiet.

**Ged** Y'have, 'aven't you? Y'ave. You mighta lain 'im down.

**Phil** Excuse me, Sophie . . . (*He opens the trunk, places the doll on Ged's stomach, closes it again.*) Ladies and gentlemen, we *were* going to start with a song . . .

**Ged** (*to the girl doll in the trunk, voice warm and sexy*) Hello, love. (*Carries on flirting and laughing – as though being tickled.*) Hey, what you doing down there, hey, what you doing . . . (*etc.*)

> *Phil abandons his attempts to entertain the audience, begins to get Ged out of the trunk. It's a painful floppy process. They flounder to the tall stool by the mic. Their patter throughout is serious, desperate.*

**Phil** (*fixing him on his thigh*) Right, now sit there and sit still.

> *Ged's dressed and made up as a ventriloquist's dummy, in Manchester City supporter's colours, sky blue and white scarf, woollen hat, rattle, rosette. His blue and white half football boots are tied to his ankles, i.e. not on his feet. He slips off Phil's knee, is dragged back, all in one movement. Perches finally.*

Can't you stay up?

**Ged** Longer than you can, if your wife's to be believed.

**Phil** That's enough.

**Ged** (*from side of mouth*) Face front and keep smiling. *Smile*, you fool. They might go away.

**Phil** Where have you been then?

**Ged** Evening. Nice out, sir, I might get mine out in a minute. (*to Phil*) That didn't go over too well. You were moving your lips, you dummy.

**Phil** I said, where have you been?

**Ged** (*deliberately posh*) Where have I been? Where have I been? I've been to the football match, haven't I, you daft pillock, where do you think I've been? Manchester City. (*Waves rattle, own voice.*) My dad were a City fan. (*rattle*) My dad said if he came home and found Colin Bell in bed with the old lady he'd brew him a cup of tea. (*The joke dies. Ged waits for Phil to throw the next line at him*) He said, if he came home and found Colin Bell in bed with me mother he'd brew him a cup of tea . . .

**Phil** (*suddenly diverting from the act; no warning*) Look, if you're so funny, why don't you tell us all a joke?

**Ged** (*turning his head to look at his brother and blinking a question*) What?

**Phil** (*uneasy at once, but insistent*) Tell us the one about the Pakistani up on a rape charge.

**Ged** (*half out of the act, trying to think, looking in Waters's direction, as if for help*) What you talking about?

**Phil** (*faintly desperate*) Tell the joke.

> Ged turns his head slowly, stares at the audience, stands, very slowly, puts his hands on Phil's shoulders, removes him from the stool, takes his place, draws his brother mercilessly down on to his thigh, repositions the mic. stand.

**Ged** (*in character*) *You* tell it.

> Phil blinks, thinks.

**Phil** (*terrified, struggling for confidence*) There's this Pakistani, see, up on a rape charge. So the coppers decide they'll have an identity parade. And they get eight or nine other Pakkies and they put this one at the front and explain what they're doing. Then they bring the girl in and

the Pakistani shouts (*Pakistani voice*) She is the one,
Officer. No doubt about it . . .

*Ged and Phil stare whitely out at the audience. Neither
knows where to go next. Ged gets up, repeats the
procedure in reverse until he's back on Phil's knee.*

**Ged** (*finally*) How about the song?

**Phil** Why not?

**Ged** A song entitled 'If I had it all to do over again, I'd do
it all over you'. How'd you like being the dummy?

**Phil** (*a nightmare: wholly dependent on Ged now*) Not a
lot.

**Ged** No. It's not funny, is it?

**Phil** How d'you mean?

**Ged** Shall I tell you some'at. There's two fellers like and
they're both crippled. One hasn't moved his hands for
twenty years and the other's in a wheelchair paralysed
from the neck down. And they go to Lourdes for a miracle
cure. And they get to Lourdes and the priest calls for the
one with the hands and he goes down and the priest
immerses his hands in the water and he says, In nomine
domine homine womine, like they do you know and
suddenly the feeling comes back to his hands and he can
use them again. He says, It's a miracle. For twenty years I
haven't been able to use my hands, and he helps to push
his dear old friend in the wheelchair into the water up to
his neck and the priest says, In nomine homine womine
and they pull him out and there's four new tyres on the
chair.

**Phil** Maybe we should sing the song?

**Ged** Have a look at your watch.

*Phil looks.*

What's it say?

**Phil** Time for a song.

**Ged** (*back in the act's groove at last*) I'm not going back in that box after.

**Phil** Sing the song.

**Ged** All right, but I'm warning you, you *walk* me off, sod your hernia, I'm not going back in there with her and that cricket stump . . .

**Phil** Maestro, please.

**Both** (*sing*)
He's my brother
Our kid
Don't want another
Our kid
He watches over me
When things get tough
He pulls the strings
That wipe the tears away on my cuff
He's my brother
Our kid
And there's no other
Our kind
He is my friend, my mate and my mucker
He is my brother
Our kid.

*They take bows like automatons, Ged striding off first,
Phil following whitely, lugging the basket. Pianist
covers.*

**Concert Secretary** Another Irishman now –

*Ged and Phil explode into violent recriminations in the*

*wings. The Concert Secretary looks frowningly behind him.*

– from Belfast, this one – good job we kept them apart – hands together, please, for . . . George . . . McBrain.

*McBrain on, carrying a hand-mic. The mania glands sweating freely. He wears a fine maroon evening jacket, horn-rimmed glasses on nose end, frills at chest and cuffs of royal blue shirt.*

**McBrain**
In the garden of Eden lay Adam
Complacently stroking his madam
And loud was his mirth
For he knew that on earth
There were only two – and he had 'em.

I had a hundred jokes standing back there, now I can't remember a one of 'em. (*He looks at the audience: stares.*) Never mind, I'm good to look at. There's this coloured feller on his way to work. (*Stops.*) Don't you think that's funny? There's this very honest Jew. No favourites here. There's this very brilliant Irishman. From Dublin. I tried to get the wife to come. It gets harder, I dunnit though. I don't say she's jealous but she's the only woman I know. If music be the food of love, how about a bite of your maracas? I was in bed with the wife last Thursday. The wife lay there, very quiet, smoking her pipe. I leaned across and I said, Do you fancy anything, heart? And she said, Yes, I fancy an African about six-foot-three with a big fat . . . cheque book. (*to audience*) Don't get ahead of yourselves! Naughty! I said, Yeah? And what do you reckon he'd make of that great fat idle bum of yours? And she said, what makes you think we'd be talking about you? Doesn't say a lot, my wife. Talks all the time but doesn't say a lot. I took her to the zoo. Belle Vue, to see the orang-utan. Enormous. Great painted whatsits, like

245

rump-steak. (*Bunching hands, stomps a bit, pulls a face*.)
Like Willie Whitelaw having a shower. She falls right over
the wire, as sure as I'm standing here, she trips clean over
the wire and lands on her back with her legs parted, her
skirt up and her drawers flapping in the wind. I couldn't
look, it was horrible. The big feller kinda sniffs and ambles
towards her, and . . . he ends up poised above her like
that, and the wife whispers, (*breathless terror*) George,
what shall I do? What shall I do? And I said, (*whisper*) Tell
*him* you've got a headache. . . . Had a look at the
alligators. Just floating handbags really. She's been a goer
in her time, I tell you. Fast? I met her at a dance in Belfast,
I said, Excuse me. She grabbed me by the lapels and stuck
her tongue half-way down me throat. I was only asking
for a light. We had a whirlwind romance, I wined her and
dined her every week for a fortnight, bean soup, pie and
peas, whirlwind. Then I plucked up courage enough to say
the words I never imagined myself saying in a million
years: You're *What*? And she was. God, what a slut. I
went to see her father . . . out to the Maze prison . . . him
and his six lads all in there together . . . I never saw a
family like it. Ugly? Listen, they wore hoods before they
joined the UVF, safact. The neighbours made 'em, protect
the kids. First thing he says, You're not a mick, are you?
Certainly not, says I. So why didn't you use something,
says he. Use something? says I. Listen, the first time I met
your daughter she was wearing a notice pinned to her
chest saying, I am an epileptic and will die unless you lie
on top of me, there wasn't time for anything like that . . .
Seamus, big friend of mine from Cork (*ape gestures*) . . .
Oh no, that's the monkey . . . (*Straightens into
Frankenstein*.) Seamus, not very bright . . . He got a pair
of water-skis for Xmas, spent the next three months
looking for a sloping lake. True. Joined the IRA. Tried to
blow up the Queen Elizabeth. Couldn't get his mouth
round the funnel. But see my wife, God she's a slut though.

Every time I go for a leak the sink is full of dishes. And the food, instant pollution. She gave us rabbit for a fortnight once, every meal. Rabbit pie, rabbit stew, rabbit rashers, rabbit pâté, rabbit trotters . . . rabbit eggs . . . After two weeks I was done in, I collapsed holding my stomach. She said, I'll send for the doctor. I said, Sod the doctor, see if you can borrow a ferret. But . . . Let's face it, few of us are perfect. Not even the Irish. I was in Belfast the other week, there's a feller lying out on the pavement with a bullet hole in his forehead. There's an old lady walks by, she stops and looks down at yer man for a minute, then she crosses herself and she says, Well, thank God it missed his eye. You can't hate 'em can you. Listen, I've gotta go, I'm wife swapping tonight. I gorra bloke's greyhound last week, made a change. So listen, I'll see yer, all right?

*He takes his bow, sweating, a bit concerned, stiff with tension now, not looking in Waters's direction. McBrain catches Waters's eye, in a bow: a still moment. McBrain breaks, disappears.*

**Concert Secretary** (*mic.*) Last, this evening, a young man from Clayton making his first appearance before an audience, I'm told . . . a warm hand for . . . Gethin Price.

*Price emerges, carrying the tiny violin and bow. He wears bagging half-mast trousers, large sullen boots, a red hard wool jersey, studded and battered denim jacket, sleeves rolled to elbows, a red and white scarf tied on to an arm. His face has been subtly whitened to deaden and mask the face. He is half clown, half this year's version of bovver boy. The effect is calculatedly eerie, funny and chill. He takes out a deeply filthy handkerchief, spreads it carefully, expertly across his right shoulder, slowly tucks the tiny violin on his left, stands perfectly still, looks for the first time at the audience. Cocks the bow, stares at it intently, apparently sinking into process. Notices a very fine thread of gut hanging down. Shakes the bow. Shakes it again. The thread hangs on. He brings the bow finally to his mouth, tries to bite the thread off, his teeth are set on edge, he winces mutely, tries again, can't. He thinks. Tries, bending oddly on one leg, to trap the thread under his huge boot. Fails. Thinks. Takes out a lighter. Sets fire to the thread. Satisfaction. Makes as if to play. The cocked bow slowly begins to smoulder at the far end. He waves it about, horrified. The violin now begins to play unaided in his other hand a piece of intricate Bach. He's trapped for a moment between the two events; finally he places the spent bow on the stage, puts the violin under his boot, dimps it like a cigarette until it's thoroughly crushed.*

**Price** (*to himself, not admitting the audience's existence*) Wish I had a train. I feel like smashing a train up. On me own. I feel really strong. Wish I had a train. I could do with some exercise.

*He does a complicated kata, with praying mantis footsweeps, a tan-fui, pa-kua dao, and other Kung Fu exercises. A spot suddenly illuminates larger than life-size dummies of a youngish man and woman carried on by a club-hand. Well dressed, beautiful people, a faint unselfconscious arrogance in their carriage. The man wears evening dress, gloves, etc., the girl, a simple, stunning white full-length dress and wrap. Her arm is looped in his. They stand, perhaps waiting for a cab to show after the theatre. Price has continued his exercises throughout this 'arrival'. Becomes aware of them gradually: rises slowly: stares. Turns to the audience, slowly smiles, evil and childlike. Sniffs. Ambles over. Stands by the man, measuring, walks round to stand by the girl. We sense him being ignored. He begins to inspect the girl minutely. Takes a cigarette from pocket.*

Cigarette? (*Nothing. He offers it to the man.*) No? (*He pockets the cigarette, turns, calls 'Taxi!' sharply out front, shakes his head as it disappears. Moves round to the man's side again.*) Are you the interpreter, then? Been to the match, have we? Were you at t'top end wi' lads? Good, wannit? D'you see Macari? Eh? (*Silence.*) P'raps I'm not here. Don't you like me? You hardly know me. Let's go and have a pint, get to know each other. Here, don't you live in Salford? I swear I've seen you at the dog track. (*Nothing. He takes a cigarette out of the man's top pocket.*) Very kind of you. Ta. (*He lights the cigarette, blows the smoke in slow separate puffs across the man's face.*) Int this nice? I like a good chat. (*intimate, man-to-man*) Eh. I bet she's a goer, int she, sunshine? She's got a fair pair of knockers on her too. Has she been around? Does she ever go dancing at Belle Vue, Satdays? I think Eric Yates took her home one night. If it's her, she's a right goer, according to Eric. (*Pause.*) I don't know whether to thump you or what. I suppose I could just give you a clout, just to let you know I exist. (*He blows smoke into the man's face.*) Is that hair dyed? Looks dyed. Are you a puff? Are you a pufter? (*Sniffs. Front, fast*) Taxi! (*Pause.*) That's not a taxi, lady, it's a hearse. (*evilish grin*) You're getting confused, lady. Unless you were thinking of a quick fun funeral before retiring for the night. (*to man*) Say something Alice? She's calling hearses, he's talking to himself. (*He turns back to the man.*) You do *speak*, do you? I'm trying to *talk* to you. Say some'at. Tell us what kind of day you've had. Are you on the buses? Eh. Shall I make you laugh? This feller pays twenty pounds for this whore, right? Only she dunt fancy him and runs out of the room. He chases her, stark nekkid, down t' street. Cop stops him, says, Where's the fire, lad? Feller says, I've no idea, but if you see a nude bird running down street, *fuck* her, it's paid for. (*Pause. Nothing.*) You can laugh, you know, I don't mind you laughing. I'm *talking* to you . . .

There's people'd call this *envy*, you know, it's not, it's hate. (*now very fast*) Are you a bi-sexual or is that your sister? You'll never get a taxi here, they're all up at Piccadilly waiting for t' last train from London. Ask me how I know. I work there that's why. And don't interrupt when I'm talking, dint your mother ever tell you, it's rude? (*He does a kung fu thrust, missing the man's head by inches.*) Bruce Lee, do you like him? God, he is. You're a stuck-up bastard, aren't you? Give me a kiss, then, go on Alice, give us a kiss. I love you, give us a kiss. (*He halts his burble. Blinks. Pads round to stand at woman's side.*) Say something? (*in her ear*) Listen . . . I've got a British Rail delivery truck round the corner, ditch Alice and we'll do the town. (*He notices a folded copy of* The Times *in the man's hand. Passes behind the figures, pops his head between them.*) Crosswords? (*Thinks a moment.*) Election. Nine across. Big poll in China, question mark. (*Chinaman*) E-lection. (*Price looks from one to the other, laughs suddenly. He takes hold of their handles, begins to lift them up and down, to indicate their mirth.*) Election! Election! Big poll in China. Laugh you buggers, laugh! (*Price exhorts them to laugh, squeezing their bodies up and down and voicing their laughter for them. Then, very suddenly*) Here. (*He takes a flower out of his pocket, offers it to them.*) For the lady. No, no, I have a pin. (*Pause. He pins the flower – a marigold – with the greatest delicacy between the girl's breasts. Steps back to look at his work.*) No need for thanks. My pleasure entirely. Believe me.

*Silence. Nothing. Then a dark red stain, gradually widening, begins to form behind the flower.*

Aagh, aagh, aagh, aagh . . .

*The spot shrinks slowly on the dummies, centring finally on the red stain. Price's 'aaghs' become short barks of laughter. Innocence.*

I wonder what happened. P'raps it pierced a vein.

*Their light goes out altogether. We're left with his single chill image.*

I made them laugh, though. (*depressed*) Who needs them? Hunh. Who needs them? We manage. (*chanting*) U-n-i-ted. Uni-ted. You won't keep us down there for long, don't worry. We're coming up there where we can gerrat yer. (*Chants.*) Lou Macari, Lou Macari . . . I shoulda smashed him. They allus mek you feel sorry for 'em, out in the open. I suppose I shoulda just kicked him without looking at him. (*Pause. He looks after them. Calling*) National Unity? Up yours, sunshine. (*Pause. He picks up a tiny violin, i.e. another, switched, uncrushed, and a bow. Addresses it. Plays 'The Red Flag' – very simple and direct.*) Still, I made the buggers laugh . . .

*Price walks off. The Concert Secretary, probably shocked, embarrassed, not wishing to dwell. Lights fade. Waters stands, face gaunt, grey. Challenor tosses down a scotch, sheafs his notes, pockets pen.*

**Concert Secretary** That's the lot, ladies and gentlemen. You have your cards, I think. Charlie Shaw has 'em for them that hasn't, and we're starting right away, settle yourselves down, now. And it's eyes down for a full house . . .

*Lights fade gradually.*

Always look after . . . Number One.

*Lights fade to black.*

# Act Three

*Classroom. Time: 9.43. Empty.*

*McBrain, Samuels and Connor return slowly, to sit in their respective places, though an almost deliberate distance apart. Phil Murray in. They sit, glum, drained, separate.*

*Simple exhaustion underpins the low, tense, anxious, angry, baffled mood of the four. No eye contacts. People sit or fiddle. Samuels sits in his coat, ready for away. Connor is again pretty wet. McBrain has changed back to his parka and jeans, his bag on the desk in front of him.*

*Price, off, suddenly starts up with 'There's no business like show business . . .'*

**Phil**  Listen to that stupid cunt.

**Samuels**  There'll be no pigging business for *him*, that's for a certainty. Did you ever see owt like it? He's bloody puddled.

*Price in, dressed as in Act One: smells the mood of the others; dwells for a moment in the doorway.*

**McBrain**  Did you see that Challenor feller? He smiled twice all evening, and both times it was at some'at the sodding concert secretary said.

**Connor**  (*low*) I don't reckon it was much fun for Mr Waters either.

**Phil**  (*checking door with a look*) Look, sod Mr Waters. He's not handing jobs out, is he, Seamus?

**Connor**  (*dangerous, suddenly, very deliberately*) My name's Mick.

*Silence.*

**McBrain** Take it easy, Michael . . .

**Connor** (*ignoring him*) Mick.

**Phil** All right. Mick.

*Ged Murray has appeared wet through in the doorway, in time for the last exchange.*

**Ged** (*finally*) Fish and chips. It's teeming down.

**McBrain** About bloody time. Did you nip home to make 'em?

**Ged** (*giving them out*) Ha bloody ha. There was a queue a mile long. It's next t'British Legion, innit. (*He's with Samuels.*) They dint have any silver hake. I got you a pie.

**Samuels** A pie? What d'you get a pie for?

**Ged** (*handing it to him*) I thought you might be hungry.

**Samuels** (*opening package*) A pie? I don't eat pies.

*Ged moves back towards his seat, taking in Price with a wave on the way back.*

**Ged** (*to Price*) Hey, that was great, Geth . . .

*Price winks.*

**McBrain** They're stone bloody cold.

**Ged** (*on way*) It's a long bloody way.

**Samuels** (*staring at the pie he's broken*) It's a bloody *pork* pie!

**Ged** Is it? Don't you like pork?

**Samuels** God almighty, I ask for silver hake, he brings us a pork pie . . .

**Price** (*about dressed, approaching: Revivalist voice*) Holy pig. Here, give us it here.

*He takes the pie, carries it over to the desks.*
    *Ged moves to Price's chair very deliberately, passing his own on the way, sits facing out, his back to his brother: Phil stares at Ged with hostility. Price notes the change in seating, takes up the centre position between them, stands for a moment, leaning on the chairback, regards the other five very carefully for a moment without speaking.*

Dearly beloved, we are gathered here in the sight of Mammon to mourn the passing of several very promising careers in the comedic arts. For those who live on . . . the words of the great and holy musical *The Song of Norway* will be of special comfort: De cuntibus minibus tuum, rectum anus mirabilis est. Which loosely translated means: It's easy to be a bit of a cunt, you've got to work to become a shithouse. Here endeth lesson one. (*He blesses them gravely, sits down.*)

    *Silence.*

**Samuels** (*finally, ugly*) You got anyone . . . special in mind, Charlie?

*Price gets up swiftly, crosses to the dais, picks up a chair leg left by the Caretaker, holds it in two hands a foot or so from his forehead, breathes very deeply three or four times, then smashes it cleanly with his forehead. He carries the two ends to Samuels, puts them carefully on his desk.*

**Price** You're gonna crucify the man, do the job properly.

*He turns, walks away, resumes his seat. Samuels grasps the two ends, McBrain takes them from him with gentle power, carries them to the wastepaper basket.*

**McBrain** There was this feller, see . . .

**Connor** (*fraying*) No more jokes, George. All right?

*McBrain deposits the ends, returns to his seat. Silence.*
*Ged finishes his chips, wipes his hands on the paper.*

**Ged** (*casual, innocent, knowing*) You'll be all right,
George. You knew what to do all right.

**McBrain** (*a freak of anger at the vent*) So when do I get
the thirty pieces of silver? (*He bangs the desk with his fist,*
*a harsh, half-self-punishing gesture.*) I don't want inquests,
I want work.

**Samuels** Right! Who the fuck does he (*Price*) think he is
anyway! (*to Price*) What about your . . . performance
then, Coco the bloody clown? It was bloody
embarrassing . . .

**Ged** It were different.

**Samuels** Different? It was putrid. Different from bloody
comedy, that's for sure.

**Connor** Look, for Jesus Christ's sake, it's over, will you
forget it . . .

**Ged** Hey, *you* were good, Mick, what I could hear of it.
You got most of 'em in too, dint you.

**Connor** Yeah. I went down like a fart at a funeral.

**Phil** What a bleeding audience. Thick as pig shit.

**Price** A bad lover blames his tool.

**Samuels** So why didn't the great Lancashire Lad do a
warm-up then, eh? He sent you out cold, and I had to
follow you.

**Ged** Oh, *you* found your feet all right, Sammy . . .

**Samuels** What does that mean then?

*The Caretaker comes in, a large battery lamp in his hand.*

**Caretaker** You lot still here? I'm waiting to lock up you know. I've got a home to go to. Somebody left that thing . . . (*He points to the muslin sack.*) . . . Meat.

*He leaves, turning into Waters.*

**Waters** We won't be long now . . .

**Caretaker** I hope not. I'm not on overtime you know . . .

*He leaves. Waters stands a moment in the doorway looking into the room. They stare, some of them half-turning, at him. He's white, drained, tired and old. He walks, less spryly, to the desk. Sits down. Stares at the desk top. Silence. Some looks round the room.*

**Ged** (*holding them up*) There's a packet of chips if you want them, Mr Waters.

*Waters looks at him, makes no answer. Challenor in, shaking his coat.*

**Challenor** Sorry, gentlemen. Several calls of nature on the way. You won't have reached your prostates yet, but you will. Mind if I use the desk, Eddie?

*Waters relinquishes the desk, goes to lean by the windows, an onlooker. Challenor places his case down, opens it, removes notes and forms, flicks through them, sniffs. Looks at Price covertly once or twice. Gathers.*

Right, there's not much time, so I'll get cracking. Interesting evening. Lot of promise. I'll take you one by one so we don't get mixed up. Mick Connor.

**Connor** Yeah.

**Challenor** Aye. You've not done a lot, have you?

**Connor** No, I've done nothing. Concerts, works do's.

**Challenor** I quite liked it. One or two quite nice jokes, quite nicely told. (*studying notes*) Bit old-fashioned. I thought, you know, following a single topic through your act. It mighta worked even so, if you'd taken something more up the audience's street. I mean, you might find being an Irishman in England fascinating, there's no reason we should, is there? (*Pause.*) Had a sort of . . . earnestness about it I didn't much take to. You know, as if you were giving a sermon. One thing you've gotta learn, people don't learn, they don't want to, and if they did, they won't look to the likes of us to teach 'em. You've got to be very good indeed to patronize your audience, I can tell you. (*Pause.*) The sex was crude. I've nothing against it, but it requires taste, if you see what I mean, I've never heard a good joke yet about coitus interruptus. Still, you had your moments. Some promise there. (*Turns Connor's sheet on to its face.*) Sammy Samuels?

**Samuels** Himself.

**Challenor** I thought you'd never get started. First thing you want to do is ditch the first half of your act.

**Samuels** Yeah, it's stuff I've been shedding, you know . . .

**Challenor** S'too Jewish. What's a Jew nowadays eh? Who wants to know I mean.

**Samuels** Yeah, I can see that.

**Challenor** Same mistake as the Irishman. (*Looks at notes.*) Fortunately, you pulled out of it and got very good. It was a different act, the wife, blacks, Irish, women, you spread it around, you can score, keep it tight they'll fall asleep on you. (*Pause.*) Liked the Women's Lib bits. (*Pause.*) You need an ending, you were just sticking one after another till you'd done. No climax. People want a climax.

**Samuels** Yeah, I er . . . got off the rails a bit actually . . .

**Challenor** Stay on 'em. Phil and Ged Murray.

**Phil** Here.

**Challenor** Aye well, what went wrong there?

*Phil and Ged look at each other briefly.*

There was a distinct smell of cock-up on the air about half-way through. (*reading notes*) I've got a note about a Pakistani on a rape charge . . . Aye, that's it. What happened then?

*Phil looks at Ged. Finally.*

**Ged** (*very quietly*) We got lost.

**Challenor** What, was it new material or something?

**Ged** Yeah. Something like that.

**Challenor** Well it was horrible. The cardinal sin for any performer is embarrassing the audience. *You* had 'em doing up their shoelaces and picking up old beer mats. (*Pause.*) I don't know. It's a nice idea, but you need the material, my God, if you're gonna carry it off.

**Ged** We missed a lot out, after we got lost.

**Challenor** (*interest faded*) I'm sure you did. I'm sure you did. Liked the song, nice sentiment. Quite catchy really . . . (*He slashes his pencil across their page of notes, turns over.*) George McBrain.

*McBrain shows.*

Cracking opening. Bang. No messing. Liked it. Lot of sex but well handled, if you see what I mean. Near the knuckle but not half-way up the armpit. A question of taste.

Knowing when to draw back. Even with yobbos like that lot down there. (*Pause.*) Quite subtle but not too subtle. 'Tell *him* you've gotta headache . . .' 'Floating handbags' . . . Yes, yes . . . Good character, I believed it, it was all of a piece. Confident, a bit aggressive, like that. Like the joke about the thick Seamus. (*to Connor*) See, that's what I mean, don't push your own particular prejudice, you're there on *their* terms, not your own. (*Notes again*) Good ending. (*nodding in Samuels's direction*) See, it was *down*beat, but it was firm. You know, diminuendo. Well thought out . . .

> *There's a long pause now, as he stares at Price's notes. People make sweating faces on their own chances. Waters leans, half sits, against the window, staring nowhere, withdrawn, remote. Price leans almost horizontally back in his chair, staring at the ceiling. He remains like this throughout most of the following.*

(*Finally*) Gethin Price. (*Another pause.*) Mmmmmmmm. Mmmmmmmm.

> *Looks across at Price finally, no nonsense, man to man . . . Price is about to levitate. Challenor looks in Waters's direction, seeking guidance. Waters purses his lips, looks out of the window.*

Not a lot to say about your piece, Price. You have a certain talent maybe as a mime, something like that . . . What you did tonight just . . . won't do. Music hall maybe, but there *is* no music hall . . .You wanna be a comedian, you'd better start somewhere else, there's no way you'll get started with what you've got. Not viable. You've got to speak to the audience, for God's sake. (*Pause. Studying notes*) Personally, I found the content of your act . . . how shall I put it? . . . repulsive.

> *He stares on at his notes. Price slowly resumes an*

*upright position in the chair.*

And aggressively unfunny. (*He looks at Price, practisedly kindly.*) If you want to get on, lad, you'd better sort a few problems out first. Get some distance, see what I mean. Don't give us your hang-ups straight. Too hot to handle. (*Closes note-file decisively.*) Four golden rules. For all of you, though some more than others. One. All audiences are thick, collectively, but it's a bad comedian who lets 'em know it. Two. Two laughs are better than one. Always. Three. You don't have to love the people, but the people *have* to love you. Four. Sell yourself. If you're giving it away, it won't be worth having. (*Pause.*) All right, I coulda left this till I got back south, but I'm not that sorta person. At the moment, on tonight, I'm interested in just two of you . . . you (*McBrain*) and you (*Samuels*) . . . I've got forms here (*Holds them up*) . . . enrolment. When these've been received, there'll be an agent to look after your business and develop your career. Don't give your jobs up just now, mind. There'll be time enough for that when you're getting the bookings. (*He gives forms to McBrain and Samuels.*) For the rest of you, I'll see you again. Drop me a line, I'm approachable. Just as long as you've learnt your lessons from tonight, that is. It's not the talent's lacking, it's application of a few basic rules of professional life. (*Turns to Waters.*) Thanks, Eddie. Nice evening. Some good lads. Few wild notions mebbe but . . .

*Waters walks towards him, takes the proffered hand.*

I'm down at the Midland. How about a drink?

**Waters**  Still full of shit, Bert. Fuller than a large intestine.

**Challenor**  How's that, Eddie?

**Waters**  You wouldn't know a comedian from a barrowload of crap.

**Challenor** (*light, unruffled*) Meaning you disagree. Oh. Send in a report.

**Waters** I don't belong, remember?

**Challenor** What do you expect? A hundred per cent?

**Waters** They were nobbled, Bert. They're great lads.

**Challenor** Your opinion. Don't be ungracious . . .

**Waters** Yeah. Enjoy the Midland.

**Challenor** (*smiling evenly*) Always do, Eddie. *Like* the best.

*He picks up his briefcase, leaves with what dignity he can salvage. A deep, uneasy silence. Price tosses and catches the pork pie, rhythmically like a juggler.*

**Price** (*without venom*) There goes nothing. A man who doesn't rate Frank Randle, what does *he* know?

**Waters** (*deliberately*) He knows enough, Mr Price. He knows where the door marked In is.

**Price** Yeah, but you know where it leads? (*looking at McBrain and Samuels*) It leads to a room with a notice on the wall and the notice says 'Kindly ensure that you leave this room as you found it'. A shitheap.

**McBrain** No need to be bitter, Geth. You'll make out . . .

*Price laughs, hard, unpleasant, remote.*

**Price** (*perfect Ulster*) Thanks, George. S'very good of you. Just you remember now – stand you your ground.

*McBrain stands up, a little uncertainly. Picks up the bag.*

**McBrain** A comic's a comic. Ain't that right though. (*sniff. Pause.*) Thanks, Mr Waters. It's been a great great pleasure. I'll never forget what you've done for me . . .

**Waters** (*with effort*) Yes. Enjoy yourself, George. I'll watch out for you.

**McBrain** We'll have a drink sometime.

**Waters** Yes.

**McBrain** Look after yourself. (*turning*) And you lot. Scrubbers. (*Going.*)

**Samuels** (*standing*) Hang on, George. I'll give you a lift, we can stop off at the club for a drink.

**McBrain** No good, Sammy. I'm late as it is. The wife's not bin too good lately . . . I'd best get off.

**Samuels** She'll not begrudge you a celebration pint, surely to God?

**McBrain** (*steel suddenly*) She begrudges me nothing, Sammy.

*Small silence. He leaves, kiln-fired, hard inside the compromise.*)

**Samuels** How about you, Phil?

*Phil shakes his head whitely.*

Well . . . Cheers, Mr Waters. A pleasure to know you. (*offers hand.*)

**Waters** (*taking it*) Aye.

**Samuels** Hard work, by Christ. Lost me script completely tonight. Don't know how I kept going . . .

**Waters** No.

**Samuels** Couldn'ta done it without you, Mr Waters, that's for a certainty.

*He treks the lonely walk to the door. Leaves. Everyone
stands, preparing to go. Phil Murray suddenly stands,
lifts his bag, slams it down on the desk.*

**Phil** (*to Ged, smouldering*) You coming?

**Ged** (*turning slowly*) No. I'll catch a bus.

**Phil** It's pissing down.

**Ged** Yeah well . . . I need the air.

**Phil** (*vicious*) Suit yourself. (*He turns to leave. Turns back
again.*) Are you going up the Infirmary Sunday?

**Ged** Yeah. Why?

**Phil** (*pulls a quid out of his back pocket, hands it to Ged*)
Give him this will you? Some fags or some'at. Tell him I'll
. . . try and make it week after.

*Ged takes the note. Phil leaves.*

**Connor** (*approaching Waters's desk*) Sorry if we let you
down.

**Waters** Not you, son. Not in a million years. Stay that
way. Because that way is a good way.

*He holds his hand out. Connor takes it.*

I'm . . . sorry.

**Connor** (*soft*) Get stuffed. (*He winks at Price and Ged
Murray, leaves briskly, stops suddenly in the doorway.*)
Shit! I never told me copper joke! I've been working on it
all week . . . (*He bangs his temple with his palm several
times.*) Dummy, dummy. (*He's gone.*)

**Ged** Anyone fancy a pint? I fancy a pint. Or seven. Better
get me skates on. (*He crosses to Waters.*) Will there be . . .
will you be doing this again another time, Mr Waters?

**Waters** Yes, I've a few lads lined up starting May . . .

**Ged** I'd like to come back, if you'd have me.

**Waters** No no. You need to *do* it now, Ged. You *have* it, lad. Believe that.

**Ged** Mebbe, mebbe not. I wanna go solo, see. (*Exchanges look with Price.*) That cock-up . . . it weren't nerves, it weren't . . . technique . . . it were deliberate. (*pointing at door*) Him. He wanted to put some'at in for Challenor. I wouldn't have it. (*Grins, sniffs.*) I thought I were going reet well up to then. Felt good too.

**Waters** Remember it, how it feels when it's good. It's important. (*Holds hand out.*) Good-night. I'll see you soon.

**Ged** (*embarrassed*) Oh, I nearly forgot. Erm. (*Takes small package from pocket.*) We . . . er . . . we clubbed together some of us and bought you this. (*He hands him the package, smiles, leaves.*)

*In the corridor we hear the Caretaker quizzing Ged.*

**Caretaker** (*off*) It's not a bloody all-night session is it? Because if it is I'm on the bloody phone to Nalgo right away . . .

*Waters unwraps the package. It's a pipe. Waters studies it.*

**Price** No one . . . clubbed together.

**Waters** (*gravely*) That's all right. I don't smoke either.

*Waters begins to pack his things, put on his overcoat, etc. Price watches him, fascinated.*

I don't know what to say, Gethin. It's late. Maybe you shouldn't ask. It's been a funny night all round. (*He waves towards the door. Pause.*) And you. You've always been a bit wild, it's why I liked you, reminded me of me at twenty-five. Tonight . . . (*He leaves it, fastens his bag.*) I don't know . . .

**Price**  Did you like what I did? I'm asking.

**Waters**  Like? (*Pause.*) It was terrifying.

**Price**  You know what they did, don't you?

**Waters**  Oh yes.

**Price**  Do you blame 'em?

**Waters**  (*emphatic*) No. We make our own beds.

**Price**  (*angry suddenly*) I didn't sell you out, Eddie.

*Waters frowns, turns slowly, straightening, to face Price.*

**Waters**  Is that what you think I think?

**Price**  Samuels, McBrain, they're nothing. They'll just float through the system like turds on the Irwell, they sold out because they've nothing worth holding on to. You can't blame them for doing it any more than you can praise Connor and Ged Murray for not. They stayed put because they've nowhere else to go . . .

**Waters**  Listen, don't go on, we'll talk again . . .

**Price**  I just wanted it to be *me* talking out there. I didn't want to do something *we*'d worked on. You know.

**Waters**  (*lifting very suddenly, disturbed*) Look, I *saw* it, you don't have to tell me what I already know . . .

**Price**  I want you to see the *difference* . . .

**Waters**  (*shouting*) . . . I *see* the difference. God Almighty, I see it, I see it, I just . . . don't understand it.

**Price**  (*shouting*) Well then why don't you listen to what I'm *saying*, Eddie?

*Silence. Waters looks at the clock.*

**Waters**  All right.

*Pause.*

**Price**  (*quiet*) I can't paint *your* pictures. (*Points to eyes.*) These see.

**Waters**  It's not only what you see, it's what you feel when you see it.

**Price**  What *I* feel. *I* feel.

**Waters**  No compassion, no truth. You threw it all out, Gethin. Love, care, concern, call it what you like, you junked it over the side.

**Price**  I didn't junk it. It was never there . . .

**Waters**  What're you talking about . . .?

**Price**  . . . you're avoiding the question, Eddie.

**Waters**  I don't know what to say . . .

**Price**  . . . Was I good or was I crap . . .?

**Waters**  (*loud, compelled*) . . . You were *brilliant*!

*Pause. Price blinks. Waters glowers at the new terrain.*

**Price**  (*slowly*) But you . . . didn't like it.

*Waters shakes his head.*

(*soft, slow*) Why not?

**Waters**  (*eventually*) It was ugly. It was drowning in hate. You can't change today into tomorrow on that basis. You forget a thing called . . . the truth.

**Price**  The truth. Can I say . . . look, I wanna say something. What do you know about the *truth*, Mr Waters? You think the truth is *beautiful*? You've forgotten what it's *like*. You knew it when you started off, Oldham Empire, People's Music Hall, Colne Hippodrome, Bolton Grand, New Brighton Palace, Ardwick Empire, Ardwick Hippodrome, the Met, the Star in Ancoats . . . the Lancashire Lad – you knew it then all right. Nobody hit harder than Eddie Waters, that's what they say. Because you were still in touch with what made you . . . hunger, diphtheria, filth, unemployment, penny clubs, means tests, bed bugs, head lice . . . Was all *that* truth beautiful?

*Pause. Waters stares at him, blinded.*

Truth was a fist you hit with. Now it's like . . . now it's like cowflop, a day old, hard until it's underfoot and then it's . . . green, soft. Shitten. (*Pause.*) Nothing's changed, Mr Waters, is what I'm saying. When I stand upright – like tonight at that club – I bang my head on the ceiling. Just like you fifty years ago. We're still caged, exploited, prodded and pulled at, milked, fattened, slaughtered, cut up, fed out. We still don't belong to ourselves. Nothing's changed. You've just forgotten, that's all.

*Waters gathers his things about him, using the process.*

And you . . . stopped laughing, didn't you? Not even a warm-up tonight. You had nothing to say to those people down there tonight, did you?

*Waters turns slowly to face him.*

In three months or more, you never said a single funny thing. (*Pause.*) Challenor reckons you could have been great . . . he said you just stopped wanting it.

*Waters sits down heavily at the desk, the pain hurting now.*

Maybe you lost your hate, Mr Waters.

**Waters** (*fierce*) What are you, twenty-six, twenty-five?

**Price**  What?

**Waters**  Before you were born, I was touring with
E.N.S.A., the war had just ended, a year, maybe more. We
were in Germany, B.A.O.R., fooling about till we got our
blighty bonds. Somebody . . . somebody said there was a
guided tour of a bit of East Germany on offer, I got a
ticket. I saw Dresden. Dresden? Twenty-five miles of
rubble. Freddie Tarleton was with us, good comic, he said
it reminded him of Ancoats . . . Then they took us to a
place called Weimar, where Mozart had a house. Saw his
work room, his desk, piano, books. These perfect rooms,
all over the house, the sun on the windows . . . Down the
road, four miles maybe, we pulled up at this camp. There
was a party of schoolkids getting down off a truck ahead
of us. And we followed 'em in. 'To each his own' over the
gate. They'd cleaned it up, it was like a museum, each
room with its separate, special collection. In one of 'em
. . . the showers . . . there was a box of cyanide pellets on
a table. 'Ciankali' the label said, just that. A block away,
the incinerators, with a big proud maker's label moulded
on its middle, someone in Hamburg . . . And then this
extraordinary thing. (*Longish pause.*) In this hell-place, a
special block, 'Der Straf-bloc', 'Punishment Block'. It took
a minute to register, I almost laughed, it seemed so
ludicrous. Then I saw it. It was a world like any other. It
was the logic of our world . . . extended . . . (*pulling out
of the deep involvement phase of the story*) We crossed
back into West Germany the same night, Freddie was
doing a concert in Bielefeld. (*Long pause.*) And he . . .
quite normally, he's going along, getting the laughs, he tells
this joke about a Jew . . . I don't remember what it was
. . . I don't remember what it was . . . people laughed, not
inordinately, just . . . easily . . . And I sat there. And I
didn't laugh. (*He stands suddenly. Looks hard at Price.*)
That exercise we do . . . thinking of something deep,

personal, serious . . . then being funny about it . . . That's where it came from. (*Long pause.*) And I discovered . . . there were no jokes left. Every joke was a little pellet, a . . . final solution. We're the only animal that laughs. The only one. You know when you see the chimpanzees on the PG Tips things snickering, do you know what that is? Fear. They're signalling their terror. We've got to do some'at about it, Gethin.

**Price** Did you learn to love the Nazis then . . . (*He says it with soft z, as in Churchill.*)

**Waters** . . . I'm not saying *that* . . .

**Price** . . . That's what I'm *hearing* . . .

**Waters** . . . It's not as simple . . .

**Price** . . . It's simple to me . . .

**Waters** . . . It wasn't only repulsive . . .

**Price** What else was it then . . .?

**Waters** (*wrenched from him, finally*) I got an erection in that . . . place! An erection! Gethin. Something . . . (*He touches his stomach.*) . . . loved it, too.

*Silence. Price turns away from Waters, takes two precise paces towards the back of the room, turns back again.*

We've gotta get deeper than hate. Hate's no help.

**Price** A German joke is no laughing matter.

**Waters** See it.

*Price turns away again, prods the muslin sack with his boot.*

**Price** I found it in the book you lent me. The idea for the act.

**Waters**  It was Grock. I worked with him once.

**Price**  It was Grock. Thing I liked was his . . . hardness.
Not like Chaplin, all coy and covered in kids. This book
said he weren't even funny. He was just very truthful,
everything he did. (*He fiddles in his pocket, takes out some
paper, etc. Finds the piece of paper he's looking for, opens
it.*) I found this in another book. I brought it to show you.
Some say the world will end in fire. Some say in ice. From
what I've tasted of desire I hold with those who favour
fire, but if I had to perish twice, I think I know enough of
hate to say that for destruction ice is also great and would
suffice. (*He folds the paper, puts it back in his pocket,
moves to desk, picks up his bag, rather casually.*) It was all
ice out there tonight. I lived it. I felt . . . expressed. (*Pause.
Lifting suddenly*) The Jews still stayed in line, even when
they *knew*, Eddie! What's *that* about? (*He swings his bag
off the desk, ready for off.*) I stand in no line. I refuse my
consent.

*Pause. Waters fastens his coat collar.*

**Waters**  (*very quiet*) What do you do now then?

**Price**  I go back. I wait. I'm ready.

**Waters**  Driving, you mean?

**Price**  Driving. It doesn't matter.

**Waters**  Wait for what?

**Price**  Wait for it to happen.

**Waters**  (*very low*) Do you want help?

**Price**  No. I'm OK. Watch out for me.

**Waters**  How's Margaret?

**Price**  (*plain*) She left. Took the kiddie. Gone to her sister's
in Bolton.

**Waters** (*finally*) I'm sorry.

**Price** It's nothing. I cope. (*Pause.*) What do you do then? Carry on with this?

**Waters** I don't know.

**Price** You should. You do it well.

*They stay a moment longer, perhaps pondering a handshake. Price turns, leaves.*
*Waters sits on at the desk, his back half-turned to the door.*
*After a moment, Patel arrives, knocks on the open door. Waters stands without turning.*

**Waters** (*as though to Caretaker*) All right, I'm on my way . . .

**Patel** Please, I left this parcel . . .

**Waters** (*turning, standing*) So you did. Not been your night, has it. Me too.

*Patel smiles, humps the sack under his arm.*

**Waters** What's in there, anyway?

**Patel** Some beef. A big piece. I work at abattoir.

**Waters** Y'eat beef do you then?

**Patel** No, no, I'm Hindu. Beef, cow is sacred. This is for a friend.

**Waters** Oh. (*Pause.*) Don't you mind . . . handling it?

**Patel** At first. Not now. (*He puts the sack down, stares around the desk.*) All your funny men have gone home?

**Waters** Yeah. All the funny men have gone home.

**Patel** You like to hear a joke from my country?

**Waters** (*frowning*) Try me.

**Patel** (*laughing, excited*) It's very funny, it's very, very funny. A man has many children, wife, in the South. His crop fail, he have nothing, the skin shrivel on his children's ribs, his wife's milk dries. They lie outside the house starving. All around them, the sacred cows, ten, twenty, more, eating grass. One day he take sharp knife, mm? He creep up on a big white cow, just as he lift knife the cow see him and the cow say, Hey, aren't you knowing you not permitted to kill me? And the man say, What do you know, a talking horse.

*Patel laughs a lot. Waters suddenly begins to laugh too. Patel lifts the sack again.*

**Waters** What do you know, a talking horse. That's Jewish. It is. Come on, I'll give you a lift. Listen, I'm starting another class in May, why don't you join it? You might enjoy it . . .

*They leave the room. Waters snicks off the lights, one pair, two. The room is lit by corridor lighting only now. We hear shouted goodnights, the clanking of keys, the banging of a pair of doors. A torch light flashes into the room through the corridor window and the Caretaker arrives for a final check. He flashes the light round the room, teacher's desk, desks, dais, blackboard. The beam picks out the scrawled radiograph of Price's limerick: Pratt (Twat), etc.*

**Caretaker** (*finally, with considerable sourness*) The dirty buggers.

*He crosses, fishes out a rag, begins to wipe it away.*

# REAL DREAMS

# Author's Note

The text published here represents the best version of the play I can at present write. It incorporates in different layers several distinct critical inputs: the first production in Williamstown; a sustained and comradely critical discourse on the text with members of the Eureka Theatre Collective in San Francisco; and the second production in London. A theatre piece takes a long time to be 'finished', leavable; and I'm clear there's more to be done.

*Real Dreams* is respectfully dedicated to those many Americans who continue to struggle for justice and equality against all the odds in a land, long mad, whose Dream has by now become, almost literally, the rest of the world's nightmare; and if to one in particular, to the friend, comrade and writer of promise who gave me his story. Write on.

Trevor Griffiths
1987

# Characters

**B.T.**
**Ringo**
**Sandler**
**Yancy**
**Bob**
**Portia**
**Ramon**
**Arons**
**Jack**
**Karen**
**Knobby**
**Sally**

**Real Dreams** was first performed by the Williamstown Theatre Festival on 8 August 1984. The first United Kingdom production was by the Royal Shakespeare Company at the Pit, Barbican Centre, London, on 30 April 1986, when the cast was as follows:

**B.T.** Keith Osborn
**Ringo** Michael McNally
**Sandler** Adrian Dunbar
**Yancy** Garry Cooper
**Bob** Murray Ewan
**Portia** Francine Morgan
**Ramon** Vincent Ebrahim
**Arons** Hilary Townley
**Jack** Gary Oldman
**Karen** Michele Costa
**Knobby** Paul McCleary
**Sally** Helena Little

*Directed by* Trevor Griffiths
*Designed by* Russell Craig

A mute black and white video monitor, slung high in the set, carries images of late-sixties American political struggle intercut with a chronicle of Vietnam. The monitor is on before the audience arrives and remains on until it has left. Each production will decide for itself how and when to use the monitor during the action of the play.

# Act One

## SCENE ONE: THE SET-UP

*Black.*

*Lights up on yard of clapboard and brick house in poor working-class neighbourhood, West-of-the-flats, Cleveland. The light is thick, heavy, high summer pre-storm; air dense, barely breathable.*

*Two women, four men lie around the scrub of dirt and grass, stilled by the heat. A dog barks, streets off; stops. Thunder, a way away. A half-gallon jug of red wine snails hand-to-mouth among them, motion slowed on the wet air: through* **Yancy,** *27, tough, wiry, who stands gazing towards the city and the advancing storm;* **B.T.,** *20, large in cowboy hat, leather boots, denim, slumped against a box;* **Portia,** *22, long frizzy hair, prone on the dirt; by* **Sally,** *20, jeans and ribbed sweater, who drinks from a can of Stroh's and passes it up; by* **Bob,** *30, hillbilly from West Virginia, in Hawaiian shirt, who shares Sally's box and beer; to* **Ringo,** *19, thin, scruffy, book-ending B.T. across the yard.*

**B.T.** (*to air, soft*) Ho Ho Ho Chi Minh . . .

**Ringo** (*eventually; a slow chime*) Dare to struggle, dare to win.

*Silence. Thunder, closing. Crossfade to:*

*Kitchen, overlooking yard, street. Unreal light, half electric, half day.* **Sandler,** *19, short, thickset, stands at a work surface before the window, peppermill in hands, staring at the street.*

**Sandler** Summer of '69. Kids off the campuses. Fanning

out across the country. Bringing the war home. Building the Revolution. We're in Cleveland. Paulette? Paulette isn't.

*Thunder. The voice of a woman, metallic, whiney, drifts up at him from somewhere. Sandler takes a swig on a bottle of red wine, eyes fixed on outside.* **Karen** *appears, a china dish in her hand, from the cupboard below the work surface. She's 28, tall, heavyish, lipstick, shadow. Onions have rawn her eyes.*

**Karen** Fuckin' onions. Goddam, Sandler, you're not even listening . . .

**Sandler** (*not*) Listening? Sure I'm listening. You're telling me about your ex . . .

**Karen** . . . I'm *telling* you about the formation of political consciousness in a woman . . .

**Sandler** OK. That's cool.

*She resumes the preparation of the beefburgers; considers continuing the treatise. He waits till she's almost there.*

Let me know when we get to the part where I say, 'Couldn't agree more, or as Marx would have it, When the pain ceases to be a pleasure it's time to haul some ass, baby' and you say, 'Fuck you, Sandler', will you?

*Karen's work slows in the silence. Thunder, closer, not yet theirs.*

'S that Jack?

*It isn't. Someone begins tuning a guitar in a nearby room.*

**Karen** (*quiet*) Fuck you, Sandler. You're so fucking scared of your feelings, man . . .

*Sandler takes another slug of wine.*

. . . 'Where's Jack?' ''S that Jack?' 'Hope Jack don't get caught in this motherfucker . . . you wanna know if *Paulette* was there, at the meeting, with *Reiner* . . . Fact is, you're a bigger mess than me. So tell me. I understand; who else? You already peppered that . . .

> *He stops the peppering he's just resumed. Puts the china bowl of potato salad below the work surface, heads slowly for the back door to the yard. Introductory chords of 'Sacco and Vanzetti' in next room.*

**Sandler**  It's Independence Day. I'm for gettin' drunk.

**Karen**  Sure. (*Reaches for the wine.*) Sure. Get your act together.

> *Crossfade to:*

*Living room.* **Arons**, *21, small, thin, mild, sits on the stool, guitar on thighs, in a soft spot; unreal light; sings first verse of 'Sacco and Vanzetti', quite loud, rambunctious:*
Say there, did you hear the news,
Sacco worked at trimmin' shoes,
Vanzetti was a peddlin' man,
Pushed his pushcart with his hands.

> *Chorus:*
Two good men a long time gone,
Sacco and Vanzetti are gone.
Two good men a long time gone,
Left me here to sing this song.

> *Crossfade to:*

*Yard. The almost-frieze almost as before. Arons, unseen, moves into the chorus, the sound lower, perspectived by wall and window. Sandler arrives, barefoot. Searches out a spot in the frieze of bodies in the immediate path of the jug. Hands sift dirt, pull at grass, pick toes.*

**B.T.** (*faint contempt*) Hey, it's Sandler.

**Sandler** (*to audience*) 'The Set-Up.'

**Ringo** (*B.T.'s echo*) Yeah. How ya doin', man?

**Sandler** (*slumping down; discomforted*) OK. OK, comrade.

**Yancy** (*stormwatch*) This is one motherfucker.

**B.T.** (*from below hat*) How's it lookin', Yance?

**Yancy** Just hittin' Cleveland heights. Then it's Case Western, down Superior and Chester and Euclid, across the flats and.

*No one speaks.*

**B.T.** 'S hope it drowns a few pigs on the way.

**Ringo** Yeah. What you say, Sandler?

**Sandler** (*still waiting to*) Sure. I'd drink to that.

*B.T. makes no move to release the jug. Sandler looks at Sally, who has the Stroh's to her lips. Sees Bob next to her.*

(*offering hand*) Hi, Bob, didn't see you there, how's it going, pal?

**Bob** (*taking it*) Good, thank you, neighbour, just dropped by to shoot the breeze . . . Drink a beer?

*He indicates the can in Sally's hand. Sandler waits for her to offer it. She stands, eases damp cloth gathered between buttocks and under arms with unselfconscious fingers; resumes her seat. Arons has stopped the song to retune a string.*

**Sandler** Guess I'll stick to the wine, thanks, Bob . . .

**B.T.** (*calling to the house*) Arons.

**Arons** (*unseen*) What?

**B.T.** Will you shut the fuck up with that hootenanny liberal crap . . .

**Ringo** We had a meetin' about that . . .

*The retuning stops. Silence.*

**Sally** (*from nowhere*) Let's hear it for male supremacy.

**B.T.** Bullshit.

**Portia** (*honest, friendly*) It's a perfectly valid point Sally's raising, B.T. . . .

**B.T.** Bullshit.

**Portia** (*patient*) The meeting didn't say Arons couldn't sing, the meeting decided we weren't interested in a sing-along.

**Ringo** Bullshit.

**Yancy** Bullshit nothing. (*Looks at Ringo hard, though the voice is soft. At B.T.*) The women're right. You guys're outa line.

*Thunder bangs and rumbles, almost theirs. Yancy swings to look at it.*

Jesus, it's comin' in fast.

*Air cools at speed. People grow sharper, in the expectant freshness. The light is dark; violet. Ramon has arrived unseen with the thunder: neat in shirt, slacks, shoes. When he speaks, it's as if out of shot.*

**Ramon** I lookin' for Jack. He here?

*People find him, startled; greet him with warmth: 'Hey Ramon, good to see you, man', 'Happy 4th', etc.*

**B.T.** He ain't back yet, man. Got a meeting across . . .

**Yancy** . . . You're a mite early for supper, Ramon. You got a problem . . .?

*Ramon scans them a moment in silence.*

**Ramon** No. I got no problem. I wait inside.

*Thunder, fast, close. They swing to look at the sky. Ramon's gone. Yancy returns to his street vigil.*

**Sandler** Jesus, what's with Ramon?

*People shrug, uncertain.*

Any signa Jack, Yance?

**Yancy** Uhunh.

**Portia** (*fingers in hair*) That was *so* scary.

**Yancy** Feel it?

*They feel it, some fear at the edges.*

**Bob** Big as a mountain. Oh boy.

**Yancy** Feel it. This one's all the way from Hanoi.

**B.T.** (*across the yard*) Sounds like old man Anderson humping his wife back at fuckin' Kent State, don't it, Ringo?

*Bob covers his mouth at the language, chuckling.*

**B.T.** I bet Anderson's old lady's pubes're like Brillo, man.

**Ringo** No, man. SOS, man. Dig? SOS?

*They chortle, embracing a past they didn't actually share.*

**Sandler** (*tentative, desperate*) You finished with that thing, B.T.?

*He points to the jug. Thunder whacks above them. Soft splashes of rain, early spillage.*

**Yancy** (*looking up, arms out*) Hey.

**Sandler** Shit.

**B.T.** Yahoo.

*The rain arrives in hoppers. They take it open-mouthed,
on faces, shoulders, bellies, as the sky debouches.
Without warning, Yancy rockets his hard body through
a series of perfect gymfreak flips. They cheer, applaud,
excited, released. B.T. stands, half in macho response,
half self-parody, tries the same series, lands ludicrously
on his arse first time of asking. Ringo follows; others,
Portia, earnest, Sally, clean, easy; Bob claps his hands
repeatedly, as if to music, hooping and yipping; Sandler,
a gentle declension to earlier compulsions; children of
the storm. Begin slow crossfade to:*

*Kitchen.*

**Karen** (*through window*) Are you guys crazy'r what? Get
the fuck in here will you . . .

*They troop off for the house, laughing, hugging, joshing
as they leave the light. Karen gathers towels and paper
rolls, ready to repel. Rain pounds the house, almost
drowning the trail of their loony laughter as they round
it.*

*Fade in yard area, now the living room. Emblematic
images of revolutionary summer, 1969, define the space.
Arons sits at the window watching the storm. Ramon
stands, remote, swaying, watching her. People begin to
pile up in the kitchen doorway.*

**Karen** Keep those feet outa this goddam kitchen. Get. Get.

*She throws the towels and rolls, bars the way with a
broom. They stream into the living room, spraying*

*water from heads and limbs as they go. Karen watches
through her wide window-hatch, envying the fun she's
missed. Yancy crosses to her, the only one allowed in;
gives her a hug.*

**Ringo** Hey, Yance, man, where the fuck'd you learna do
those fuckin' flips, man?

**Yancy** (*through hatch; Gable smile under Gable
moustache*) Did gymnastics in the marines, it's nothing
man. What d'you say, Bob?

**Bob** (*opening six-pack*)Looked pretty neat to me, pal.

*Sally and Portia towel each other down. Sandler
watches Sally, Portia mutters something, Sally laughs,
Sandler looks away, crosses to Arons in the window.
Stands behind her, looking out.*

**B.T.** (*jug still in hand*) Fuck, see that? Flat on my fuckin'
ass.

**Ringo** Great.

*The high's already fading. Karen comes in from the
kitchen, unclipping her hair; short skirt and top. Yancy
follows.*

**Karen** Oh shit, just look at this place, will you?

**Portia** You wanna dance, Karen?

**Karen** I don't care. I guess this takes care of the goddam
barbecue . . . You gonna stand holding that thing all night,
B.T.?

*B.T. hands her the jug, a touch offended. She drinks,
while Portia sorts 'The way you do the things you do'
on to the Motorola. Lightning, long moments of it.*

**Arons** God, this is really going crazy, Geoff.

**Sandler** Fuckin' storm, man.

*The Temptations' Greatest Hits gets under way. Karen and Portia funk around, best friends, rarely more than adjacent to the music. People lounge to watch, clapping the floor. Sally joins them, after a moment, effortless and faultless Beaver Falls; slowly takes the stage. Sandler looks in, drawn by the wet grace and power of the movement. Ramon edges in, eyes agleam. Portia and Karen sing along, arm in arm. B.T. and Ringo yeahyeah her on. Thunder, lightning, fast, devastating. Room lights go, come back, several times. The stylus stops, slides, starts, slides again. Karen crosses to lift the arm, the only one to move.*

**Yancy** (*father*) 'S OK. 'S OK. Just a good old Cleveland lightning-ball.

**Karen** Holy shit.

**Yancy** I seen worse. You all's living in a mean town.

**Arons** (*at window, quiet*) Holy shit's right. It's Jack. That crazy boy.

*People crowd over to look, lifted by the news. Ramon drifts towards the jug, collars it, retreats to a wall.*

**Yancy** Jesus.

**B.T.** Hey, Arons, your aunt's VW looks like a fucking U-boat . . .

**Ringo** No, man, a submarine.

**B.T.** Whadda you think a fuckin' U-boat is . . .?

**Ringo** I dunno, man . . .

**Yancy** Goddam, the man's gonna drown out there . . .

**B.T.** It's a fuckin' submarine . . .

**Ringo**  So I was agreein' . . .

**Yancy**  Get the door, somebody.

*Sally's almost there. Calls to Jack up the path. People shift to greet him, Arons to the fore.*

**Arons**  Hey, Jack.

*Jack's in, poncho gleaming. He's tall, messy, not shaped; 24; stands, shaking water, as he scans the room.*

**Portia**  God, you're really *wet*.

*Jack ducks for Portia to help him off with the poncho.*

**B.T.**  Hey, Jack, how was the meeting, man?

**Jack**  (*half-crouched*) Everything all right here? (*Nobody follows*.) Tremont's got no phone or electricity. The storm is kicking the shit outa this city. The radio said four people killed already . . .

*A bubble of 'Holy Shits'. and 'Jesus Fucking Christs' around the room.*

**Yancy**  We got no problems, Jack.

*Jack claps his hands, exuberant now.*

**Jack**  Outta sight. (*Strides in, hand extended to Ramon.*) Hey, Ramon, man, good to see you. How's it going, man?

**Ramon**  (*nothing*) OK, man, OK.

**Jack**  Hope I'm not too late to eat. I'm fuckin' starved.

**B.T.**  (*insistent for attention*) Hey, man, what about the meeting?

*A small silence. Jack looks at him levelly for a moment.*

**Jack**  (*flat*) Meeting was outta sight. (*up again*) What about  dinner? You gonna take a bite with us, Bob?

**Bob** I gotta eat later, Jack . . .

**Jack** We got enough, Karen?

**Karen** Well, we were hoping to grill the burgers outside
. . . But I decided to put hot dogs on the stove, and there's
salad and stuff . . .

**Jack** (*bellow*) Fuckin' right on! The correct line on dinner
is definitely dogs, salad and stuff . . .

*He strides for the kitchen, sucking Karen, Sandler and
Arons in his tailstream. The room's minimally reordered
for eating: B.T., Ringo, Bob. In the kitchen, Jack doles
out dogs and salad on to the china Karen provides,
Sandler cuts a French roll, sticks a slice on each plate,
Portia brings salt, pepper, mustard, paper cups and red
wine to the cleared space. Yancy and Sally take laden
plates, two at a time, from hatch to people or places in
the room. They work fluently, easy, absorbed; little
chat.*

**Karen** Go easy on the china, B.T.

**B.T.** That still the line on the china, Jack?

**Jack** Never mind the fucking china, B.T. Why's everybody
so goddam wet?

**B.T.** We bin doin' flips and fuck knows what in the yard,
man. You missed something, man. I fell on my fuckin' ass.

**Jack** (*a critical look at Yancy*) Fourtha July, hunh?

*Yancy keeps his eyes steadily down on the plates in his
hands. Thunder. The lights bobble again, settle down.*

(*advancing back into the room*) Let's do some eatin'.
While we can see. Come and eat, Ramon, you're the guest
of honour . . .

*They settle on the floor, a rough circle, to eat and drink.*

289

*Ramon perches on a box, outside the group, drinks deep, picks at the plate of food.*

**Portia** Fourtha July.

**Ringo** Right.

*They eat.*

**Yancy** (*mouth full*) Hey, Sandler, you make this potato salad?

**Sandler** (*tense*) Yeah, I made it, Yance.

**Yancy** This fuckin' potato salad is insane, man. *Insane.*

**Portia** It's really *good*, Geoff.

*Sandler basks a little in the gathering praise.*

**Karen** Sandler's an excellent cook.

**Jack** Great salad, Geoff.

**Sandler** Well, if you must know, the real credit goes to Arons, who ripped the bacon off of Fisher Fazio's . . . It's bullshit without the bacon.

**Jack** Then I guess we'd better raise a glass to Arons . . .

*Cartons are refilled. 'Arons, for the bacon' is toasted. Thunder, already someone else's.*

**Arons** (*a shrimp*) I got the jug, too.

**Jack** (*holding it*) You got the jug?

**Arons** Sure. And a carton of Kools.

**B.T.** Yeah, but they're non-filters. Like smokin' a fuckin' blowtorch.

**Jack** You'll smoke them anyway, B.T. Nice work, Arons. Fish in the sea.

**Karen** Anyone got views on the macaroni salad, I made that.

**Sandler** Perfect.

**Yancy** Absolutely.

**Karen** Yeah.

**Jack** How's the family, Bob?

**Bob** Kids're fine. Just too many of 'em . . .

*Laughter. A stool crashes to the floor, as Ramon struggles upright. He takes a few rubbery steps, to free himself, stands with the china plate in his hand, food slipping and sliding from it. People spread out a little, out of his path.*

**Ramon** I got an announcement. (*He sees the food fall, tries to rectify, almost drops the plate.*)

**Karen** Hey, Ramon, watch the china, man . . .

*He stares at them, broods from face to face.*

**Ramon** Tonight. You gonna off the A. & P.

*Silence. Nobody knows much what to say.*

**Ringo** (*low*) What'd he say?

**Yancy** Take it easy, Ramon . . .

**Jack** (*quick*) Leave it, Yance. OK? (*slow, clear*) What d'you mean, man?

**Ramon** I mean, man, you gonna rip off the A. & P. tonight. It's orders from the S.P.I.C.s. To you. (*Wobbles. Sits on a box.*) A. & P. got to burn tonight.

*They look at each other. B.T. sits upright, chuckling to himself. Eyes turn to Jack. Jack sits, head in hands, as if weighing things.*

**Portia** (*sotto*) This guy is really drunk . . .

*Jack's head flicks up, silences her.*

**Jack** The Spanish People in Cleveland organization told you this in person, Ramon?

**Ramon** (*punching himself*) Ramon, me, right.

**Jack** Fine. We've got to talk about it, man.

**Ramon** You've got to talk about it? You bin talkin' for weeks, man. 'S all you people ever do . . .

*Ramon jerks upright, grabs a wall to stay on his feet.*

**Jack** Hey, Ramon, cool it, man, OK?

**Ramon** (*slow*) OK. I be back in a while give you the rest of the orders. I gotta go get cigarettes.

*He leaves; gathers himself by the back door for the prolonged walk; is gone. Thunder, receded. They look at Jack. Jack sits on, in thought.*

**Sandler** (*low*) What's goin' on, Jack? This for real?

*Jack lifts his head; reads his company.*

**Bob** (*out of it, can to lips*) That guy's crazy. What the hell's he talknabout anyways? The S.P.I.C.s're crowda Spanish kids kickin' butt on Detroit Avenue . . . They're younger'n you people . . .

*He laughs, drinks, at ease. Jack finds the moment.*

**Jack** (*gentle; simple*) Listen, Bob. We're gonna hafta talk . . . among ourselves, you know?

**Bob** Hey, listen, sure thing. Denise an' the kids'll be waitin' supper anyways . . . Thankye all kindly for the . . . eats . . .

**Yancy** (*an excess of empathy*) You wanna look in later,

you're welcome, Bob . . .

**Bob**  Sure thing.

**Jack**  (*quick*) Better still, Bob, we finish our business, we'll give you a call.

**Bob**  Couldn't be better. Thank you all kindly . . .

*He leaves by the kitchen door; a decent, courteous man. People begin to gather inwards for the talk.*

**Knobby**  (*off; in side path*) Hey, cousin, I just lef' your place, Denise's hollerin' like a mountain cat . . .

*Bob starts talking to him off, explaining.* **Knobby** *claims he's expected, it's OK.*

**Jack**  (*on his feet, the move*) What the fuck's goin' on here? (*Turns on them; hard suddenly.*) Who invited Knobby?

**Karen**  (*remembering, in panic*) Oh my God. I promised him a reading lesson tonight.

**Jack**  Great. Outta sight, Karen. The day of the regional meeting with national leadership? Pretty unlikely we'd have anything to talk about, even in the normal run of things . . . Where's your *head* at, Karen?

*She's withered. He glares on at her. People are scared of his mouth, like this.*

Listen . . .

*Three bangs on the door and Knobby's in, a book in one hand, a parcel in the other. He's short, well muscled, a touch flash-macho, ducktail haircut.*

**Knobby**  Happy Fourth, ever'body.

**B.T.**  Hi, Knobby, how's it goin', man?

**Knobby**  Quite nicely, thank yer.

*Karen moves to remove him. He deflects her with the
parcel.*

Brought these, I thought they'd look nice in the house . . .

**Karen** What are they?

**Knobby** Flowers.

*She inspects the parcel for the breathing hole; finds
none. He takes it from her.*

I'll do that, why don't you get a vase or sumpn?

*Karen looks for help, finds none, heads for the kitchen.
Jack joins her there. Knobby unwraps the heap of
sodden flowers – lilies, gladioli, dahlias, the odd rose –
from the brown paper.*

Some fuckin' storm, eh? Morgan's Flower Market got
washed clean out . . . Fuckin' flowers everywhere, man
. . .

*He shows the draggled swatch of ex-blooms. Some
pallid nods and smiles around the group. Holds them
out for Sally to smell.*

**Sally** Great.

**Sandler** What's the book, Knob?

**Knobby** (*checking reading*) It's er . . . On . . . New . . .
Democracy. By Mao Tse-tung. 'S in English, course . . .

**Sandler** Sure.

*Silence. He stands with book and flowers. Jack's
muttered critique of Karen in the kitchen carries
through the window-hatch, indistinct but unavoidable.*

**Knobby** (*polite*) 'M I interruptin' sumpn?

**Karen** (*decisive, from hatch, showing vase*) Bring the

goddam flowers, will you, we'll work upstairs tonight . . .

**Knobby**  Sure will, miss . . . (*He smiles at the group, winks, leaves for the stairs by the front door.*)

**B.T.**  You have yourself a good time, Knobby . . .

**Ringo**  (*leering*) Yeah.

**Portia**  (*defensive*) What's that supposed to mean?

*Jack returns to the main room. they take their places to face him. He stands for a moment, quiet, quite bleak.*

**Jack**  Arons?

**Arons**  Yes, Jack?

**Jack**  What do you think?

*She sits, a shrimp in the spotlight, unexpectedly on the line.*

**Arons**  I don't know, Jack. I mean, I know the S.P.I.C.s've bin asking supermarkets to honour the Farm Workers' boycott of Californian grapes . . . an' I know for a fact the A. & P. haven't agreed, cos the one I ripped off yesterday were Grade A Delano . . . I don't know. Doesn 't it seem kinda sudden?

*Jack waits, impassive, but she's finished.*

**Jack**  Portia?

**Portia**  (*stickling*) I just don't think we should let Ramon'r anyone else . . . hand out orders like that, Jack. I mean, to me it sorta sets a bad precedent.

**Yancy**  Too fuckin' right it does. I mean Ramon's an outta sight motherfucker – dig? – but comin' in here givin' us fuckin' orders? (*Holds his hand out flat, miming the anger he's controlling.*) No fuckin' way, man. No way.

**Portia** Exactly.

**Arons** I'll go with that.

*Jack looks towards Sally, who shrugs, unfussed. At Sandler, who says nothing.*

**Jack** Everybody see it like that?

**B.T.** (*sudden, standing*) I fuckin' don't. I ain't no chickenshit and I ain't scareda trashin' no fuckin' A. & P. and I don't want no fuckin' Ramon sayin' I am, man.

**Ringo** Right on.

**Portia** B.T., man, you're so damn tough. Who're you trying to impress . . .?

**Jack** (*quiet, depressed*) B.T.'s right.

*Silence. A thin film of dread begins to settle on the room. Sandler has it on his palms. Furtively tries to dispose of it. Fails.*

What the fuck are we here for? Mm? Anyone remember? This is the S.P.I.C.s' turf. They live here; they've *been* living here. This shit is *their* shit. We come in off our campuses, setting up our . . . SDS collective . . . right? . . . on our fuckin' summer programme . . . trying to organize city kids for the National Action in Chicago in the fall, right? . . . and fulla shit about how we're willing to put ourselves at the disposal of black and brown leadership, and the first order we get, what do we do? We say no, we'll follow black and brown leadership when we feel like it. What the fuck are they gonna think of us? We've got four hundred years of white imperialism to lick before they're gonna trust us and this is the first shit we pull? For weeks we've been pushin' Ramon to get 'em to meet with us face to face; this is recognition they're offering. OK, I don't like the action, I don't like the timing, not one fuckin' bit, but we can't just say no. If Ramon tells them we're bullshit, you'd better believe it, we *are* bullshit. And we'll have nothing. Not a single fuckin' contact. That's it. (*Watches them carefully, gauging where they are.*) Leadership made it clear in the meeting this afternoon, the National Action in Chicago takes priority over everything, study programmes, cadre development, learning from the people, whatever. They see 50,000 working-class kids out there in Lincoln Park, bringing the war home. Leadership wants action, dig? (*Fixes on them again.*) So maybe it's time we started earning a bit of *respect* around here. Read me?

**B.T.** I fuckin' read you, man. What d'you say, Ringo?

**Ringo** Let's fucking do it, man.

**Jack** Sally?

**Sally** (*cool*) It's cool.

*Jack nods, looks at Yancy.*

**Yancy** I got no problems *doin'* it, I don't like the relationship . . .

**Jack** (*nodding*) Sandler?

*Sandler's arrested, half-way to the kitchen, glass in hand. (gentle, devastating)* You wanna give us the benefit of your doubts, man, while you're around . . .?

**Sandler** Mouth's kinda dry, Jack.

**B.T.** (*scorn in the grin*) 'S only fear, man. Passes.

**Sandler** (*quiet*) OK. I think this is fucked up.

**Jack** Tell us.

**Sandler** I got no problems trashin' the fuckin' A. & P., OK? Clearly, black, brown and poor white people get

297

trashed by the A. & P. every day of their fuckin' lives with
the lousy habit-forming overpriced fuckin' 'food products'
they dump on 'em. And there's nothing wrong with the
S.P.I.C.s tellin' us to do it, Yance . . . I mean, that's what
following black and brown leadership's gotta mean. I can
dig on that. When and how is the fuckin' issue. Let's say
we got an alliance goin' with the S.P.I.C.s, OK? They come
to us and say, 'Blow up the fuckin' A. & P.', we say, 'Outta
sight, let's plan it together; What night, who goes, what we
use.' This shit has got to be planned. Not on a couple
hours' notice after we're all fuckin' drunk, for Christ's
sake, including Ramon. And I don't see why this can't be
laid out to Ramon, Jack. 'The action's cool, but not
tonight. Let's plan the fucker.'

**Sally** (*in the silence*) Dig.

*She looks at Sandler; he looks away, pleasured by the
favour. Arons, Portia, Karen agree.*

**B.T.** Dig shit. What's the fuckin' big deal on trashin' a
fuckin' A. & P.? You gotta be sober to mix up a few
fuckin' molotovs, for Christ's sake . . .

**Jack** (*flat*) Who's drunk here?

*Hands go up, Jack's included. Sandler's goes up, then
comes down.*

You drunk or what?

**Sandler** I drank. I'm not drunk.

**Jack** (*sitting down*) OK. We do it Sandler's way. But we
can't lose Ramon. I just hope to fuck I can convince the
motherfucker.

*Air is released from taut lungs, as they absorb the
decision. Above, the sound of bedsprings, under use:
echt* whambam thankyou ma'am.

**Sally** (*deadpan*) *On New Democracy.*

*They relax into chuckles, bits of laughter.*

**B.T.** (*to ceiling, mock loud*) Watch the fuckin' china.

*A few choked-back calls of tense joy from Karen.
Silence.*

**Portia** (*serious, concerned*) Oh God, here we go again . . .

**Jack** (*eventually standing*) I'll be on the stoop. Waitin' for
Ramon. We need to talk about the meeting later . . .

*He leaves by the back door, Arons in his wake.*

**Yancy** Who's on KP?

**B.T.** Yeah.

**Ringo** Yeah.

**Yancy** Tell you what, you bring the stuff through, I'll start
in on the washin' up . . .

**B.T.** Dig it, comrade.

*They begin clearing up. Yancy goes to the kitchen,
stands framed in the hatch rolling up his sleeves. Sally
finishes her can of beer. Looks at Sandler briefly,
expressionless; leaves by the back door. Sandler stands
on, as the lights cross fade to:*

*Stoop. Faded light; haze and vapour over the street. Kids
play the firecrackers at the far end of the block: cannons in
a faraway war, Jacks sits on a box, staring at his feet.
Arons squats on a step, below him, chin on knees.*

**Arons** How'd those people die, Jack? In the storm?

**Jack** (*grave, remote*) Three in boats out on the lake, one
hit by lightning over near Lorain.

**Arons** (*catching his tone*) God.

*Jack says nothing.*

Don't you love that smell?

*He says nothing, plays with a pebble between his shoes.*

Reminds me of my grandmother.

**Jack** (*flat, retruded*) Brian Jones offed himself. Did you hear? Yesterday. In his pool.

**Arons** God.

*Sally comes round the side of the house. Approaches slowly, sits on the steps by Arons. Leans back, breathing, eyes closed. Jack watches her a moment.*

**Jack** You fitting in OK here, Sally?

**Sally** Sure.

**Arons** (*hugging her, kissing her cheek, fond*) She's fitting in fine. Doesn't miss Penn State hardly at all.

**Sally** What do *you* think?

**Jack** I think you're doin' OK. I think you should start sayin' more.

**Sally** (*finally; unmoving*) OK.

*Sandler arrives, lacks confidence to rupture their circle, stands by a box on the edge, scans the street.*

You want to talk about that?

**Sandler** Maybe he won't even come back. Could be in his bed on Detroit right now, sleeping it off . . . We gotta get a new line on this cheap red wine . . .

**Arons** He's such a gentle man. I hated seeing him drunk like that . . .

**Jack** (*back with his pebble*) I just hope to fuck we covered all the bases back there . . .

*A firework rocket erupts from the street, trails weird light across their space.*

**Sandler** (*to Jack; carefully*) So, who was at the meeting, man? Reiner show . . .?

**Arons** (*undeflectable*) You know, I just remembered . . . he quoted Che to me the other day. (*finding it*) 'Riesgo de ponerme en ridiculopero, un revolucionario verdaero es dirigido por sentimientos de amor.' 'At the risk of sounding ridiculous, a true revolutionary is guided by feelings of love.'

*A shout in Spanish, loud, challenging, from down the street: 'Compañeros'.*

**Sandler** Shit. He's back.

*Jack stands, stares down the street.*

**Jack** What's he doin'?

**Sandler** I don't know. He fell down.

**Sally** Jesus.

*More shouting in Spanish. Knobby and Karen appear at the front door. Approach the stoop.*

**Ramon** Vamonos.

**Knobby** You people need anything, I'll be next door at cousin Bob's . . .

**Jack** Thanks. Knobby. It's under control.

**Knobby** Ain't afeareda no fuckin' spics, no sir.

**Karen** Just go, will you . . . and watch your mouth.

**Knobby** I'll see you later, sweet potater. (*book in left hand,* *raised*) Thanks for the er . . .

*He shades off into the near dark, whistling a hillbilly tune. Another shout, closer.*

**Karen** (*standing a moment*) The things we do for the revolution . . . (*Makes her way back in.*) I'll put the coffee on. Doubtless you'll fill me in when you have a moment.

**Jack** 'S he coming?

**Sandler** He appears to have lost his way.

**Jack** Call him.

*Sandler looks at Jack carefully.*

**Sandler** Ramon! Over here, man.

**Jack** We'll get this over with.

*Ramon arrives, several drinks down the road. They think he might speak. All his energy appears to be needed to control the movement of his body.*

(*Eventually*) Hi, Ramon.

**Ramon** You people ready for your orders?

**Jack** Have a seat, man.

*Ramon sits, frowning.*

Listen, we think it's outta sight the S.P.I.C.s want us to off the A. & P., really outta sight . . .

*Ramon says nothing, lifts his head a little, focusing.*

But shit like this gotta be planned, man. Together, you know what I mean . . .? We'd like a meeting with these guys, talk it out with 'em . . .

*Ramon squints at Jack, careful, dangerous.*

**Ramon** What you sayin' here . . .?

**Jack** I'm saying the action's cool, comrade . . .

**Ramon** OK, let's do it.

**Jack** But not tonight, man. You talk to the S.P.I.C.s, you tell 'em we want a meeting . . .

*Ramon stares at Jack, the others.*

**Ramon** You goddam fuckin' *pussies* is what you is. You fuckers. Pussy faggots. You wan' me to talk to the S.P.I.C.s, I talkin' to the S.P.I.C.s and then you fuckin' *dead.*

*He goes wild, sudden, frightening. Tears stream down his cheeks and nose, spitballs dance from his mouth. The people on the stoop are very still, paralysed by the scale of his anger and humiliation.*

(*demonic*) Coño. God damn you fuckin' pussy faggots. I put my ass on the line for you with these people, you pussies. Some fuckin' revolutionaries. You comin' in here . . . An' we supposer *trus'* you? My word is my life, you faggots. Chickenshit. (*He swings off into darkness, slashing the air with his arms, coils of heavy Spanish unwinding behind him.*)

**Jack** Ramon, come back here, man . . .

*Rafts of Spanish scream in from the dark.*

(*looking hard at Sandler*) Oh boy, have we fucked this one up . . .

*Sandler looks down at his feet, appalled.*

We're goin' down the tubes, children . . .

*Ramon returns, pursued by new furies; picks up a box and smashes it against a wall, yelling at the top of his voice. They scatter, save Sally, who stands motionless, watching.*

(*mad*) Ramon, goddam it, come back here, man, you'll raise the whole fuckin' street . . .

*Ramon's stumbling off; falls to his knees, mutters and whimpers, almost weeping. Sally approaches the kneeling figure; stands behind him.*

**Sally** Ramon. This is Sally. Please just shut the fuck up and listen to what Jack has to say, will you?

*Yancy and Karen arrive from the house. Jack waves them still. Joins Sally. Looks down at Ramon.*

**Jack** (*distinct, depressed*) Ramon, you're right. It's OK, man. We'll do it.

*Ramon looks at him, then eyes the rest of them. They're busy eyeing each other.*

Give us half an hour. It'll be all the way dark. We'll move then, OK?

*Ramon nods, takes Sally's hand to get to his feet, wipes his face with the insides of his sleeves.*

**Ramon** Whasse call, him next door?

**Jack** Bob.

**Ramon** I sit over there.

*B.T. and Ringo round the house. B.T. has a stave in his hand.*

**Portia** (*watching Ramon leave*) Jesus.

**B.T.** Where's the fuckin' action, man?

**Jack** (*marshalling them*) OK. We're gonna do it.

**Sandler** (*off the mark fast*) Lay it out, Jack.

**Karen** (*scared, working at it*) Could I ask how this decision was reached?

**Yancy** (*tough*) 'S not material, Karen. Discussion's over.

**Jack** (*soft, steady*) Yance, take the van and fill it up.
(*Throws him the keys.*) You'll need money . . .

**Yancy** (*on the move, tapping his back pocket*) Did two
days for Manpower this week, I have it. (*Stops, turns.*)
You want me along on the action?

**Jack** You'll look after things here.

*Yancy nods, the discipline holding, heads off down the
street.*

You made that coffee, Karen?

**Karen** It's brewin'.

**Jack** B.T., Sandler, Sally and me'll do it. OK?

*Sandler nods, stiffly. Sally nods.*

**B.T.** You bet.

**Ringo** (*sitting on it*) Aw shit, man.

**Jack** We'll use Aron's VW. Questions?

**Karen** I'd like to go, Jack.

**Ringo** Come off it, Kushner, that's the stupidest thing I
ever heard.

**Karen** Fuck you, Ringo, you're just mad cos B.T.'s going
and you're not. I've got to get into heavy shit some time.
I'm 27, I've never even bin fuckin' busted . . .

**Jack** Karen.

*She shuts up at once.*

Another time, cool. This action's our first and it's not
exactly overplanned. Another time. Cool?

**Karen** Sure, Jack. Just thought I should raise it.

**Jack** Appreciate it. See everybody gets coffee. Ringo, help her.

*They leave for the house.*

Arons, check the plugs on the car, I don't want the fucker stallin' on us . . .

*Arons leaves at once, the discipline tight and holding.*

B.T., you and Portia organize Coke bottles, half a dozen, a funnel, a lengtha rubber tube, what else . . .?

**B.T.** Rags, man, we'll need some fuckin' rags . . . (*He's gone.*)

**Jack** (*calling*) Five minutes. We gotta plan this fucker. (*Looks at Sandler. At Sally. Quiet*) This OK for you?

**Sally** No sweat.

**Jack** (*to air*) Pure fuckin' farce.

*Arons tries starting up the VW; it draws, starts, putters out.*

**Sandler** (*soft*) Read it wrong, Jack. Sorry.

**Jack** (*flat*) I read it wrong. It was a collective decision. You ain't responsible.

**Bob** (*approaching, from next door; Knobby in tow, slipping into his jacket*) Jack. We're goin' with ya.

**Jack** Bullshit, Bob.

**Knobby** Bullshit, bullshit, why not?

**Jack** (*lifting slightly*) 'Cause you're not involved, fuckhead. Forget it. Who told you about this anyway?

**Knobby** Hey, waita minute, feller . . .

**Bob** (*slow, decent*) We don't know what'n hell this's all about but if y'all're gettin' into sumpin' this dangerous, we're goin' with ya. That crazy Puerto Rican you all's lettin' order you aroun' tole us, man.

**Jack** Look, you guys, thanks, we dig it, truly man, you wanning' to help, but this thing's fucked up an' you've got a *family*, Bob, are you crazy?

**Bob** (*grinning*) No crazier than you all.

**Jack** (*moved*) Forget it, OK? Really.

*Bob offers his hand. Jack takes it.*

**Bob** Awright, Jack. But we don't like it. You watch out now.

**Jack** Sure.

**Knobby** Change your mind, let us know. I'll go crazy with anyone . . .

*They wave, drift back to their house. Arons starts the car up again. It runs. Ringo arrives, mugs of coffee on a breadboard, hands them round in the near-darkness of the stoop. From indoors, the sound of Tracy Nelson, 'I just can't find another man to take your place', on the turntable.*

**Sandler** Can somebody get my sneakers? They're in the living room.

**Jack** (*to no one*) Whereof one cannot speak, thereof one must be silent. *Tractatus Logico Philosophicus.* And other inerasably bourgeois bullshit.

*The song indoors gathers, grows more intense in its despair.*

**Ramon** (*off, calling*) What you waitin' for, man? Let's go.

*He crashes around in Bob's strip of garden.*

**Jack** (*tired*) We were gonna wait for it to get darker, man, remember?

**Ramon** (*stumbling around*) It's dark, man, it's fuckin' dark, you wanna wait till fuckin' midnight or somethin'?

**Jack** Yancy's not back, he's getting gas for the cocktails.

**Ramon** We don't wait, we get gas on the way. Let's go.

**Jack** (*sudden, shouting to the house*) B.T.! Get out here, will you.

> *A call from within, a door slams. Jack lets air out slowly through tight teeth.*

Pure fuckin' farce. (*calling*) OK, Ramon. You're callin' the shots.

**Ramon** That's right man, that's fuckin' right.

**Jack** Get in the car.

> *B.T., Ringo and Karen arrive. B.T. wears a black balaclava, fatigue jacket, basketball shoes, carries a heavy torch and a bin-liner, bottles clinking inside.*

You got what we need?

> *B.T. clanks the bag, Ringo throws a pair of sneakers at Sandler's bare feet.*

Tell Yancy what happened. He's in charge. Let's go.

> *He leaves, B.T. and Sally behind him. Sandler runs after them, one sneaker on, another in his hand. Ringo follows, to see them off. Portia and Karen draw close, arms round each other, watching from the stoop. The car starts first time. Car doors slam.*

(*off; patient, dangerous*) Will you get in the car, Ramon? Get in the fuckin' car, will you, man. *This* car, Ramon. Fuckin' Jesus.

*A car door slams. The car's in gear and away down the block. The music reasserts.*

**Karen** (*finally*) No one ever says goodbye. You noticed that?

*Slow fade to black.*


## SCENE TWO: THE ACTION

*In the blackness, the fast crump of a roller-door opening. A flashing neon light on the rear wall proclaims the A. & P. Slow, edgy, arrhythmic lighting dimly reveals the side of the building and the spare lot. At the base of the wall, beyond the raised roller-door, a '64 Chevy, a* FOR SALE *sign: $800, parked under a lamp. Two street lights, left and right, define the parking lot.*
  *Over this, from inside the cruising car:*

**Sally** We still ain't got the gas, Jack.

**Sandler** Want me to ask Wittgenstein back there what we should do?

**Jack** (*Over shoulder*) We're fuckin' there, Ramon. Where d'you suggest we get the gas?

**Ramon** Pull over.

*Brakes; handbrake; engine.*

Over there. We get some gas.

**Sandler** Fuck it, Jack, you could take photographs in that fuckin' light . . .

**Ramon** (*lifting*) I give the orders, I say we get the gas over there . . .

**Jack** (*desperate*) OK, OK. Over there it is.

*Car doors bang. Traffic, street sounds, a block away. the four appear out of the dark, crouch in the shadows, stare at the building and the Chevy.*

**Ramon** (*from the car, distressingly loud*) Less go, less go.

*They cringe tighter to the floor.*

**Sandler** (*nervy*) This is our leader? Vay ist mir.

**Jack** (*sotto*) OK, I'll take a look . . . (*He moves forward a couple of crouching steps. Stops. To audience*) 'The Action.'

**Sandler** Jack, I hatea say this . . .

**Jack** (*fast, hissy*) Then don't, OK? (*flattening*) Don't make me have to deal with your defeatism, Geoff, 's that OK? Not at the moment. Would you stand up and look natural, for Christ's sake? (*He moves forward, is lost in shadow.*)

**B.T.** (*tough, hoarse*) Just shut the fuck *up*, Sandler. This's a fuckin' *action* man. You're on active service. In the People's war, man. Keep it shut. Jack wants your thoughts, he'll ask you for 'em.

*B.T.'s eyes never leave the building, the car. He's coiled like a spring, alive and arrested in the moment; filled by purpose. Sandler looks at Sally, who faces out, covering their rear, some distance away.*

**Sandler** (*tense*) B.T., believe me, man, I accept every damn word you say, I was genuinely offerin' sympathy . . .

**B.T.** (*terse; handrolled cupped in his hands*) He don't need your fucking sympathy right now, just get in line.

**Sandler** (*angering, against his instinct*) I'm in line, I'm in line, man, give me a break, will you . . .

**Sally** (*fast*) Shuddup.

*They freeze. Car headlamps play momentarily across them, curve left and cruise away.*

Clear.

*Jack's returned. Squats to one knee to confer.*

**Jack** We're gonna have to lob stuff through windows, this place is built like a brick shithouse.

**Sally** (*clear, across the distance*) Jack.

**Jack** Yeah, Sal?

**Sally** We gotta cover the corners. There's a lotta stuff around.

**Jack** Sandler, stay back here with Sally, anyone enters the street I wanna know about it. B.T. you got the stuff?

*B.T. clanks the bag.*

Er . . . everybody know the procedure for if you get busted . . .?

*They do.*

Who's on charges here?

*They all show hands.*

O.K. You gonna put that fuckin' thing out, B.T.?

*B.T. stubs the handrolled under his shoe, apologizes.*

Let's get the gas.

*Jack and B.T. approach the building, disappear into shadow, reappear eventually by the Chevy through the arch. Throughout what follows, they are seen at work trying to siphon gas into Coke bottles. Sandler watches a moment, then spreads towards the uncovered corner. Cars slide wetly by, a block away, in the silence. The two stand quite still, on the edge of their street lamps,*

*silvery outlines in the haze of light. Sandler takes a pace*
*or two forward, absorbs the light, mainly in his face.*
*When he speaks, he's on radio mic., relayed, flexible*
*acoustic.*

**Sandler** (*remote, high-school debating voice*) To be or not
to be never was, isn't now, and never could be the question.
To those who see history scientifically, we on this side of the
argument – 'commie bastards' was the charming allusion
bestowed on us by my learned opponent – to those who see
history as substantially a history of class struggle, the
critical question has never been be or not be but do or not
do. We must always first and foremost deal with questions
of power, not questions of mere existence. Let me spend a
little time illustrating our thesis. Take, for example, the
aggressive military presence of American imperialism in
Vietnam . . . (*His voice breaks in on itself, inward now,*
*flaky under pressure. Off mic.*) Fuck it, Paulette, I *need* you,
I need you a lot, when you needed me, last fall, I was there,
remember? I mean, sure we agreed we each had the right to
decide our own futures, but when did I abrogate the right to
be consulted? I'm bleeding, Paulette. Can't stop it. Thirteen
fuckin' months of mutuality, respect and trust down the
tubes for what? For Reiner? For a guy who's known
movement-wide for nothing, for *nothing*, hear me?, except
the size of his prick and his extreme readiness to give it
employment . . . ( *Begins to step from the light. Stops,*
*spectral. Speaks in own voice.*) Maybe this, after all, is what
revolution, war, history is like: unlikely people doing things
they're afraid to do and maybe don't want to do in the first
place. We wade in gasoline, who knows which match will
send it up? One. Galvanizing. Symbol. What difference will
it make then that Ramon was drunk and Sandler was
scared and spoke against the action?

*A bottle smashes under the archway. Jack curses, a*
*single expletive, Sandler and Sally look inwards to*

*check, turn back, look at each other across the dark, resume watch. Sandler picks a stone from his foot. He has only one sneaker.*

Seen anything of Ramon?

**Sally** Still in the car. Maybe he's asleep.

**Sandler** You OK?

**Sally** Sure.

**Sandler** I hope you hear by my voice that I ain't pulling no male chauvinist shit on you.

**Sally** Yeah, you're scared.

**Sandler** You got it. Aren't you?

**Sally** Some.

**Sandler** You're unreal.

**Sally** Why'd you take your hand down?

**Sandler** I dunno. It sorta came down.

**Sally** Crap, man. You wanted to come.

**Sandler** How else do I lick it? Or anybody? Do it.

**Sally** (*after pause*) Shit, Sandler.

**Sandler** What?

**Sally** I'm 20, I never even tasted Chinese food, Sandler.

*He begins to chuckle.*

**B.T.** (*from arch, calling*) Sandler. Get the fuck down here fast.

*Sandler begins to scutter towards the arch, gets caught at once in the headlamps of a car approaching the intersection 30 yards away. Brakes, a sense of scouting, the lights advance, as the car cruises circumspectly forward.*

**Sally** (*strong deadpan call*) One guy, on his own, headed straight at us.

*Brakes again. The car's quite close. More scrutiny. They stay quite still, rabbits on the highway. In the silence, Ramon staggers on, sodden with booze. Stares blindly at the lights. From behind the headlamps, the voice of a 50-year-old law-abiding Clevelander, a prototypical good German.*

**Voice** (*high Ohio tenor*) Hey. I seen what you're doing. And you better stop stealing that fella's gas, because I'm calling the police . . .

**Ramon** (*a sudden scream*) Why don' you mind your own fuckin' business, you little fuck? I gonna kill you fuckin' ass. I kill you fuckin' ass . . . (*He goes up a couple of gears, faster in Spanish, as he lunges out in the direction of the lights.*) Singao de mierda. Pon tu coche mierdero en el culo grosero, hijo de mamalon. Que haces por aquí. Debes etar in casa, mirando su maldita tele . . .

*The car crashes into reverse and creeps rapidly backwards, brakes, crashes into first.*

**Voice** I'm gettin' the police. You'll see.

*He drives off, at his version of a lick. Ramon sits down on the fringe of the car park; whistles fragments of 'America' from West Side Story. Jack and B.T. are back with the others. Jack has a rag wrapped round a bad, bloody gash on the palm of his right hand. Nobody marks it.*

**Jack** (*bleak*) Fuckin' Feydeau, man. Get Ramon in the car, we're goin' . . . Sally!

*They try to Get Ramon to his feet. He's all but out; gives minimal and unreliable help.*

**B.T.** You callin' the action off, Jack?

**Jack** (*struggling with Ramon*) This action is postponed, while we get the fuck outta here before the pigs arrive and start plastering us into that wall over there . . .

**B.T.** (*arm around Ramon's waist*) Dig it. We do it later, Yancy'll have the gas, pigs'll go back to the trough.

**Sandler** (*helping where he can*) This thing needs talkin' over again, Jack. That guy was really close. Something happens here, he'll be around to identify us.

**Ramon** Where we goin'?

*They ignore him. Help him off. They become voices.*

**B.T.** Look, Sandler, so we get busted, there's some actions worth gettin' busted for.

**Sandler** (*retreating*) OK. I just think we oughta talk it over, that's all.

**B.T.** (*bleak*) That's all you ever wanta do, Sandler.

*Sally has remained, scouring the terrain for evidence of their occupation. Picks something up. Brings it under the street light. Inspects the sneaker in her hand. She leaves. Car doors slam. the car drives away. Slow fade. Towards the end, the sound of a patrol-car siren, blocks away, answering a call. On black, a sudden brilliant explosion of festive fireworks throws lurid flickery red light over the A. & P. For a moment, it burns. Dies to black again.*

# Act Two

## THE LESSON

*Black.*

   *Sounds of police siren, fire engine, en route.*

   *Living room. Karen, Portia, Arons and Ringo stand motionless staring out. A fierce, deep red glow lights their faces. They're held; silent. Dull sucks and rumbles, as fire eats air. A slow, iconic moment. Behind them, room and kitchen area are sparely lit by storm lamps and candles. There's a sofa in the room, handsome, proudly set.*

   *Fire engine gets closer, a block away. Arrives, settles down at once.*

   *Jack, Sandler, B.T., Sally in fast by kitchen door, unseen and unheard by the watching group.*

**Jack**  Anyone mind telling me what the fuck's goin' on here? Shit. (*He's thudded against the sofa.*)

**Karen**  Oh, Jesus, Jack, I'm sorry, it's my sofa. Larry brought it over, he was looking after it for me . . .

**Jack**  Later, Karen, OK . . .?

**Yancy**  (*fast, in through the back door*) Pigs. Get away from those fuckin' windows, how many more times have I gotta tell you, you assholes.

   *Portia, Arons and Ringo move back fast into the shadows, as the patrol car screams in and stops across the road. Doors slam, some shouts, some shouted replies. The fire's already ebbing away, under control. Yancy crawls into the room.*

**Jack**  (*desperate suddenly, hoarse*) Yancy, who the fuck sent for the pigs? Are we being set up or what, man?

**Yancy** (*across the darkness, patient, patently more in control*) Someone set that old DeSoto parked in front of Gordon's front yard on fire. I don't know who sent for the pigs, Jack. We bin right here, all of us, as ordered. I've been out back hidin' stuff. They coulda bin comin' here, after you . . .

*Silence. The cops stand by the patrol car, radioing a preliminary report on the fire. On the response, it's mainly static.*

**Portia** (*from darkness*) You hurt your hand, Jack?

**Jack** (*flat*) It's OK.

**Yancy** (*deliberately*) So what happened, man? You get hit? Let's hear . . .

**Jack** (*fast*) 'S Ramon here?

*He's not.*

Sandler?

**Sandler** (*tense, from shadow*) I left him in the yard, Jack. Said he wanted to take a piss.

**Jack** (*in a scathe of air*) You left him out *there*? With the place swarmin' with fire pigs and fuck knows what? I don't believe this is happening . . .

*Silence. Sandler bites his lip, chidden. They sit or crouch in the shadows, barely there. The red orange of the fire has all but gone. In the dark, the storm lamps gradually assert themselves, beacons against the night.*

**Sandler** Want me to go look for him, Jack?

**Jack** (*slow, tired; slumping on Karen's sofa*) No. Leave him where he is. Maybe he went home. (*Beat.*) OK, listen, people. We fucked up. Some asshole good citizen saw us syphoning gas and we split.

317

*It's depressing news. They search out each other's faces in the gloom.*

**Ringo**  So what you sayin', man, it's over?

*Jack doesn't answer. Doors slam, an engine starts, the patrol-car siren starts up.*

**Ramon**  (*off; on the stoop*) Hey. You hear me in there?

**Jack**  Jesus fucking God.

*Banging on the door, loud, mad.*

(*lifting; fierce*) Ramon, this place is crawlin' with pigs, what the fuck d'ya want?

**Ramon**  (*eventually; reasonable*) I splittin'.

**Jack**  (*controlled; weary*) Why not wait till the pigs split, man?

**Ramon**  (*fast, up*) I splittin' now. (*Pause.*) Action cancel.

*The fire engine leaves. Karen gets up, crosses the room raising lampwicks and lighting more candles.*

**B.T.**  What's the fuckin' line on the candles?

**Karen**  In case you think I thought this one up, my idea of some fuckin' bistro in the Village, we had a power failure, Jack. It's the best I could do in the fucking circumstances. Phone's still working'.

*Jack has his head in his hand; collecting his thoughts. People have relaxed, begin little wanders, move bits and pieces here and there. Begin to feel perhaps they have come through.*

**Jack**  (*collected*) OK. (*Stands.*) Listen up a minute.

*They gather.*

Make sure you're around tomorrow. All day. I wanna

discuss our meeting with national leadership first thing. And I'm calling a criticism/self-criticism session for the rest of the day. Which I will lead. For tonight, we lock the doors, stay inside, get some sleep. We're in one piece. Next time we'll be better. Right, Ringo?

**Ringo** (*not wholly gung-ho*) You bet, Jack.

**Jack** B.T.?

**B.T.** Yeah, you bet, Jack.

*Jack walks towards the staircase by the front door.*

**Arons** I'll get some stuff up, clean that hand . . .

**Jack** (*not looking*) Thanks, Arons. I'd appreciate it.

*He leaves. Arons has gone to the kitchen, puts water in a bowl, finds cotton wool and iodine. Karen joins her. Eventually sends her on her way. Looks exchanged, as Jack leaves; worried, concerned, a touch embarrassed. Portia hovers by Yancy. Sandler and Sally squat crosslegged on the floor, each in the other's eyeline.*

**Ringo** I shoulda gone, B.T. I fuckin' offered, man.

**B.T.** (*flat on the floor, eyes closed*) Wouldn'ta made no difference, Ringo. It was a fucked-up action.

**Ringo** Yeah?

**B.T.** Never had a chance.

**Ringo** Yeah? So why the fuck'd we go on it?

*No one speaks for a while.*

**B.T.** (*as if tranced*) Fourtha July, man.

*Silence again.*

**Yancy** (*on duty still*) I was plannin' on crashin' out, but if you guys're startin' in on tomorrow's criticism session, maybe I'll join you.

**Ringo** Hell no, Yance, we weren't doin' that . . .

**Yancy** Good. Jack'll appreciate that. (*he picks up a storm lamp.*) You comin' up, Porsh?

**Portia** I need to talk with Karen.

**Yancy** OK.

*He leaves. Portia joins Karen in the kitchen.*

**Ringo** Fourtha fuckin' July.

**B.T.** (*flat again*) Fuckin' fourtha July.

**Ringo** Fuckin' July fourth.

**B.T.** July fuckin' fourth.

**Ringo** Fourth Ju-fuckin'-ly.

**B.T.** (*stumped*) Inde-fuckin'-pendence Day.

*They're amused.*

That's all she fucking wrote.

*He gets up, waves, leaves for the stairs. Ringo waits, checks the room for askers, finds none, follows.*

**Karen** (*through hatch*) You people want anything? Arons got some nice Earl Grey . . .

*The phone on the window-hatch ledge begins ringing.*

'S OK, it's probably my ex about the fuckin' sofa, let it ring . . .

**Sandler** (*to Sally*) Tea?

*She shakes her head. Earl Grey has been a foreign language.*

One tea. (*serious*) You're a fuckin' security risk, Karen,

320

givin' the fuckin' number out like that, you know that?

**Karen** (*waitress*) One tea.

*The phone stops. She gives Sandler a finger. Watches him covertly eyeing Sally.*

Did you ask Jack yet whether Paulette was at the meeting, Sandler?

*Sandler squirms, deflated. Karen chuckles. The phone rings again.*

This bastard's gonna wake the whole house . . . (*Picks up the phone; in improbable ansaphone voice.*) The number you have called has been temporarily disconnect . . . What? (*Listens, stopped.*) Er sure. Hold on a minute, will ya, I'll go get him . . . (*Lays the receiver down, crosses from kitchen to front-door area. Urgent; calm*) Jack. Could you come to the phone, please? I think it's the S.P.I.C.s.

*Jack comes in quickly, shirtsleeves, heads for the phone, picks it up from the room side of the hatch. Yancy appears, without shirt, lamp in hand; B.T. and Ringo, shorts, undershirts, socks; Ringo has their lamp.*

**Jack** Yeah, this is Jack. (*Listens.*) What? (*Listens, cuts in.*) Listen, who is this, is Ramon there? Lemme call you back, what's your number . . . OK, OK, OK, you call back in five minutes. Right. (*Replaces the receiver slowly, turns to face them. To ceiling; controlled call*) Arons?

**Arons** (*on the move*) Here, Jack. On my way. (*She arrives from upstairs, bowl in hand, towel over shoulder.*)

**Jack** You use the phone tonight?

**Arons** Yeah.

**Jack** Who'd you call?

**Arons** My aunt. Why?

**Jack** (*dead*) Your aunt. Why'd you call your aunt, Arons?

*Arons looks around the uncomprehending room for help.*

**Arons** I was nervous. About the action, I guess. She's a good person. I just wanted to talk to her.

**Jack** Did you tell your aunt about the action, Arons?

*A mutter of 'What's, exhalations of bafflement.*

**Arons** No. Are you crazy? Acourse not, Jack, Jesus.

**Jack** Are you sure? You didn't say anything about the car?

**Arons** Jack. Stop it.

**Jack** (*rubbing his face*) I don't even know what the fuck we're talking about. They didn't even say anything about your goddamned aunt. Did you call the Fire Department?

**Arons** (*disbelief crescent*) You're asking me if I called the fire pigs?

**Jack** (*lifting*) Did *anybody* call the fuckin' fire pigs, I gotta know, people. I wanna know. I swear this has gotta be on the fuckin' line. (*Stares at them.*) Did anyone?

*No one speaks.*

**Yancy** (*gentle*) Cut the mystery shit, Jack. What the fuck is this about?

**Jack** (*slow*) The S.P.I.C.s say Arons called the fire pigs. The little chick is what they said. And they wanna know how come? And I'm goin' fuckin' nuts or somethin' cos I don't fuckin' get it. They say they saw her and they heard her. I don't know how they achieved this. Maybe they had someone out back watching saw her on the phone and just assumed she was talkin' to the fire pigs, I don't *know*, I don't fuckin' know.

**Karen** They sure sounded mad.

**Sally** This is bullshit. What's the deal, Jack?

*The phone rings. They listen.*

**Jack** (*remote*) They're calling back, Sal. (*Crosses, picks up the receiver.*) Yeah, this is Jack. Listen, comrade, you got it all wrong . . . (*Listens, for some time, stopped cold.*) No, hey, hold it, man . . .

*They've hung up. He drops the receiver on its stand. Picks it up again. Dials a number, fast, urgent. Waits.*

Come on, Ramon, man. Be home. (*Waits, then in a voice barely more than a murmur.*) They want us to turn Arons over for interrogation by midnight. Cornera 25th and Detroit.

**Yancy** (*dazed*) Fuck *them*.

**Jack** (*same level*) Or they say they're coming over to kill us.

*He gives up on the phone. People absorb what they've heard.*

**Yancy** Fuck them.

*Silence again.*

**Jack** (*drained*) What time is it?

**Yancy** Eleven. Minute after.

**Jack** Lock the doors, Yance. I gotta check something out.

*He leaves for upstairs. Yancy starts locking doors.*

**Arons** Maybe I should try to talk to them.

**Sally** (*distinct, decisive*) Forget it. No way.

**B.T.** (*mainly shielding Jack's leadership*) Yeah? Who fuckin' died around here? This ain't gonna be no fuckin' joy ride, these fucks don't piss around . . .

**Sally** (*into light, hard, direct*) We don't piss around either, B.T. No way. I've seen shit as heavy's anythin' *you*'ve seen, only I got no balls to rattle, so maybe you think I know nothing, and maybe I don't know much at that, but I learned some things that can't be otherwise: like, if we don't defend each other, who defends us? No way Arons goes outta that door. *I* say so. You got it?

**Ringo** Fuck, Sally. B.T. wasn't sayin' that . . .

> *Jack's back in the room, an address book in hand, watching.*

**Sally** (*back in the shadow again*) Fine, Ringo.

**Jack** O.K. Here's what we do. I found another number for Ramon he's sometimes at, we keep trying both till we get him, we've got about an hour, we get him over here and work this thing out. In the meantime . . . (*he looks at Yancy.*)

**Arons** Jack, we were discussing if I should try and talk with them.

**Jack** (*simple, dismissed*) Forget it. OK (*on*) In the meantime, we get our shit together. Yance?

**Yancy** (*on the move*) Two minutes.

**Jack** B.T., Ringo, give him a hand.

> *They leave, quickish. Jack crosses to the phone, begins dialling. Gets no answer. Tries the second number. Sandler, Sally, Portia, Karen scan the street outside the front windows. Arons follows Jack to the phone, continues bathing and cleaning the wound.*

**Portia**  This is really awful.

**Karen**  It'll be OK, baby. We'll get it together. Jack'll sort things out . . .

*Silence. Jack curses at the back of the room. The four peer on.*

**Portia**  Fourtha July.

**Karen**  We're still gonna smash the fuckin' state.

**Sandler**  Onea these days.

**Karen**  (*quiet*) Fuck you, Sandler.

**Sally**  Nice couch, Karen.

**Karen**  You like it?

**Sally**  'S nice.

**Karen**  It was my mother's, she gave it me when I got married. Never move without it. 'S Louis-seize or something.

*Sally looks briefly at it over her shoulder.*

**Sally**  'Louie says'?

**Karen**  'S what they say.

*The back door bangs. Yancy, B.T. and Ringo in quickly, laden. Yancy lays down his load to relock the door. B.T. and Ringo lay down the heavyish boxes they carry in the centre of the room. Yancy carries his heavy sacking over, lays it down between the boxes with a clunk. They gather round, silent. Jack puts the phone down, approaches the rough circle of people. Arons tags along behind. Jack goes on one knee, flips open the box lids, then lays bare the contents of the sacking: five guns – an M-3 carbine, an M-1, two .22 rifles, a shotgun. Looks up at them carefully.*

**Jack** Anyone got anything to say, say it now.

*He waits. No one speaks.*

**Yancy** (*soft*) Ten after, Jack.

*Jack nods. He's calm; deathly.*

**Jack** It's possible nonea this is real, the S.P.I.C.s won't show. Ramon'll talk with them and straighten them out about us, maybe they're testin' us out or somethin', maybe the whole fuckin' evenin's bin a test . . . An' it's possible they're comin' to us. Figurin' we're a buncha pussy faggots in the paya of the fuckin' FBI. So. We gotta be as heavy as the traffic. An' I'm not talkin' about bein' discredited, I'm talkin' about being wiped out. (*Looks around, suddenly boyish. Grins.*) Nobody said learnin' to live the life of the people was gonna be easy.

*People smile, work on the rigor in their cheeks.*

**B.T.** (*half self-parody*) Gimme the fuckin' shotgun. Nobody calls me a pussy faggot and lives.

*Tension eases a touch. People smile at B.T., warmed a bit. Jack watches them; loves them all.*

**Ringo** Fuckin' A. Goes for me too, man.

*They look at him; pale, neglected, unlovely, trapped inside his acne and his asthma; are saddened back into the present.*

**Jack** Yance, lay out how you think we do this, will ya, I gotta try . . .

*The phone rings. Jack's there fast.*

Hello, yeah . . . No. No, she ain't. No, she ain't expected back tonight, she's er . . . she's spending a few days with her mother. Her father then. What can I say, she ain't here. Terry called, I'll give her the message. OK.

*He puts the phone down. Stares down the room at Karen. She goes to speak, gets smart, lowers her eyes.*

Let's do it, Yancy. I'll try Ramon.

**Yancy** Right. B.T., you used anya this shit?

**B.T.** (*defensive*) Sure. I handled stuff. Sure.

**Yancy** Take the M-1. Back bedroom.

*B.T. Takes it; fishes in a box of clips, begins filling his cowboy hat.*

Anyone else?

*They shake their heads.*

OK, I take the big feller upstairs, rest don't matter so much anyway, so long as whoever's got the shotgun got good nerves. It's gotta be point-blank range.

*He scans them. Sandler tries to look tough; fails. Karen passes: no question. He holds on Sally.*

**Sally** Cool. (*She dips for the gun, puts cartridges in a china bowl.*)

**Yancy** Kitchen.

**Ringo** (*off the hook*) Fuck it, man, I ain't scareda no fuckin' shotgun, man . . .

**Yancy** (*on*) Sandler, take a .22. Living room.

*Sandler dips for his.*

Ringo, B.T.'ll need you upstairs for back-up, the M-1's a motherfucker.

*Jack's given up on the phone. They know it.*

You used anya this, Jack?

*Jack shakes his head, headed back.*

Karen, you spell Sandler down here; Arons, with Sally . . .
Portia, you're with me.

**Portia** Fine, Yance.

**Yancy** (*handing him a .22*) I figure you should move
around, Jack . . .

**Jack** You gonna show us how to use these things?

**Yancy** I'll do that when we got people in position, Jack,
we gotta get a move on.

**Jack** OK. Here's what we do. Only shoot if you *see*
someone shoot first, or getting ready to throw a cocktail.
*See*. Dig? Anybody rushin' the house without a cocktail or
a gun firin', just holler out. I fuckin' don't want anyone
shot unless it's absolutely necessary. If they try to come in
the door without shooting, we'll take care of them inside.
And nobody needs to go freakin' out, all we're doing is
bein' prepared. Let's go.

> *Jack rounds the room, dowsing the candles. Ends up at
> the phone, dialling Ramon. Pairs move off to their
> assigned posts. Sally and Arons move to the kitchen; we
> lose them. Sandler and Karen move the sofa closer to
> the windows. Sandler draws the bolt of the .22
> experimentally, fiddles a 9 mm. from his pocket, slides it
> in, closes the bolt. Fear edges the movements; makes
> them sharp, arrhythmic. Karen sits on the couch.*

**Karen** I've bin hoping against hope we're gonna get outa
this in one piece, but watchin' you with that fuckin' thing,
Sandler, I know we're in deep trouble.

**Sandler** (*grim*) Shut the fuck up, Karen, would you?

**Karen** Why'd they wanna kill us, tell me that, they never
even fuckin' met us.

> *He says nothing. She watches his tense frame by the*

*window, gun clutched to his chest like a teddy.*

Was it bad tonight, down the A. & P.?

**Sandler** Karen. Compared to this. It was fun.

**Karen** Shit. You think we're going to die?

**Sandler** If I thought it mattered, I'd give you an answer.

**Karen** What does that mean?

**Sandler** I don't know. I just thought it sounded good. Give me a break, will ya?

**Karen** (*sad*) Poor Sandler.

*Silence. She watches him watch the street. An owl hoots, end of street; a second. Jack puts down the phone; listens. Nothing. He takes a window, book-ending Sandler. Karen's face is a dim glimmer behind and between them.*

**Jack** (*sotto*) Fuckin' owls already.

**Sandler** So how was the meeting, man?

**Jack** The meeting. (*blank*) Heavy. Still lotsa trouble with the Running Dogs about the National Action. They've still got this United Front bullshit stuck up their ass. Katzen says they're actually talkin' to the Mobe-Fucks about a fuckin' *peace* march in Washington. Walker thinks they're ready to split.

**Sandler** Jesus. I hate splits.

**Karen** Let 'em split. Dahlberg an' Alman're shits. I hate 'em.

**Sandler** (*dogged*) So who was there anyway? Barry and Hamer from Columbus?

**Jack** Linda came instead of Hamer. God, she's getting

heavy. She fuckin' creamed Reiner around women's militia. It was outasight.

**Sandler** (*casual*) Reiner was there, hunh?

**Jack** Ahunh.

**Sandler** Anyone else from Akron?

**Jack** Doug and Sue.

**Karen** (*great timing*) I think Geoff wants to know if Paulette was there, Jack.

**Jack** Oh Jesus. Sandler . . . We're sittin' here with fuckin' guns in our laps praying to Christ the fuckin' comrades don't blow us away by sun up and you're worried about fuckin' *Paulette*? (*Pause.*) She's in San Francisco, Alan took her with him to meet with the Panthers.

**Karen** What?

**Jack** I'm checkin' upstairs. Keep an eye on the fuckin' street, OK?

> *He leaves. Sandler takes it in image by image, bowels burning, brain aghast.*

**Karen** (*at his shadow*) Fucking San Francisco. Jesus.

> *An owl hoot, close; another; silence. Metallic sounds of B.T. and Ringo upstairs being put through gun drill by Yancy; they dismantle, reassemble and load the M-1.*

**Jack** (*from the darkness*) Fuck. Anybody remember to turn the light switches to off?

**Arons** (*from darkness*) It's done, Jack.

**Jack** Thanks, Arons.

**Ringo** (*puzzled*) Lights *are* off, Jack.

**Jack** (*deadpan*) Thanks, Ringo.

*Clicking upstairs, the snap of a clip. Karen watches
Sandler's trembling frame in the gloom.*

**Karen**  (*soft*) Geoff?

**Sandler**  What?

**Karen**  Let her go. Can't you see that staying with you was
just holding her back? Geoff?

**Sandler**  Fine, Karen. Fine.

**Karen**  This personal shit holds us all back, Geoff. We've
got more important things to deal with. The Man wants us
hung up in love and romance so we won't fight him.

**Sandler**  (*not wanting this*) Listen . . .

**Karen**  I'm not like somea the others. I understand love.
You know, after Leroy – the sax player usedta beat me up
all the time? – *I* was destroyed, you know. And I thought
Harold would pull me together. Because he loved me.
That's why I married him. But my alienation was too
heavy . . . I don't know. I tried to die. Something went. It
was Yancy and Portia helped me through. The movement
gave me something to live for again.

**Sandler**  Let's do our job, Karen.

**Karen**  Men hold women back, Geoff. That's how it is.

**Sandler**  Listen, when I met Paulette at counter-orientation
at Oberlin, she had the politics of fuckin' Bambi. She
didn't know Stalin from Trotsky, she didn't even know
Snic from Core. I *made* her, Karen . . . And now she's
fuckin' her way to the top . . .

*A slow volley of hoots rings the house, very close.
Another, returning down the loop.*

**Jack**  (*off*) Great. They can't even wait till fuckin'
midnight. You see anything up there?

*Bring up upper-right bedroom. Yancy, with gun, and Portia.*

**Yancy** Nothing, Jack.

**Jack** (*off*) B.T.?

*Bring up upper-left bedroom. B.T. with M-1, and Ringo.*

**B.T.** Not a thing, Jack.

**Jack** Anything, Sal?

*Bring up kitchen-door area: Sally, with shotgun, and Arons.*

**Sally** Nothing.

*The four dim images of the defence of the collective hold for some moments. More hooting, sudden, encroaching. All lights cut, save Sandler's.*

**Sandler** (*on radio mic*) So this is what happens when you leave me, hunh? You go to San Francisco with the most famous and sexiest man in the whole revolutionary movement to meet with the Panthers. While the rest of us are stuck in Akron, Columbus, Cleveland . . .

**Karen** (*hoarse, from the darkness*) What do you think they're gonna do, Jack?

**Jack** (*hoarse, from dark*) Karen, how the fuck am *I* supposed to know?

**Sandler** (*on*) Those of us who prefer to deal with history scientifically might want to account for Paulette's political development somewhat differently. A year before she met me she was getting herself gassed at the Pentagon. Gassed and cut. Barbed wire. I saw the scars. Later, through sheer black tights. As it happens, I was there too. But I turned back. On the Memorial Bridge. It was getting late and the

Pentagon was still fuckin' miles away and my aunt had a special dinner waiting for me over in Chevy Chase. (*Trembles slightly, living this present and that past together.*) I didn't *make* her. I held her back.

   *Owl hoots. Silence. Hoots and stick-clicks.*

**Karen** (*from the dark; sotto; an attempt at scorn*) This is so fuckin' corny, you know, I saw Randolph fuckin' Scott in this movie, who're they tryin' to scare?

*Upper right. Yancy, gun, window. Portia crouched behind.*

**Yancy** (*blank*) 'Weapons are an important factor but not the decisive factor in war. People, not material, form the decisive factor. War cannot be divorced from politics for a single moment.'

**Portia** (*blank*) 'The people are like water, the revolutionary army are like fish.'

   *Hooting, fast, penetrating. Jackal calls; answers.*
   *Crossfade to:*

*Upper left. B.T., gun ready, Ringo behind.*

**Ringo** (*as if Joplin*) 'It's all the same fuckin' day, man.'

**B.T.** (*sings, as if Dylan, stone-faced; gun-guitar*)
Gas in the streets
Napalm in the park
Bombs in the airways
Turning day into dark.
And there's blood on the moon.
Going underground. Underground bound.
Got a message for the man
With the shadow on his jaw:
America ain't my fatherland
And the president ain't my pa.

Blood and bone. Gonna sink like a stone.
Hanoi lovers sitting out in the park
Making love and revolution in the noontime dark
Feel a dripping on their shoulders
Feel a trickle on their hair:
Blood on the moon.
Going underground. Turn my heart to stone.
Underground. Gonna bring the war home.

> *Take out B.T. light. Black. A flurry of hoots, circling the house. Bring up:*

*Sally and Arons, dimly framed in kitchen window. Sally has the gun. Arons is quite scared.*

**Arons**  Oh God, here we go.

**Sally**  'S OK. These fucks're havin' themselves a good time just *scarin'* us to death, they won't need to come in.

**Arons**  You think so? (*Works it out.*) I guess this is the first time I realized dying's a part of it.

**Sally**  Yeah.

**Arons**  An ' I was sort of wonderin' if it ever happened in my parents' lives.

**Sally**  I sorta knew in Chicago.

**Arons**  Oh sure, pigs, the State, I guess I knew that. I mean, now it's . . . we're anybody's, anybody could just . . . rub us out, you know, like even the people we're solid with, I mean, the people. I mean, we're waiting here with shotguns and fuck knows what to kill our brown brothers who're out there somewhere planning how to off *us*, it's a fuckin' unfunny joke . . .

**Sally**  We go no *choice*, Arons. We put choice behind us when we started this thing. All we gotta do now is what's necessary. Maybe this is the people's first lesson for us: respect grows from the barrel of a gun.

**Arons**  Oh shit. I wish you hadn't said that. And I absolutely know it's true.

*Take out light. Owl calls, dispersed, slightly less close. They continue in black.*

Where you from, Sal?

**Sally**  Beaver Falls.

**Arons**  Where's that?

**Sally**  Nowhere.

*Owl hoots, less threatening, spaced.*

*Lights on, upper right. Yancy, on a box, gun cradled. Portia sleeps, next to him.*

**Yancy**  (*listening, then interrupting*) . . . Listen, man, you don't believe it, you've spent twenty-seven years on a Ford assembly line, getting broken down to what you are now, deaf, lame, arthritic and goddam nowhere, man, I know it, man, I lived through it, I watched it growin' up, gave me my first politics, watchin' what capitalism did to its people. This is a pig society: we behave and think and feel like pigs. So why should we behave any different in South-East Asia? I've been *in* the fuckin' military, for Chrissake, I know what it's like and what it's for, and I'm telling you, its sole purpose is to enforce White Racist America's foreign policy, which is to reconstruct the world in its own fuckin' image. Pig world. A worlda pigs, snuffin' at the trough. (*Pauses. Grins, softens.*) Didn't go down too good at my court martial, that speech . . . but er . . . as it was my whole line of defence . . . I had no choice. Listen, Dad, you look a lot better, stronger, than you did last week, how're they treatin' you in here?

335

(*Listens. Pulls out a pack of Camels.*) Fuck it, Dad, you just had a lung removed, you're asking for cigarettes, are you crazy're what?

*He chuckles, fond. Crossfade to:*

*Karen on couch. Tracy Nelson again: 'I'll never find another man to take your place'. Karen joins the song briefly, as if in her sleep. Crossfade to:*

*Kitchen. Sally in special, gun vertical, check on barrel.*

**Sally** (*interior letter-voice*) 'Camp Superior, Ohio, 4th July. Dear Mom, Your letter arrived the day I left Ohio State for the summer-camp job and I've been worked off my feet since I got here. Thank Pop for the 25 dollars and tell him I'll write when I get a chance – it's appreciated. By the way, I wrote Grandma but got no answer – is she OK? She sent me a Navajo bracelet, coral and silver, for my birthday: beautiful.

'Mom, you don't say it, but I sense you're still upset I'm not coming with you and Pop on the camping trip this year. Don't be. It's only that I need to spend the time working out what I want to do with my life, now my teens are behind me. It doesn't mean I don't love you both, really. And how long is it since you and Pop spent free time together, away from the store and all that goes with it? You owe it to each other. Oh yes, I'm short on shirts, pants, T-shirts and sneakers – could you raid my bedroom and see what's there? And could you send them to me care of Karen Kushner, 10 Michigan Avenue, West-of-the-flats, Cleveland. We've been told not to use the camp address until the leader finds out which hut's intercepting the mailman and pocketing the goodies. Karen's a friend who comes out waitressing weekends and she'll see I get them.

'OK. I'm due at the pool in five minutes – life-saving drill. Tomorrow canoeing. Otherwise, I'm fit, well and pretty happy. A kiss for Pop, a tickle for Brandy and a special hug for you. Sal.'

*Crossfade to:*

*Upper right. Yancy at window, gun slung across shoulder. Portia sits watching him, awake again, a blanket round her shoulders.*

**Portia**  Hi. What time is it?

**Yancy**  Three. Sleep.

**Portia**  Oh God. Is everything still as awful?

**Yancy**  No, they've quieted down. They ain't gone.

**Portia**  Did I tell you Jack's wife called?

**Yancy**  No.

**Portia**  She's in Pittsburgh.

**Yancy**  Still in the movement?

**Portia**  Stronger than ever. And having a really good time.

**Yancy**  Ahunh.

**Portia**  Anyway. It set me to thinking maybe we should have that talk you said we should have about us as a couple an' things.

**Yancy**  (*a beat*) OK.

**Portia**  I sense a lotta resentment from the others, us bein' the only ones an' everything . . .

**Yancy**  Yeah?

**Portia**  An' I think, like, ideologically it's a bit suspect, you know what I mean?

**Yancy**  I can dig that.

**Portia** Anyway. Jack asked me a couplea days ago if I'd be interested in goin' over to Akron, they're openin' up another house . . .

**Yancy** Yeah? What'd you say?

**Portia** I said I'd like to. I think I have to. What do you think?

**Yancy** Do it.

**Portia** Yeah?

**Yancy** Sure. Any move that frees you as a woman for the revolution gotta be objectively correct. Your voice ain't heard here.

**Portia** That's right. You speak for both of us, even when you don't.

**Yancy** OK. You tell Karen yet?

*She shakes her head.*

She'll be a problem.

*Portia grunts, relaxing back towards sleep.*

I'll miss you.

**Portia** It's crazy. Why would anyone wanta leave a guy as OK as you?

**Yancy** That's the fuckin' dialectic, baby.

*She laughs. He puts an arm around her. They cuddle. Lights out. Black. Owl hoots still there, dispersed: a fainter presence, but not lost.*

*Special up on Jack, living room, behind the sofa, gun in one hand, a crumpled page of type in the other. He scans the page briefly, looks at his audience.*

**Jack** 'Report on West-of-the-flats Collective to National Leadership. Comrades. The collective – then five men and three women – set up base here June 5th. A fourth woman joined us last week. All nine have committed to the programme until the fall.

'Internal Development: In four weeks, the gains have been few and painstakingly gathered. Daily criticism self-criticism sessions have raised awareness on aims and objectives, strengthened collective discipline, shaped chains of responsibility and established lines of command and generally increased our cohesion as a group. On the down side, the assault on cultural and psychic formations in group members has met with very limited results (see attached reports on individual members). Realistically speaking, the smashing of the liberal under the skin is likely to take some time. The key-text reading programme helps, though the shortage of copies (two Mao, one Fanon, three Lenin) slows us down.

'Outreach: Significant gains here have yet to be made. We have established a relatively unquestioned presence in the neighbourhood. Contact with working-class youth has been so far confined to recruitment drives at schoolyards, playgrounds, parks and beaches, with as yet little tangible yield. But though this is clearly not good, a recent strong contact with a member of the Puerto Rican Socialist Party holds realistic possibilities for a significant advance in this field. The man in question spends a good deal of time in the house, accepts our programme and is currently negotiating a meeting with the area's most militant youth section (S.P.I.C. – see note attached).

'Personal Comments: (*Long pause.*) None. Yours in struggle, Jack Stone. July 3rd, 1969.'

*Upper left. Ringo dreams of food. B.T. listens, impassive.*

**Ringo** Hostess Twinkies, Cheeseburger-Deluxe with

onions, a chocolate milk shake, right, a T-bone steak with mushrooms, yeah, and a Big Mac, French fries and a peanut-butter and jelly sandwich, yeah, and some flapjacks with real maple syrup and Frosted Flakes and yeah a fucking great Pepperoni pizza . . . oh and hold it, how about a . . .

*Very slow crossfade to:*

*Living room. Pre-dawn, dark, dank. Karen sleeps on her matrimonial sofa, body as untidy as sacking, mini-skirt rucked and rumpled. Her glasses hang from her face. Sandler sits on a box, gun still in hands. A single owl hoot. A second, much later. Sandler pays no heed. Sound of water-closet being flushed. Jack appears. Sandler starts.*

**Jack** 'S Jack. 'S OK.

*He draws up a box to join Sandler, looks briefly at Karen. Then stares at floor. Sandler watches him. Jack becomes aware of the gaze. Looks up.*

How're you doin'?

**Sandler** OK. How 'bout you?

*Jack puts his head down, looks at his boots.*

**Jack** (*serious enough to cry*) Sandler. I'm goin' outa my fuckin' head, man.

*Sandler says nothing, disturbed, embarrassed a little.*

I mean, what the fuck is happening, man? This is fuckin' *Wagon Train*. (*Looks up.*) I shouldn't be talkin' like this . . . I don't know why I'm fuckin' tellin' you . . . Probably cos you're an asshole intellectual. Like I used to be. Regression in the face of crisis.

*Sandler tries to smile; can't.*

Here we are, man, what are we doin'. We're protecting our goddam womenfolk. From the savages. Only what we're sup*posed* to be doin' is *joinin'* the savages. It wasn't supposed to turn out like this. For Christ's sake, Sandler. (*almost at a whisper*) It wasn't supposed to turn out like this . . . What was I supposed to do? Maybe I shoulda told Ramon to fuck off in the first place . . . but what would that have done? I mean . . . (*Stops; can't find what he means.*)

**Sandler**  There was nothing you could do, man. Except what we're doing.

**Jack**  (*bitter, not looking*) Don't give me that shit, Sandler, just look at the fuckin' mess we're in, we're supposed to be forming an alliance wi' these people . . .

**Sandler**  (*fast*) What the fuck *are* we, man? We're just fuckin' kids. Doin' the best we can with what we've got, which ain't that much . . .

**Jack**  (*harder, more desperate*) We're supposed to have a theory, a strategy and a tactic, Sandler. We're supposed to know what we're doing. 'Do the best we can'? This isn't the Oberlin–Kenyon homecoming game . . .

**Sandler**  (*sudden*) Wait one fucking minute, man, Who in hell *ever* knew what was goin' on and what the fuck to do about it? Lenin? After twenty years of practice underground, overground and all around town and the greatest fuckin' genius political mind of all time he got shit right mebbe two out of three times. Unless you listen to Rosa Luxemburg, in which case it was a lot less than that. (*Gathering*) Leadership ain't about gettin' it right every time, it's about gettin' it right more often than most. (*Pauses.*) What do you expect from us, Jack? Sure it ain't no fuckin' football game, but we're still fuckin' college kids . . . All we can do is try, and fuck it, we're trying. Just like Ramon. He ain't no Fidel, man: let's face it. Who knows what crazy shit's goin' on with them out there . . . maybe they're doing us a big favour, teachin' us what it feels like to play for keeps . . . Maybe they just don't like us honkeys and want to mind-fuck us a little. Maybe they want an excuse to kill our asses. We've gotta take it as it comes and right now it comes like Ramon. But there *is* a revolution goin' on out there, and there's not a part of the world can't feel it. We didn't start it, we're not gonna finish it, and we're not gonna have a lot to say about what happens in between. But we know what it's for and what it's against. And we know who's gonna win. All we can do is push. In whatever direction looks like the right one. Hard, and as long as we can. And we are, man. We are.

> *He gets up, walks over to Karen, props his rifle on the couch, gentles her hair with his fingers.*

All of us, man. And if we fuck up all summer long, no one's gonna tell me Dahlberg or the Mobe or PL or any other buncha white commie college kids is gonna do any better either. And no one's gonna tell me there's anything better to *be* in this pig world than what we're tryin' to become. After we're all dead, maybe someone will know if any of us were worth anything . . . What we've gotta worry about now is *not* doing it. All the shit that holds us back and fucks us up – the personal, the comfortable, the safe, the neurotic, the racist – you know, everything that feels natural – well, that shit's there, it's gonna fuck us up, but we gotta make sure it doesn't stop us, man, drive us back to bein' good citizens or hippies or junkies or pigs. I know what *I'm* workin' on . . . It's a list as long as your arm, man . . . But we're only gonna get as far as we get, man.

> *Jack gets up. Sways a little, adjusting.*

**Jack** (*ironic*) Thanks, Geoff, I needed that. Now let's see if you can explain all that to the Comrades.

**Sandler** Comrades're gone, Jack.

*They listen to the silence. Faint dawn light deepens the room. A dog barks. Jack stifflegs slowly off into shadow.*

**Jack** (*yawning*) National leadership need to know by next week whether you agree to leave Oberlin and work for us full time . . . If the answer's yes, they wanna put you in a leadership cadre . . .

*Sandler's left. The question hangs. He kneels, buttocks on heels, begins to strip down to a a sort of white judo suit, the loose jacket tied at the waist. Dawn light continues to grow.*

**Sandler** Ramon called next day to say things were cool and offered no explanation. We didn't press. We figured it must've bin some sort of test. Four weeks later, after a few dozen failed attempts to recruit a single working-class kid to the National Action, and half a dozen reports of Paulette going round the country with different members of the leadership, I left the collective. For New York. Where with the help of some Lebanese hash and amphetamines, an empty apartment belonging to a friend of my sister, and the three all-night TV stations, I set a personal record for uninterrupted television watching: eighty-three hours. (*Begins tying a red sash round his forehead.*) But these are dreams that will not go away. These are real dreams.

*The others – all eleven – have emerged, in the judo garb and the red head-sash, from the gloom. Arons carries a huge, fine NLF flag, which she waves menacingly, side to side. They walk on their bare heels, arms in karate state of preparedness; but the pace is slow, dreamlike. They form a knot of bodies, looking out, nuclear, unified. Light brightens, whitens, dreamlike (Bergman's*

Dream). *Their movements soften into slow early morning Tai-Chi, disciplined, graceful. Cohere, eventually, into a group, a collective unity, in the bright unreal light.*

**Arons** 'Prison Poem': Ho Chi Minh.

*They deliver, a phrase each, with perfect timing, tone and meaning, Ho's poem written in prison.*

The wheel of the law turns
without pause.

After rain, good weather.
In the wink of an eye.

The world throws off
Its muddy clothes.

For ten thousand miles
the land

spreads out like a brocade
Light breezes. Smiling flowers.

High in the trees, amongst
the brilliant leaves

all the birds sing at once.
Men and animals rise up reborn.

*They stop. Arons salutes the auditorium with the flag. Raises it again.*

**Ramon** What could be more natural? After sorrow, happiness

*Fade down to flag; a single image: it's now Sandinista. Above it, the TV monitor's alive with images of victory.*